Jayne Torvill was born in Nottingham in 1957 and, with her partner Christopher Dean, she won the gold medal for figure skating in the 1984 Winter Olympics. They subsequently turned professional, before helping train the contestants in the successful TV series *Dancing on Ice*.

Christopher Dean was born in Nottinghamshire in 1958 and became a police constable before winning Olympic gold in figure skating in 1984 with his partner Jayne Torvill.

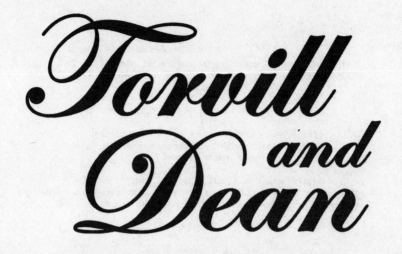

OUR LIFE ON ICE
THE AUTOBIOGRAPHY

**SIMON &
SCHUSTER**

London · New York · Sydney · Toronto · New Delhi

A CBS COMPANY

First published in Great Britain by Simon & Schuster UK Ltd, 2014
This paperback edition published by Simon & Schuster UK Ltd, 2015
A CBS COMPANY

1 3 5 7 9 10 8 6 4 2

Simon & Schuster UK Ltd
222 Gray's Inn Road
London WC1X 8HB

www.simonandschuster.co.uk

Simon & Schuster Australia, Sydney
Simon & Schuster India, New Delhi

A CIP catalogue record for this book
is available from the British Library

ISBN: 978-1-47113-870-6
eBook ISBN: 978-1-47113-871-3

Typeset in the UK by M Rules
Printed and bound by CPI Group (UK) Ltd, Croydon, CR0 4YY

JAYNE:

I would like to dedicate this book to Chris for being my inspiration and best friend; to Phil for his love and support; and to my beautiful children, Kieran and Jessica.

CHRIS:

I want to dedicate this book to the person who has been by my side on and off the ice for the last 46 years, Jayne; and to my two boys, Jack and Sam, who have shown me the love a father can have for his children.

Contents

Preface

JAYNE & CHRIS:

When we were first approached about writing this book it's fair to say we were sceptical. We'd already written one autobiography, about 20 years ago, and were at a loss as to what else there would be to say. We were the same people – who'd want to read the same stories again?

Then, as we began going through the first book we realised that actually things had changed. We'd changed. Perhaps we could deliver something different and original after all.

As we discussed the idea further it became apparent that we did indeed have a story to tell. That 20-year period had presented us with countless new experiences – the majority of which we've never discussed in detail before. But we also now see the past through different eyes, and our memories seem to be full of what really matters to us.

So, much of what you're about to read will be completely new to you. And even the events you may be familiar with have been told by us as we are today, not as we were two decades ago, and that's a very different proposition.

1

Growing Up

CHRIS:

I was born in Calverton, which is a small mining village on the outskirts of Nottingham. My parents, Colin and Mavis, and I lived on an estate that had been built by the council specifically to house miners and their families. Home was a flat – a kind of maisonette, really. It sounds quite posh but I promise you it wasn't.

Come to think of it, the inside of the flat resembled something out of *Coronation Street*. We had lino instead of carpets and all of the furniture was either second-hand or on its last legs. If it had legs! We even had three ceramic swallows swooping majestically across the living-room wall, just like Hilda and Stan Ogden's flying ducks.

The flat was heated by coal, of course – or at least the living room was – which, despite living so close to the pit, would still be delivered by the coal men each week. The rest of the flat wasn't heated at all, except by the warm weather, and there was certainly no double glazing. I remember during the winter months getting up in the morning and scraping the ice off the inside of the window.

I had one bath a week (something my children find stomach-churning), except in the summer when I had a stand-up strip-wash – the weather being far too hot to light a fire and we had no immersion heater. We had more of a continental climate back then and having a bath seemed less of a necessity. In fact, you could say it was more like an event.

Believe it or not, throughout my young life I only ever had one pair of shoes at any one time. There were no trainers or plimsolls then, or at least not in our house, so it didn't matter if I was playing football or going to school, I always wore the same shoes. We often went to ridiculous lengths to make them last – usually sticking the soles back on with glue – but I do remember going to school once with my shoe wrapped in black tape. The glue obviously hadn't worked so plan B was brought into operation!

All I wanted to do when I was young was climb. That was my thing, and from the age of about four I would shimmy up the side of our building, clinging on to the old pot drainpipes that ran down the side. You had to be careful as they could be quite fragile, but I always managed to get up on to the roof and into the garret. Funnily enough, my mother didn't share my enthusiasm for climbing and would stand at the bottom of the drainpipe trying to make me come down. 'You get down from there. Get down!' Which I did, of course, although very slowly. Somewhere slightly easier to negotiate was the outhouse, which we shared with the other three flats. That was a far less dangerous proposition and didn't scare my mother nearly as much. Once on the roof I would sit there cross-legged, surveying all that I thought was mine and looking out for new things to climb.

Despite never falling off a roof (thank goodness) I seemed to have a 'hate-hate' relationship with bicycles. I was a bit of a daredevil and could only go anywhere fast. Slow was just something you had to go through to get there!

Accidents became an almost daily occurrence at one point, with my mother spending half her life patching me up and mending my clothes. I always got straight back on, though; in fact, it was impossible to stop me. I saw it as some kind of challenge, even then. It was up to me to master the bike, not the other way round. It definitely stood me in good stead for what was to come.

As much as I loved exploring our garret, the one place in Calverton I visited on a regular basis but never wanted to leave was the local Co-op food store, where my mother worked full-time behind the meat counter. In those days professional childcare hadn't really been invented (we wouldn't have been able to afford it, anyway); so, if your parents didn't have a family member or a reliable friend close by, you were picked up, taken along, put down out of the way somewhere and told to behave. Had my mother worked in an office, I expect it would all have been quite boring; but the Co-op had a storeroom at the back, and in the storeroom there were boxes – hundreds of them. To me, it was like having my very own adventure playground.

Something else that hadn't really been invented in the early 1960s was 'health and safety'; at least, not like it is now. These days there are thousands of people all over the country busily enforcing billions of pages of rules and regulations. Back then, you got a finger wagged in your face and a warning: 'Remember, Christopher, no climbing on the boxes, OK?'

'Yes, Mum.'

Despite being ordered to stay at ground level, I was allowed to build dens with the boxes – not to mention cars, planes, rockets and battleships; a fair compromise, I thought. None of the other mothers who worked there brought their kids in with them, so I had the whole place to myself for the entire day. I only wandered through to the shop on the rare occasions I was either hungry or in need of some company.

I've never really been one for reminiscing or hankering after the 'good old days', but about 20 years ago I decided to go back to the Co-op while on a visit to Calverton – and, after explaining myself to the manager, was allowed to have a peek inside the storeroom again. I was ushered through a door and there it was, my old adventure playground. I'm not really sure what I was hoping to see – I was probably trying to reignite my imagination – but all the magic had gone. It was simply a concrete floor and about a hundred boxes. The imagination of a child is a very precious thing.

At about the age of five I was evicted from my adventure playground and forced to attend Manor Road Infant School, together with lots of other cruelly abandoned climbers and den builders. Crueller still was the fact that I could see the Co-op through the fence in the playground. I was in mourning for months.

I'm afraid to say I hated school. I could never understand why I was there. My parents never encouraged me to learn so I just saw it as some kind of punishment. It wasn't until I was in my teens that its importance began to dawn on me; by which time it was too late.

I always yearned for the days when I was required to pack my sports kit. I was what you might call a good all-rounder: running, football, swimming, gymnastics, I honestly didn't mind, and seemed to have a natural aptitude for most. The event I really looked forward to was the 100-yard dash, which was the one I was always most likely to win. Nobody could keep up with me when it came to running.

Looking back, I wish I had been encouraged to do well at school, been made to understand the importance of education. But like the majority of boys at Manor Road Infants, I was expected to leave school at 15 and follow my dad down the mines. People's lives seemed to be almost preordained in those days, especially in working-class communities. It was a rite of passage.

I have a definite thirst for knowledge, though – I always have – and I think I would have taken to university life quite well. It may not have been for me, of course, but not having been given the opportunity is one of my few regrets.

So the first six years of my life were a mixed bag. Before going to school I was fairly happy. We never had any money and home was basic to say the least, but I was always well-fed and got lots of fresh air and freedom.

But then things started to go downhill, and not just at school. Home was to become unhappier still.

I don't often talk about this part of my life. In some ways it draws a bit of a blank, and I only remember certain parts. A psychologist would probably tell me that I block out the memories, and perhaps I do.

But on the few occasions that I have discussed what happened with my parents I'm always asked if I saw it coming. I can say in all honestly that I had no idea. When I wasn't at school I was playing outside, and when I wasn't outside I was in my bedroom reading comic books or playing with my Corgi cars. I was totally oblivious to anything going on outside my bubble.

Then, one day, my mum and dad took me to see some friends of theirs. Or at least I always thought they were friends.

When we arrived at their house I was told to sit down in the living room. Soon after, I remember an almighty row ensuing. All four of them seemed to be shouting across the room at each other and I was sitting in the middle. Even at six years old I understood what had been going on. Apparently my dad had been having an affair with Betty and my mum and Betty's husband must have found out. This was obviously the aftermath.

When they stopped shouting, it was as if a conclusion had

been reached, although I didn't know what. Something had changed, though, and I remember the atmosphere during the drive home being pretty awful.

Sometime after that my mum took me to see some friends of hers. I didn't think anything of this; it was just a trip out. Then all of a sudden she sat me down: 'Christopher, I'm afraid I'm going away,' she said.

There was no reason or explanation given, although I knew it must have had something to do with the row at Betty's house. I asked her why but she just deflected the question. Then I started to cry. I pleaded with her not to go but she didn't say a thing. No answer. I remember holding her hand as we walked home, still crying and pleading with her not to go.

After about a week, with nothing further having been said, my fears had all but disappeared. Children tend to live in the moment, and I was no different. Then, one morning, I went downstairs to find my mum standing by the front door with a suitcase. I don't remember her saying goodbye. One minute she was there, and the next, gone. Then, later on the same day, Betty arrived with a suitcase.

Again, there were no explanations given, and no opportunity to ask questions. It seemed that I just had to get used to the idea. I remember looking at my dad, hoping he'd sit me down and explain, but he never did.

I didn't know of any other divorced or separated parents, so for a long time we were like the 'black sheep' of the estate; there was lots of staring and whispering. Nothing said out loud, of course. It was very much a taboo subject. Gossip fodder, really.

It was never suggested that I should make contact with my mother, and I certainly never asked. She had just seemed to disappear and I was never once given any news as to her whereabouts or wellbeing. She was never far away from my thoughts, though.

A couple of years later, on my way back from school, I saw my mum walking into a flat above the local hairdresser's. It turned out she'd moved back into the village and was now living there. It was a strange moment seeing her after such a long time. I was excited; relieved even, yet scared of the trouble it might cause at home. That was the overriding thought: What would Dad and Betty say? I was actually in fear of getting in touch with her.

I didn't know for sure that they would have had a problem with me seeing my mum again; but I always assumed that because it was never mentioned, it was off limits.

So, for a time, my mum's return to Calverton remained my secret. I didn't tell anybody I'd seen her. I just remember slowing down as I passed her flat each day, hoping to get a glimpse of her. And I did some days, but usually just the top of her head.

After a while we did make contact, although I forget how and why. I just remember being allowed to go and stay with her once or twice. Again, nothing was said from either side. I was simply delivered to her. She enjoyed the visits, but I found them quite difficult. I was afraid to show any emotion, probably for the same reasons I'd kept quiet about seeing her.

Then, as quickly as it had started, it all came to a halt and I was no longer allowed to go. I've no idea why or from where the order came; all I know is that Mum and I were to go back to being strangers again. In a funny sort of way I was relieved, as my going to stay had caused arguments at home. Nothing directed at me, thank goodness, but it was reason enough for me to yearn for a return to normality.

It wasn't until the mid-1990s that I started seeing my mum again on anything like a regular basis: over 30 years since she first left home. She used to come and watch me skate back in our amateur days, but only very rarely, and I was never made aware of it at the time. In fact, it was Jayne's job to make sure I didn't find out. It would have been too much of a distraction.

I know it took a lot for her to come and see me in those days, as we weren't actually in contact with each other then. After she'd seen me skate, that was it, she'd be off – there was no popping backstage afterwards for a chat. My dad and Betty often attended competitions, so it would have been too dangerous.

Much later, when we were making *Dancing on Ice,* she used to come to the studio sometimes and watch. Occasionally I'd look up to where she was sitting and, regardless of what was happening on the ice, she'd always have her gaze fixed on me, as though she was frightened of losing sight of me.

These days my mum and I get along fine. She's well into her eighties now and I think would sometimes like to talk about what happened, try to offer closure, perhaps. But if I'm honest it's not something I crave. For a start, my dad is no longer with us, and I suppose I'm afraid that if we start going into detail, I may learn things about him that might taint my memory of him. In addition to this, I'd only ever get one side of the story. What would be the point? I don't hate my dad for having an affair, the same as I don't hate my mum for leaving me. I prefer to look forward rather than back.

My dad was my constant in life, he was my hero. The one person I knew who would always be there for me. That alone was monumentally important after my mum left. Dad and I never had an especially deep relationship, but that wasn't exclusive to me. If anything it was a generational thing. He was the strong, silent type – a typical miner. We never hugged or said that we loved each other, but I knew he did. With him it was a quick handshake, a ruffle of the hair and a 'Well done, Buster'. That was enough for me, though.

But what little bits of his character my dad was prepared to share are very dear to me, and so, as tempting as it occasionally is to find out the full details of how and why my parents split up, the pull isn't nearly strong enough for me to want to have the conversation. Not just one side of it; it wouldn't be fair. As I've mentioned, I'm not a nostalgic person. What's past is past. That said, I do miss my dad very much.

He didn't want much out of life: a packet of cigarettes and a few beers once or twice a week – and to be able to work on his car on a Sunday. He was just a very normal, decent, hard-working man. I remember watching him hand his wage packet in as soon as he got it. 'There you are, that'll keep us going for a bit.'

He loved cars, but could never afford anything decent. He used to choose them by rust: how much it had and where it was. He would have loved a new car, and I'd have loved to be able to buy him one. Unfortunately, he died before I could afford to. He was only 59.

People used to say to me, 'Oh, your dad must be so proud of you', but I don't think the word 'proud' was part of our vocabulary at home. When we first started winning championships he used to shake me by the hand and say, 'Well done, Buster', or 'Well done, Bud'. Proud was not part of his lexicon. But again, he didn't have to say it. I knew full well that he was proud of me, just as I knew that he loved me. That's what kept me going.

With my own children it's very, very different. I can't help hugging them and hanging on to them. As much as they go, 'Dad, stop it now', I can't imagine not doing that; not being connected to them. Is that a result of what happened to me as a child? I don't think so. I'm not compensating for anything by being tactile. They're my children and I love them very deeply. I need to have that bond. I feed off it. What parent doesn't these days?

Losing my mum and being an only child definitely went some way to making me who I am today. I've always been very independent and emotionally quite self-reliant. I'm very much a 'that's just the way it is' kind of person. I don't let things fester and tend to just get on and make the best of it. Yes, I'm driven, and if I get it in my head to do something I'll always give it my best shot. But everything I do, I do with consideration. I don't go into things lightly, but when I commit, I commit.

I never had any heroes as a child, apart from my dad. There were no posters of footballers or pop stars on the walls. I didn't aspire to be like anybody else and focused all of my attentions on doing what I wanted to do. It sounds a bit selfish, perhaps, but I had to channel my independence into something worthwhile. So, as skating became more important, I became totally focused. It was the only thing that mattered.

So, how else has my slightly unorthodox childhood affected who I am today? Well, I did become a bit of a cleanliness freak at one point, which is something that has stayed with me. After my mother left it kind of became my job to clean the house. My dad worked seven days a week and wasn't the tidiest person on earth. Betty worked, too, which meant it was down to me to keep the place in order – cleaning, hoovering, dusting and washing up – and I brought a whole new meaning to the word 'fastidious'. My enemy throughout all this was undoubtedly our coal bucket, which had a great big hole in the bottom of it. I used to try and cover it up with newspaper but it didn't make much difference; the floor would still end up covered in coal slag.

My relationship with Betty, who is also no longer with us, was naturally quite difficult at times. We definitely had a love-hate relationship, especially in the first few years. I always felt like I had to go out of my way to please her, and I couldn't always do that. After all, I was a six-year-old boy, and children of that age can be quite testing. Being in almost constant search of her approval was a challenge, and not one I particularly enjoyed. I was walking on eggshells a lot of the time, never really knowing what her mood was going to be. Anything could set her off – the slightest thing. You had to be very careful.

To be fair, it must have been very hard for her taking on a new family. She had two grown-up children of her own when she moved in with us, so having to go through all that again, and with somebody else's child, can't have been easy.

The one thing I'll always be grateful to Betty for is introducing me to ice skating. She'd been a recreational skater in her teens and had talked my dad into buying me my first pair of skates. That must have been a huge outlay for them at the time, but it was quite a masterstroke.

She also pushed me towards ice dancing, which you'll read about later – so I've a lot to thank her for.

JAYNE:

I grew up on the Clifton council estate in Nottingham. It was all very new when I was young but these days it's one of the most troubled estates in the city. The singer Jake Bugg also grew up there.

According to my mum, the first thing that ever interested me as a child was music. It didn't matter what kind of music, so long as there was a rhythm attached to it. Then, when I was old enough to get up on to my feet I'd try and twirl to it. It was obviously something instinctive and I still remember doing it – getting up off the floor and going round and round on the spot. The only downside was that this put me at eye level with most of the windowsills in the house, which resulted in one or two collisions, and ultimately a few tears. It never stopped me, though. The pull was far too great.

Like Chris, I was a very active child, always out and about – although I couldn't be doing with climbing. That was far too dangerous. We used to have a coal shed at the side of the house, and once a week the coal lorry would arrive outside, always full to bursting with sacks and sacks of the stuff. I remember watching the two coal men jump out of the front, absolutely covered from head to toe in dust. As they poured the sacks of coal into our shed, small pieces would fall on to the ground where I was sitting, watching them. I'd obviously still not cottoned on to what coal was actually for at the time, and as the stray pieces fell on the ground I'd pick them up and eat them. Don't ask me why. It just seemed like the right thing to do. As I tucked in, the coal men would pause and have a bit of a giggle, before my mum came racing out to stop me, shooing the coal men on their way and carrying me indoors.

Being quite a girly girl, I was always into dresses – especially new ones. Once, when I was about five years old, my mum asked me if I'd like to be a bridesmaid for one of my aunts. It was a rhetorical question, of course. What self-respecting five-year-old girl with a penchant for dresses and twirling wouldn't want to be a bridesmaid?

I was so excited. 'Will I get a special dress?'

'Yes, of course you will.'

'Great, what colour will it be?'

'Yellow.'

'Oh, OK.'

Although yellow wasn't my favourite colour in the world, it didn't really matter. I was getting a new dress!

The day the dress arrived was a huge event in our house. Well, for me at least; like all my birthdays rolled into one. I'd never had such an important job to do and I was taking my role very seriously indeed.

When I tried the dress on my mum looked at me. 'Now, our Jayne, you must look after this dress. Whatever you do, don't crease it. Try and keep your arms away from the sides a little bit so that you don't squash it.'

Rather than keep my arms out to the sides a tiny bit, as my mum had actually advised, I took what she'd said a little more literally. In fact, for the entire day I insisted on holding both my arms straight out at the sides – not just for the service but during the photos, the reception, the throwing of the bouquet, even the journey home. As long as I was in that dress I carried that position. I don't remember much about the day itself – I was far too busy concentrating on the job in hand. There's a photo of me somewhere, standing there in that odd pose. Every time I see it, it makes me smile.

Like Chris's dad, my parents, George and Betty, had a tremendous work ethic. They never stopped, and that definitely rubbed off on me. Dad worked for Raleigh Bicycle Company when I was young. They were an institution in Nottingham, and Mum was a machinist up at the Lace Market. She used to work all kinds of funny hours and sometimes wouldn't get home until past ten. But it was the only way they could both have a job and still be able to look after me. When I was a bit older they bought a newsagent's business.

Although my dad's very active, he's an extremely laid-back sort of person, very placid and not easily fazed; whereas my mum, who is also very active, is far more forceful. Even now in their mid-eighties they have fairly busy routines to stick to and are still totally independent. I'm definitely a cross between the two: I'm like my dad when I'm off the ice, and like my mum when on it.

They'd first met in the early 1940s, at a dance at the school they'd recently attended, Adela Roscoe. My dad had been taking ballroom lessons and eventually became quite good. Being able to dance was the best way of finding a girlfriend back then, as the better you became, the more girls there were who were willing to dance with you. It was always their big thing, ballroom dancing, and I remember very vividly how my dad would pick me up and stand me on his feet at the local British Legion club, then he'd take my hands and we'd dance the foxtrot together. It was my first introduction to movement.

At about 8.30pm, me and all the other kids would go outside and play for a while, before coming back in and being greeted by this huge cloud of cigarette smoke. Everyone smoked in those days. Then, when I eventually became tired I'd fold my arms and fall asleep at the table, before being picked up and carried by my dad when it was time to go home.

Holidays were usually spent at a B&B in Cornwall – that was our destination of choice, and such a beautiful part of the world. I was often a bit of a nightmare while we were there, especially as I was such an active child. Sitting still for more than two minutes was virtually impossible, and, boy, did my mum know it: 'Jayne, will you come and sit down!'

'But I want to go outside.'

'Why don't you read a book?'

'But we're on holiday. Can I go out and play?'

Most parents will have had similar conversations with their kids at some point. At home it wasn't a problem because I was always surrounded by friends and cousins. Boredom was almost unheard of! But on holiday it was just the three of us, so I was far less easily entertained. In the end they usually relented – it was either that or watch me fidgeting all day – and off I'd go and practise my cartwheels.

Cartwheels used to get me into all kinds of trouble, especially with my mum, and especially on holiday. On one occasion we were sitting down to dinner at the B&B. I'd wolfed down my food and had finished way before everyone else – so began pleading: 'Mum, can I go out and play?'

'Not yet, we're still eating. Can't you just wait for a few minutes?'

'No, I want to do something.' And on it went ... (I have exactly the same running battle with my daughter, Jessica, today. Even though she's adopted, she's very much like me when I was a child, and I'm exactly the same as my parents: 'Will you just sit down!')

Within about a minute I was waved on my way, and took myself off into the hall just outside the dining room. I could do cartwheels undisturbed there. Well, not quite: I remember having to try and avoid kicking some fellow guests once or twice. But it was fine; better than sitting in our room. Everything was going swimmingly, in fact, until the next load of food was ready to be brought in. I didn't see the kitchen door open, or the landlady walking out carrying a two-storey tray. All I remember was starting a cartwheel. I was getting good now and could cover quite a distance from start to finish. Well, within about three seconds the landlady and I were covered from head to toe in steak and kidney pie, potatoes and peas. She just stood there, aghast, still clinging on to the tray, minus its contents. My mum knew instinctively what had happened. She came out and didn't even bat an eyelid.

'Our Jayne, this hall's not big enough for cartwheels, and you're too big to be showing your knickers in public. Get up those stairs and clean yourself up. I'm most dreadfully sorry, Mrs . . . ' It didn't put an end to my cartwheeling.

Although I didn't have any brothers or sisters, I was surrounded by family. My mother was one of eight children and three of her siblings – a brother and two sisters – also lived on the estate. They had kids of their own so I was never short of company, and we were always in and out of each other's houses. It was a bit like having four homes.

When I was at primary school my cousins and I used to walk home for lunch, and I remember once, in my final year there, being confronted by the school bully on the way to my house. 'I'm gonna get you, Torvill,' he said. 'The next time we see you about, you're for it!'

I'm not ashamed to say that I was absolutely terrified at the time. He had a gang – about six of them – and they were all quite tough-looking. Sure enough, the next time they saw me, they began to run towards me. I tore off, as fast as my legs would carry me, straight into the schoolhouse. As soon as I was inside I headed straight to the staffroom and banged on the door. 'Please let me in, they're going to get me, they're going to get me!'

'Off you go back to the playground, Jayne, and stop being so silly!'

The next day the same thing happened, except this time I was on my way to my aunt's house with my cousins. 'Hey, Torvill, we're *really* gonna get you now!' came the familiar cry, and so once again I set off as fast as I could, my cousins close behind. We made it back in the nick of time, with only a couple of seconds to spare. It was terrifying! As soon as the door was shut we pulled down the lock and breathed a huge sigh of relief. That wasn't the end of it, though. We could still hear them shouting outside. Eventually we plucked up enough courage to peep through the side of the curtains, and there they were, prowling around the front of the house, looking menacing. In the end they got bored and walked off, but it seemed to take an age!

The only teacher I remember clearly from primary school was Mrs Fitzhugh, who organised the skating trip that first got me hooked. She was one of the younger ones and always seemed pretty all right to me. The majority of the teachers were quite old, as I remember, so having one even a bit closer to your own age was a novelty. Mrs Fitzhugh spoke to us like grown-ups, not like children, so we also tended to respect her a bit more.

I remember that, on the way back from that first trip to the ice rink, there was some problem with my parents picking me up – I think our car had broken down – so Mrs Fitzhugh took me back to her house and her husband gave me a lift home. Going to a teacher's house was *really* cool! She was very laid-back; a lovely lady and a great teacher.

There were three senior schools in Clifton, and going to the grammar school meant you were top of the pile, at least educationally. My passing the eleven-plus was a big thing for my parents, because their schooling and education had been quite limited. Both of them had left school at 14, which you could easily do in those days, and I think they were secretly quite excited that I was doing well. The fact that I never made it to university was never an issue with them. I think they were just pleased that I did as well as I did for as long as I decided to do it. Their support has always been completely unconditional. Ironically (or fate-driven, as Mr Dean might say), the uniform at the grammar school was purple – a colour that, from 1984 onwards, would become almost synonymous with us.

I was very well behaved at school, and seemed to have a halo permanently fixed around my head. In fact, in all my years at both primary and at grammar school I don't ever recall incurring the wrath of a teacher. How horribly square! This didn't always go in my favour, though: several times I had naughty children put next to me in class. I presume the teachers thought I might be a good influence on them. I remember thinking I wish they'd asked me first.

A question I'm often asked but find difficult to answer is what I might have gone on to do if I hadn't become a skater. Apart from working as an insurance clerk for a while (which I was sort of forced to do, as at 16 you had to get a job) all I've ever known is skating; it's all I've ever wanted to do. Thinking up alternatives would be pure fantasy: an astronaut or a film star? I honestly don't know. I never really tried when it came to exams, my heart wasn't in it, and I came away from school with just two O levels, in Art and English, so maybe an artist or a writer? I could have been Nottingham's answer to Jackie Collins! I actually wanted to stay on and do A levels in those subjects but you had to have a minimum of five O level passes to do so. All I know for sure is that every form I've ever had to fill in that has required me to declare my profession has always ended up with the words 'Ice Skater' written on it.

2

Ice

JAYNE & CHRIS:

This chapter was originally going to tell the story of how we both became skaters, and we'll get on to that. But we've decided that, given the title, we should perhaps dedicate a few words to what it's like to work on ice. After all, we've spent a total of about five years of our lives on it.

This is only a rough estimate, which was worked out on a bit of paper, but during those five years we think we must have skated at least 250,000 miles. That's almost ten times around the earth!

The fact is we feel at home on the ice. Even when we're not working we still have to put our skates on once every few days and feel the ice. It's kind of essential. Like an amphibian needing to get into the water. We have to get back to it again.

During rehearsals for *Dancing on Ice*, we'd often stand there holding a cup of coffee, chatting to contestants about moves or routines. Then, without thinking, we'd begin to demonstrate the moves while still holding our coffee. We'd never spill a drop, mind you. We're like pursers on a ship in high winds; totally comfortable in our environment.

Everyone assumes that ice is always the same, but it's not that simple. Ice is a strangely complicated surface to work on. First of all, there are many different kinds of ice. There's soft ice, hard ice and rough ice; as well as something called Jet Ice. Jet Ice is made with distilled water and therefore has no minerals in it. This makes it faster to skate on and is primarily used for ice hockey.

On a rink the ice is constantly moving (although very slowly) and can change temperature by the minute. It doesn't just sit there, solid. It has to be treated with care and respect. It also changes after use, of course. For instance, during the compulsories (which we would have to perform at every competition), where everybody performs the same dance using roughly the same pattern, you naturally start to get grooves forming. As they usually tend to resurface the ice after two groups – and there'll be five or six couples in each – you could end up, if you're the 12th couple, following a pattern that has already been skated over 33 times (as each couple completes three circuits). Imagine – 33 edges close together. If you're unlucky enough to get caught on an edge, you're likely to fall. You can be perfectly in sync one minute and on your backside the next.

We'd always look at the pattern first, and if we were on towards the end of the second group we'd see if we could alter things slightly so as not to get stuck in a rut, so to speak.

When it came to the free dance, things were a lot more unpredictable – the two main culprits, as well as the ice itself, being debris and traffic. Think about some of the costumes we had to wear, all covered in sequins, feathers and heaven knows what else; many of which could fall off during the routine. But the biggest offenders were always hairgrips. If you went over anything like that it could easily spell disaster. In fact, it could cost you a championship. Imagine if we'd gone over a hairgrip in Sarajevo! It was the same with skating traffic, though.

Before the warm-up for the free dance every couple would be split into groups. These would then take to the ice one by one and practise different parts of their routines. Having so many people on the ice at the same time would naturally result in a few bumps and collisions, not to mention countless near-misses. On one quite famous occasion, during the warm-up at the 1984 World Championships, Jayne came very close to being floored by another couple. Watching it back now makes us flinch.

That's why, pre-competition, we'd always try and get time in the main building so that we could become used to the condition of the ice there, not to mention the environment – especially surrounding the rink. This can be crucial, as during practice you begin to notice particular objects at certain points in the routine, and they become markers; reminders of exactly where you are – or perhaps where you should be – in the dance. The more familiar you are with the building, the more comfortable and confident you feel.

It's hardly surprising that the most comfortable we've ever felt on the ice is at Nottingham Ice Stadium, which was demolished and replaced by the National Ice Centre back in 2000. From our early teens until our early twenties we probably spent as many waking hours there as we did at home. In fact, in many ways it still is a kind of home – the home of so many memories and important occasions: our first time on the ice, falling over and trying to pretend we didn't care; meeting our first partners, then meeting each other; winning our first British Championship. We could probably go on for hours.

The man whose job it was to look after the ice was very passionate about what he did and soon tuned into how passionate we were about skating. His name was Norman Beckett and he always made sure the ice was perfect for us. We can't stress enough the importance of having good ice to skate on.

Something else you have to worry about is getting your

blades right – and, as with ice dancing itself, you have to really work on your timing. Once you've had your blades sharpened they will probably be at their optimum sharpness for only two routines' worth of ice time. The problem is that you're never exactly sure when that will be. If your blades are too sharp you end up having to fight with them a little bit, which can easily result in a fall; and if they are too blunt, you get the opposite effect and go too slowly. Either way it can be very hazardous. We probably became slightly obsessed by it at one point and used to alternate between two sets of blades each. We did manage to gauge it pretty well in the end.

JAYNE:

You'd also think that rinks are all completely flat but that's not always the case. We usually prefer not to perform on a rink where there's a slope, for obvious reasons, but on the few occasions that we have it's produced a nice bit of dramatic comedy. The last time was at Aberdeen Exhibition Centre while we were on tour with the Russian All-Stars. When we arrived we realised that the floor was on an angle. There was talk of fitting a false floor on to the sloping side so as to balance things up a bit, but the cost of that would have been astronomical, so we all said we'd carry on regardless and work with the slope. It probably wouldn't have been visible at first glance but it made a big difference when we were skating. We had to skate harder going against the slope, easier going down it – and all in time to the music!

Shortly after the crew had finished laying the ice we all trooped out for the press call. 'Line up in the middle of the rink facing the cameras, would you?' asked whoever was coordinating the call. So the company did as we were asked, taking our place in the middle of the rink, and as we all got into position and the cameras started flashing and rolling, several hundredweight of skaters started moving involuntarily towards them. There must be a photo of that somewhere?!

Another thing people often forget is that ice is clear; they don't realise that the ice as seen on television or at a live show has taken many hours to prepare and has a thick layer of white paint running through the middle of it. If it didn't, you'd be forced to see us skating over a concrete floor and several miles of piping, which would probably take away some of the glamour. There's an art to making good ice, though, and it takes time, patience and skill.

First of all you put enough water on the surface to cover the pipes and let it freeze, then once you've repeated that a few times you cut the ice and clean it, making sure the surface is smooth. Next comes the paint, which is applied using a huge spray bar stretching the entire breadth of the rink. After two or three coats you then apply a mist, wait for it to freeze, and then start layering on the water again. Once you're about three-quarters of an inch above the paint, you're ready to go.

Start skating when there's less than that and you're in trouble. We had that problem many years ago while performing at an ice hockey stadium in Chicago. It was during our *Face the Music* tour. For some reason they'd only gone slightly over the paint, and so when it came to our first rehearsal we were skating on paint, which can be quite dangerous. It's like skating through butter. At one point it was touch and go as to whether the show would go ahead and, up until an hour before we were due on, the entire company were out on the ice trying to scrape off the paint. We made it in the end, but only by minutes.

CHRIS:

The first time I ever set foot on the ice was in January 1969. I was ten years old at the time and had already been the proud owner of some skates for two weeks. Betty, my stepmum, had suggested buying me some for Christmas. She'd skated in her teens and figured that as I was so active, the chances were I might enjoy it. It might also help me burn off some energy. Betty was also keen for me to take up ice dancing, as she and my dad were always very fond of ballroom dancing, which is where ice dancing originates from.

On first setting eyes on those skates that cold Christmas morning, I was thrilled, but also slightly confused. It was quite unexpected really; not what you'd normally get for a ten-year-old boy. Excitement soon got the better of confusion, though, and I set about badgering my dad and stepmum about trying them out.

Slight problem there: Calverton was eight miles from Nottingham, which was the equivalent of around a hundred in my dad's old banger. A special trip was out of the question, so it would have to fit in around a shopping expedition; something which usually happened around once every couple of weeks – car permitting.

It was going to be about that long before the next trip. We had to get Christmas and New Year out of the way. I'd just have to be patient. How many ten-year-old boys do you know who can practise patience?

In the end we reached a compromise. If I promised not to moan, I was allowed to wear the skates around the house, as long as I kept the guards on the blades. So, for the next two weeks, whenever I was indoors, I wore my skates. The movement was a bit of a struggle, especially on the lino, but at least I managed not to break anything. That would come, though.

Finally, those two weeks elapsed and off we set to

Nottingham. It was touch and go for a moment ... or at least I thought it was.

'The engine's a bit cold. I'm not sure it'll start, Buster.'

'What? Oh no, Dad. Please make it start!'

'Only joking, Buster. It's fine. Let's get going.'

After what seemed like an eternity we finally arrived at Nottingham Ice Stadium.

What happened next was, I suppose, my own version of *The Lion, the Witch and the Wardrobe*, as on walking through the heavy, glass-fronted doors I was suddenly faced with this enormous wintry kingdom. Winter has always been my favourite season, so this was just blissful.

The stadium itself was cavernous, with a great arched roof and yellow walls, one of which bore a mural of a picturesque scene from Davos, up in the Swiss mountains. And there, in the middle, was the ice; this vast oval of brilliant white, with around a hundred or so people on it, all swishing round at what seemed like a hundred miles per hour.

I'm sure that if I could see that moment again now, the expression on my face as I first took to the ice would make me smile for a week. I had a grin so fixed it would have been impossible to move. The anticipation had been almost unbearable. Two weeks of walking around the house with my guards on, and at last I was let loose.

What happened next was typical me. As opposed to doing what most people did, which was hold on to the barrier and work your way round, I decided to just go for it. Patience was still eluding me.

Well, it wasn't pretty, but it was certainly the right thing too. I probably fell over around a hundred times in those two hours, but then I knew I would. Betty had warned me. That said, I'd spent more time on my feet than on my backside and by the time I was called in I could skate forwards quite happily.

'Can we come again next week? Please!'

Dad and Betty could see how much I'd enjoyed it; in fact, it probably gave them as much pleasure as it did me.

'All right then, Buster.'

As it turned out, they started bringing me every Saturday.

Everything about Nottingham Ice Stadium appealed to me, but especially the atmosphere, which was always cheerful. One of my favourite things was watching them resurface the ice. These days they use something called a Zamboni, which slices off a very thin layer of ice, before covering with water which is then frozen. But at Nottingham Ice Stadium, circa 1969, things were a little more primitive, not to mention comical.

When the ice was ready for resurfacing, a tractor – which actually resembled one of the old aircraft towers from the Second World War – would be driven on, towing a contraption that had a blade fixed to it – a blade, incidentally, that was being guided by an elderly gentleman on skates. Once the blade had skimmed off a good pile of snow, the man driving the tractor would make his way to the side, at which point the elderly man on skates, who looked like he was waterskiing behind the tractor, would push a lever, making the blade rise. Then (and this was my favourite part) he'd be towed off again, straight through the pile of snow. While all this was going on, another chap would be following them with a hose pipe, spraying on a fresh layer of what would eventually become ice. Simple. A Zamboni might be quick and effective, but they're not nearly as much fun.

After a few weeks I was able to skate not just forwards, but backwards too. Then I started to teach myself turns, each new trick bringing with it a fresh batch of embarrassments and bruises. But none of that really bothered me; it was my challenge, and I was aware even then that it was all part of a process.

By this point I was actually skating twice a week, adding Thursday evenings to my now indispensable Saturday mornings. This was hugely demanding for my dad and stepmum, but their commitment was unfaltering. In fact, it was my dad who suggested I take lessons. I wasn't keen at the time; I was shy and didn't like the idea of not being able to do my own thing, but it was definitely good for me.

As well as mastering my first dance steps, I also learned how to move to music, which meant I had to listen to it carefully. It might sound strange but that was probably the first time I'd ever properly listened to music. Of course, I'd heard it before, in the background, but I'd never actually *listened* to it or had to move to it. Now I had to listen to the beat, or find it.

So, when it came to having to choose between learning free skating or dancing, the decision was an easy one, which pleased my dad and stepmum enormously, as they'd always been very keen ballroom dancers.

At 13, I was teamed up with my first ever partner, Sandra Elson, who would later become a friend of Jayne's. Sandra, who I'm very sad to say is no longer with us, was strong for a 13-year-old; not just in body, but also in mind. She was headstrong and had a temper on her. I was shy but at the same time stubborn, and didn't like being pushed around, so when sparks flew, it would usually be followed by a firework!

Despite the odd difference of opinion, Sandra and I stayed together for over four years and in that time won both the British Primary Championships and the Junior Dance Championships. The Primary Championships were the kiss of death, apparently, as those who came out on top rarely lasted more than another year. I'm pleased to say we bucked the trend, but not by long.

I clearly remember the thrill of winning the Primaries, though. I was wearing a navy blue cat suit with a pink samba shirt underneath, which had the biggest sleeves you've ever seen. It resembled the costumes Morecambe and Wise wore during their sketch with Angela Rippon. Very 1970s!

There's a photo somewhere of Sandra and me holding the

cup. Fortunately, it's in black and white. It's fair to say that from a fashion sense it wasn't one of my finest hours.

After that we even competed abroad once, visiting Czechoslovakia. It was there that I first met the Russian skaters, Andrei Bukin and Natalia Bestemianova, who would later become great rivals, winning multiple European and World Championships. The first time Jayne and I ever competed against Bukin and Bestemianova, the officials got our medals muddled up. They had won silver and we had won bronze, but they gave them out back to front. After the ceremony Bukin came up to me and started pointing at my medal. At first I thought he was just trying to congratulate me, and it was only after his several attempts to take it from round my neck that I realised what he was getting at. I'm glad it didn't happen eight years later, though, when we won the European Championships and they came second!

In 1974, Sandra and I came sixth at the British Championships, which was to be the pinnacle of our four-year career. You'll find out later on how it all came to an end, but despite us not being a perfect match (we were obviously far too similar in temperament) it is a time that I look back on fondly, and with a great deal of nostalgia. Sandra was an excellent skater and I think we learned a lot from each other.

JAYNE:

I'd already been skating for a couple of years by the time Chris took to the ice. I'm about a year older than him and had started when I was eight. Mrs Fitzhugh, who was always my favourite teacher at primary school, said one day that she'd like to organise a skating trip, and would we all ask our parents if that would be OK? I don't think there was any question of our parents saying no (we wouldn't have let them!) and the next day she went ahead and booked it.

We were due to go on the following Friday, and as the day approached the excitement started to build. Getting us to concentrate on anything other than skating was impossible.

The first thing we did when we arrived was get fitted up with skates. I may have only been eight, but even then I knew what looked good and what didn't. They were all a horrible brown colour, and had obviously been worn (and scuffed) thousands of times before. Those people who'd been on the ice a while had obviously bought their own skates, but these were white. They looked wonderful. I hadn't been on the ice yet but I already knew what colour skates I wanted.

Laces tied, we all stepped on to the ice in a line holding on to a long rope, each one desperate not to be the first to fall. When the lady looking after us decided the time was right, she pulled away the rope and we were free to skate. I took to it like a duck to water. I felt completely at home. My sense of balance was quite keen and I managed to stay upright during the entire session.

The excitement of doing something which, to watch, seemed almost impossible was intense – even for an eight-year-old. I felt like I was flying, and never wanted to have to walk again. I wanted to skate everywhere.

The skating teacher could see that I was obviously enjoying myself and suggested that I might like to come back the following day – Saturday – and take part in something called Ice Cubs, which were basically classes for the under-12s.

From the moment I got home that afternoon I began badgering my parents about going again. It wasn't just nagging, though; I was really thrilled by what I'd done just a few hours earlier and I wanted to tell them all about it.

They seemed really pleased that I'd taken to something, so the following morning we all set off to the Ice Stadium. Once again, the moment I hit the ice I felt as free as a bird – the best feeling ever. And the more I improved, the more rooted that feeling became. Ice skating already felt like it was a part of me.

After a bit more persuading, my parents bought me some second-hand skates (white ones, of course) and arranged for me to start having lessons.

My first teacher, Miss Thelma Perry, was like Mrs Fitzhugh on ice. She was a lovely warm woman, tall and inspiring, and a superb teacher. First she taught me some spins and jumps; followed by some of the preliminary dances. I was a happy student, but I also listened to her every word, which meant I progressed quickly, and within a year I was having two lessons a week – one on Friday and one on Saturday. My Saturday lesson was with a male coach, as Miss Perry had said that if I ever wanted to take any tests I'd be asked to dance with a man, so I'd better make sure I was ready.

In my lessons with Miss Perry she used to play actual gramophone records, or 78s, as I think they were called. She had a pile of them that she'd obviously been using for donkey's years, and when it was time for me to have a programme for competition, she would take me to where they were kept, look me up and down, pick one out and say, 'This is the one for now.' Then it would be played over the loudspeaker, complete with scratches and jumps – it sounded like a cat being strangled!

Choreography didn't seem too important at this point; in fact, we were asked to perform a jump at a particular point in the record. 'Listen for the cymbal crash, Jayne … now … jump!' *Swan Lake* at the Royal Opera House it was not, but neither was it meant to be. Choreography was a thing of the future; unlike Miss Perry's record collection.

I was definitely more into music than Chris; I had a flute recorder at home and listened to the radio all the time. My parents will both be able to confirm this, although probably through gritted teeth. By the age of ten, I'd already been a music lover for around eight years and, as I mentioned earlier, whenever I listened to music I danced. Nothing had changed since I was a toddler. But when you added to that some skates, a brilliant teacher and a little bit of natural talent, you were left with the makings of a good, and extremely keen, skater.

The next rung on my skating ladder would be the National Skating Association Tests – skating's equivalent of a cycling proficiency badge. These held no fear for me whatsoever, as I was always well prepared, and luckily I ended up passing almost all of them first time. Tests actually became a bit of an obsession of mine for a while. I enjoyed taking them. They tested my ability and I always wanted to push myself.

Although a very shy little girl, who usually lacked any kind of confidence, I became a different person on the ice. I was never arrogant, though. Discovering something you're good at is an exciting moment for a child, and it can awaken all kinds of emotions. For me, it was confidence.

At 12 years of age I was teamed up with my first partner, Michael Hutchinson. Not as ice dancers (that would happen later, with somebody much blonder than Michael), but as pairs skaters, which includes incorporating some of the different elements of free skating.

The transition from skating alone to skating with a partner was relatively smooth for me, the main difference being psychological. All of a sudden you have a responsibility to your partner, as well as yourself. But it was fun, and Michael and I got on well.

He was a very good-looking boy; in fact, he was just about a man at the time, being roughly four years older than me. He always had girls flocking round him, which I always rather enjoyed. He was skating with me, after all, not them.

Like Chris and Sandra, Michael and I did well together. We had an advantage, however, in that we were one of only around four couples competing in the UK, so were almost always guaranteed a good finish. In 1970 we became British junior champions, then runners-up in the seniors! As I said, the field wasn't very big. The best part of coming second at the seniors was that it won us automatic entry to an international event in Oberstdorf, Germany; somewhere that, in a few years, would become like a second home.

Believe it or not, there were only two couples in our section, and we came second (not last, as somebody had suggested). Nevertheless, it was a great experience. I'd never been abroad before so was just pleased to be there.

The following year we won the British Championships and were selected for the Europeans. This was a big step up, of course, and although we finished last overall, competing in the event was a privilege; not to mention a thrill, as I got to see many of my early skating heroes in the flesh. I was only 14 at the time.

There was only one downside to our trip to the Europeans, and it came in the shape of a good telling-off from the then number three ice dancer, Rosalind Druce. She was my roommate for the duration of the trip, and I woke her up after coming in late one evening. I'd only been watching some skating, but it was still after 11pm by the time I got to bed. In the morning Rosalind tore a strip off me. It was like being told off by my mum.

Not long after the Europeans, Michael told me that he'd started to become bored with skating, and that he intended to break up the partnership. He was 18 now and had a good job in Nottingham. He also had a steady girlfriend and wanted, quite naturally, to devote more time to her and to his job. He was so nice about it. We always got along well and had become good friends. For my previous birthday, he'd even bought me a pair of golden skate-shaped earrings; the first present I'd ever received from anyone other than family. I used to wear them at every performance, until I lost one of them about ten years ago. The one remaining earring is safely locked away now.

I admit I was upset by his decision. Also, the break wasn't immediate, which just made it worse. Prolonging the agony.

It was like we were winding the relationship down. We

stopped training as hard and subsequently had a string of bad results. I even had a fall during one of our last British Championships, which wasn't like me at all. What I should have done was just say, 'Right, Michael, I respect your decision. You go off and do your thing and I'll find a new partner,' but I wasn't particularly driven, and I was still only 14. That was also an off-the-ice matter, and all my confidence was reserved for when I was on the ice. I loved skating, but I didn't see it as anything long-term. I was simply doing something I enjoyed. Had I appreciated then that I might be able to continue skating into adulthood, I'd probably have seized control and finished it immediately.

Rather bizarrely, the partnership came to an end when Michael started skating with a new partner in London. So much for spending more time with your girlfriend! Perhaps he needed somebody older than me, somebody closer to his age. It's all academic now, of course, but whatever happened in London didn't affect his relationship with Janet, his girlfriend, as they ended up getting married and moving to Canada. Last I heard he was teaching at an ice rink there.

So, there I was, on my own. It never occurred to me to begin looking for a new partner, so I began skating solo again. I'd got a little behind by that point, but it didn't take me too long to catch up. I was too old to skate in junior championships now – you had to be 14 or under – so I decided to concentrate on the seniors. For this, I would have to take another test. Brilliant! The trouble was, I was never really very strong at compulsory figures, and so failed the test twice. I was down, but I wasn't yet out. My then teacher, Mrs Bowmar, suggested I take ballet lessons, as this might improve my skating. I loved the idea and so, together with another struggling figure skater, signed up.

Our teacher was a lady called Sissy Smith, who had once partnered the great Robert Helpmann, one of the greatest dancers and choreographers of the twentieth century. She must have been about 60 at the time and her husband had just passed away. This meant she was often distracted, and we all felt desperately sorry for her. She seemed to be lost without him.

'Now girls, first position,' she'd say, after which she'd just stare out of the window, eventually coming to when one of us would whisper, 'Excuse me, Miss.' This meant that lessons would often go on way longer than they were supposed to, and I found it difficult to learn much. She was a lovely lady, though.

With skating still just a hobby, and my school career coming to an end, I was forced to start looking for a job. I had no real ambitions at the time, and so decided to apply for a position at Norwich Union, working in the Motors department. My main duties were filing and form-filling.

It was around this time that I first became aware of Chris. I'd seen him around the place, but only as another regular skater, and there were loads of those. Then I became friends with Sandra Elson, Chris's partner, and all that started to change. Sandra was quite fiery and, as Chris has said, could be quick to lose her temper. This meant there were often arguments, and I was always first to hear what Chris had done wrong.

When they eventually broke up, I got the full story from Sandra. Despite their arguments, she and Chris had got along quite well together, and had been successful. As well as some logistical problems, it had just run its natural course. Luckily for me, of course, although I didn't know it at the time. Coincidentally, she also went to London to skate with another partner.

Yet, I wasn't assertive enough to suggest that we might team up. I was also a solo figure skater – albeit a fairly average one – and so was in a different category to Chris. Thanks to Sandra, though, we were now aware that each other existed, and were often in the same place at the same time.

Just before the public session on Thursday nights, they ran a dance club at Nottingham, from 6.50 until 7.30pm. What you did was put your name into a hat, and you were then partnered up with somebody. Three judges would come into the rink, and the couples all danced together. Chris and I were paired twice at dance club, winning our second outing together. Even then, though, there was no inclination to pair up properly. That suggestion would have to come from someone else, an adult.

3
Mentors

JAYNE & CHRIS:

We talk a great deal in this book about the importance of our work ethic; the years of dedication and focus. All true, of course, but what use is dedication and focus if there's nobody there to help you channel it and nurture the results?

Ever since Janet Sawbridge first paired us up back in 1975, we always seem to have met the right people at just the right time – a succession of mentors, masters in their field, all totally dedicated both to us and to our success. Some would say we've been lucky, and indeed we have, but at least one of the people we're about to tell you about used to say to us that the harder you work in life, the luckier you become.

What compels us to pay tribute to these very special people, some of whom you may recognise, is not just the guidance and instruction they imparted; it's the fact that they gave it unconditionally and in the vast majority of cases without payment. Had they not come into our lives when they did, there would be no *Bolero*, no *Dancing on Ice*, no Torvill & Dean even – and certainly no book.

This chapter is for them.

JANET SAWBRIDGE

Janet Sawbridge was our Brian Epstein, if you like; the one who got us together and made it all happen. We'd admired her for years before we actually came into contact with her, as she'd been one of the world's top ice dancers throughout the 1960s, winning a string of medals at the British, European and World Championships. On turning professional in the mid-1970s she'd been offered at job at Nottingham, and so it was a big thing when she arrived – like being taught to play football by Bobby Charlton.

CHRIS:

It was a whole new start for us. I was still skating with my first partner, Sandra, and Janet had been our coach. She used to despair at our clash of personalities. A certain amount of quarrelling is inevitable within any kind of partnership, but Sandra's temper meant she would storm off at the drop of a hat, leaving me alone on the ice. When one cross word results in the loss of an entire training session, something has to give.

'How long is this going to go on, Chris?' Janet used to say. 'If I spent as much time coaching you as I did waiting for you to get over a row you'd be world champions!'

Fortunately – for everyone concerned, I think – Janet wouldn't have to wait long, and just six weeks after we all began working together, Sandra left the partnership and moved to London. The atmosphere improved immediately, as did my ability as a skater – since, without a partner, I was left to skate with Janet.

Although this wasn't a long-term solution, the benefit of practising with a three-time British champion wasn't lost on me, and I very quickly began to get a genuine feel for movement. Janet was also very short – about 5ft, which was a good few inches shorter than Sandra – and she used to bend her knees a lot when skating, which rendered her about 4ft 5in. With me being 5ft 11in, I had to learn to bend much lower very quickly, which must have looked very strange to any onlookers. I didn't know it at the time but this would put me in good stead for when I finally got together with Jayne, who's just over 5ft tall.

Janet was constantly on the lookout for a suitable partner for me; she was like a dog with a bone. This was at a time when we didn't have the mobility that we do now, or the money. There was also no internet or social media. These days people are willing to move country to work with a new partner, but back then if there wasn't a partner in your own rink, that was that. You rarely thought of looking further afield.

JAYNE:

When Janet first approached me about pairing up with Chris I was delighted. I didn't say so at the time, that wasn't in my nature, but inside I was thrilled. My career as a solo figure skater had stalled and was coming to its natural end (I was past it at 15!), and so ice dancing seemed like the most sensible move. I loved music and dance, and was an expert in twirling, remember?

I knew that Chris and Sandra had had quite a turbulent relationship, but I also knew how fiery she could be, so figured it was probably her more than him. Anyway, it was worth giving it a go.

JAYNE & CHRIS:

Something else we mention quite a bit in this book is our shyness and timidity. We used to be famous for it. It's something
we eventually grew out of, of course, but in 1975 it was still
very much part of who we were. Janet could sense this might
be a problem, so when it came to arranging our first practice
session, she suggested the ungodly hour of 6am – a stroke of
genius as it turned out, as had we taken to the ice at 6pm, surrounded by hundreds of skate-clad onlookers, the
embarrassment might well have been too much for us.

So, the following Thursday, at about ten to six in the morning, we both arrived at Nottingham Ice Stadium, Chris on his
moped and Jayne hitching a lift with Janet. Were we nervous?
Absolutely. As well as the impending 'try-out', skating at
Nottingham was like being part of a small village, and even
though the majority of the other residents were asleep at the
time, our new partnership had been the main topic of conversation for days. Neither of us enjoyed or were used to that kind
of attention.

Several minutes later there we were, in the middle of the
rink, staring at the ice, trying our best not to make eye contact.

'Right, you two, I'd like you to stand together in hold, face-
to-face and pelvis-to-pelvis.'

'What?'

'I'd like you to stand in hold,' Janet demonstrated by getting
in hold with Chris, 'then face each other – eye-to-eye and
pelvis-to-pelvis.'

'Oh. OK.' Reluctantly we did as we were asked.

This was yet another stroke of genius on Janet's part;
absolutely pivotal. The 'elephant on the ice' at the time – our
shyness – was in danger of spoiling proceedings, and had to be
dispelled, even partially, if we were ever going to move on. That
30-second embrace prevented months of awkward hesitation

and left us free to get on with forming a partnership. It was where Jayne and Chris started to become Torvill & Dean.

After that we skated around the ice together for a while, throwing in an occasional turn, before going on our way. There'd been no 'Hallelujah' moment – no bells or celestial choirs singing. It had all been fairly workaday, apart from the elongated hold!

That evening, Janet asked us if we'd like to dance together in the interval. This was a kind of public statement, where you'd let the Nottingham skating community know that you were skating together. Thereafter our partnership was common knowledge and our relationship with Janet, and with each other, went from strength to strength.

CHRIS:

Apart from actually pairing us (which was fairly important), the most significant thing Janet taught – or, more accurately, gifted – us was how to be creatively independent.

It's slightly ironic perhaps, but she actually coached us on being less reliant on coaches. She believed there were certain things a coach was responsible for, and certain things a skater was; her reasoning was born more of a desire to watch us progress than a desire to get out of doing something.

Choosing your music, for instance, had always been something left to your coach. Janet would say, 'But I'm a skating coach, not a disc jockey. You're the ones who've got to dance to it, you choose it.'

The first time she asked us to do this we did nothing. We were too nervous.

'Have you got your music then?'

'No, we haven't.'

'OK, tonight's cancelled. Go away, listen to as much music as you can, choose something to dance to, and come back when you've found it.'

We went away thinking, Wow, she's serious. It was like being trusted with your dad's car, but without your mother knowing!

That was our first experience of somebody railing against tradition and granting us some independence – but it would by no means be our last. Once again, this was a significant milestone for us, sparking what has become a lifelong obsession with both music and, as a result, choreography; something we'll talk about later. Had we not been given that responsibility? Well, it's unthinkable.

In Janet's eyes she was there to assist only with the physical aspects of a skater's life. She was a great technician, and that was precisely what we needed at the time. She was also very hands-on. Because she was a terrific skater, she was able to demonstrate technique effectively, take hold of us physically, which helped especially when practising the compulsory dances.

JAYNE & CHRIS:

Not only did Janet give us some independence, she gave us a regime – the all-important work ethic we've been talking about. This first came about when discussing the following week's schedule:

'When are you planning to train next week?'

'Monday, Wednesday and Friday,' we said.

'What's the matter with Tuesday and Thursday?'

'We can only get half an hour on Tuesday and Thursday.'

'So what? Half an hour's better than nothing. There are people in Russia who'll be skating all day, every day.'

'OK, we'll come in Tuesday and Thursday.'

We were still unsure at the time, but during that first 30-minute session we squeezed in more than we normally would in two hours.

Learning how to work and prioritise effectively was vital.

It also meant that we were now training five days a week and that alone gave us a great boost in confidence. We felt far more capable.

This is what we mean when we talk about the significance of having the right people around us at the right time. Had Betty Callaway been coaching us in 1975 instead of Janet, it would never have worked. Betty was far more consultative and traditional in her approach, and from a different generation to Janet and us. She would never have told us how many times a week we had to train. We would be expected to be aware of that already. You might say that we had to 'grow into' Betty. Meet her at a certain level.

All this makes us wonder whether Janet could have taken us all the way. Maybe. She wasn't all that proficient in politicking, something which is, unfortunately, rife in amateur ice skating; she simply hadn't been a coach for long enough. She'd probably have learned, though, and the chances are we'd have carried on progressing. It's all academic, of course, as in 1978, after three trailblazing years together, Janet decided to call it a day.

When she first came on the scene back in 1975 we were everything to her, and we really felt that. She was totally dedicated to us, and we to her. Then she met a man and all of a sudden everything started to change. He had nothing to do with the skating world and seemed, almost from the very beginning, extraordinarily possessive of her. He started going everywhere with Janet and seemed to resent the fact that he had to share her with us. Things really started going downhill when he began turning up to meetings and to practice sessions. It was like having a fourth person in the team. Even when we were sitting down having a chat he'd be there watching Janet's every move.

The fact that Janet was devoting so much time to us obviously irked him and seemed to make him agitated. It was all extremely disconcerting, as well as a little bizarre. It also made us feel very uncomfortable, and as time went on we could feel her slipping away from us; reluctantly, we thought. Then they got married and Janet eventually fell pregnant.

A few weeks later, after the World Championships in Ottawa where we finished 11th, Janet formally told us that she no longer wished to teach any more. In hindsight we should have called time on things long before, but we were extremely naive at the time – not to mention parochial – and refused to face up to the inevitable. We even tried to speak to Janet's new husband, in an attempt to persuade him that we weren't trying to take her away, and that he should allow her to continue. It wasn't a very long or particularly pleasant conversation, and we left after only a few minutes. It was actually a very bad idea.

At first we were absolutely devastated. As well as instilling a work ethic into us and teaching us how to be creatively independent, Janet had given us the belief that we could succeed, be more than just also-rans. Losing her was like losing a close relative. Apart from reading an interview she gave in the early 1980s, we never heard from Janet again. Nonetheless, she was an amazing woman, and dedicated three years of her life to us. For that and for everything else we have mentioned, we'll always be extremely grateful to her.

BETTY CALLAWAY, MBE

CHRIS:

Betty Callaway was the grande dame of ice skating. She commanded respect without ever having to ask for it and had a matriarchal air about her, although she was never demonstrative. Beautifully understated, she took everything in her stride and was always composed. Misbehave around her, though, and you were in trouble! Not that we ever did. We respected her far too much. To us she was like royalty.

We're often asked what it was like working with Betty; what she brought to the party. After all, she's synonymous with us; or us with her. It's an easy question to answer. Betty added finesse to what we'd learned from Janet; she put a shine on it, an elegance to how we behaved both on and off the ice. Working with her was like going to finishing school.

If you have confidence in your coach and you admire them, the chances are you'll probably aspire to be like them in some way. We certainly did with Betty. She came from quite a well-to-do background, sort of upper middle class. She was classy, worldly wise, respected, self-assured; in short, the perfect role model.

That pretty much sums up how we were with Betty. By the time we approached her in 1978 we were more than ready to work with a coach again.

We first came into contact with her at the 1978 European Championships in Strasbourg. It was our first time at the Europeans; a very different experience to the British Championships. We were there as much to learn as we were to compete.

On arriving at the rink we were suddenly surrounded by people we'd only ever seen on TV before. It was a surreal experience and had a definite dream-like quality to it. We just floated around the place, open-mouthed. I remember walking into the banqueting hall where all the meals were served. It was like something out of a *Harry Potter* film. A huge room lined with tables, all piled high with luxurious-looking foods. There were bowls of exotic fruits, a hundred different kinds of meats and enough French bread and croissants to fill a football pitch. Today I can see it for what it was (a well-stocked continental breakfast!) but to two naive youngsters from Nottingham it was like walking into a palace.

The winners that year were the Russian pair, Irina Moiseeva and Andrei Minenkov, ice dancing's equivalent to Fonteyn and Nureyev. Watching them was life-changing for us; we explain why in a later chapter.

JAYNE:

Betty was training the couple who eventually won bronze that year – Krisztina Regoczy and Andras Sallay, the Hungarian title holders and future world champions who we're pleased to say became friends of ours. We knew all about Betty, of course, but never for one moment thought about approaching her for coaching. She was far too busy. Also, if our first meeting was anything to go by, I doubted she'd even agree to speak to us again, let alone coach us.

Not long after we came off the ice (we finished a very respectable ninth that year) I suddenly saw Betty walking towards me. 'Hello,' she said. 'What a nice programme. Well done!' She must have waited for a reply, although she didn't get one. I was so shy at the time, not to mention star-struck (it can happen with coaches too!), that I became completely tongue-tied. I just stood there staring at my skates, probably resembling a traffic light stuck on 'STOP'.

CHRIS:

I'd had a similar experience with Betty just the day before in our hotel. I was in the lift, on my way down to the lobby, when all of a sudden the doors opened and there she was. 'Hello,' she said. 'You're one half of the new couple, aren't you?' I had a really bad cold at the time and like Jayne was probably a bit star-struck. I can't remember exactly what I said but I'm pretty sure it wasn't coherent. Goodness only knows what she must have thought of us both.

JAYNE & CHRIS:

Several weeks later, an ice skating judge named Pam Davies told us that Regoczy and Sallay were about to retire, and that it might be a good idea for us to contact Betty. Oh my goodness, we thought. There's no way she'll agree after what happened at the Europeans.

Fortunately, we couldn't have been more wrong, and when we eventually plucked up the courage to ask Betty, she said yes straight away; after which we apologised for our behaviour.

'Oh, don't worry about that, my dears. I could see you were both shy. We'll need to work on that.'

We were in very good hands.

Although never a successful amateur skater, Betty Callaway's life so far had been an eventful one. Convent educated, she'd left home at just 16 to join the Blackpool Pleasure Beach Ice Show. According to Betty, her parents hit the roof, and it was a long time before they'd speak to her again.

A few years later she married Roy Callaway, who was the principal skater at Blackpool. Having had enough of the Northwest, they eventually decided to venture south, each landing a teaching role at Richmond Ice Rink, where they stayed for almost 20 years. Apparently, Betty coached royalty there, something she mentioned quite nonchalantly one day: 'A year with Prince Charles and three with Princess Anne, my dears.' What perfect casting! We were very impressed.

Ironically, Betty's first success as an amateur coach had been with Yvonne Suddick and Roger Kennerson (twice runners-up in the British Championships), whose main rivals at the time had been Janet Sawbridge and her partner, David Hickinbottom. Was that a good omen? We weren't sure.

A few years later Betty began coaching the West German team. At that time, not one German skater had ever even come close to winning an international championship. Within a year or so that all changed when, under Betty's tutelage, Erich and Angelika Buck – a brother and sister team – won the 1972 European Championships.

When Betty eventually began working with us she was one of the most respected coaches in the world, so our experience had to be more in line with hers. She was a woman of few words, and it was often what she didn't say that made most sense; something we'd never have understood as teenagers.

We had some amazing times with Betty over the years and achieved probably more than any of us thought possible. From 1979 to 1984 we won most competitions we entered: six British Championships, three European Championships, four World Championships, and, of course, the 1984 Olympics. Whatever competition it was, however, Betty's ritual would be exactly the same. Just before we went on the ice she would pat us on the shoulder and say, 'Skate well.' Then, as we came off, she would always say, 'Well done, dears.' It didn't matter how big the trophy or how shiny the medals, that was it. Such a wonderfully understated lady.

JAYNE:

We once became quite well known for doing everything we possibly could to avoid hearing other people's scores. We always saw it as a distraction. After taking this to ridiculous lengths at the European Championships one year – me banging about in my dressing room and Chris sitting down with his fingers in his ears going 'Lalala' (people thought we were mad!) – we actually missed the final marks, and so had absolutely no idea where we'd been placed. We didn't like to ask anybody (far too British for that) and when Betty walked in a few minutes later she just said, 'OK, onwards and upwards, my dear.' She didn't say it in any particular *way* – there was no clue in her tone of voice – which meant I was still none the wiser as to where we'd finished. Then Chris walked in and looked at me expectantly. I just shrugged as if to say, 'Don't know.'

So there we both were, perched on the sofa watching Betty go about her business, desperately looking for some kind of sign. 'She's not giving anything away,' I whispered to Chris. 'Why don't you ask her?'

'I'm not asking her,' he said. 'Why don't you?'

But before either of us could ask Betty what the result was one of the journalists walked in.

'Congratulations, you two,' he said.

'What for?' we enquired hopefully.

Suddenly Betty spun round.

'You mean you don't know?'

'Know what?'

'You won!'

We jumped up off the sofa. 'Whaaaat! Really?'

'Yes, of course. I was wondering why you were both looking so pensive.'

To say Betty Callaway was understated is perhaps understating it a bit. I'm very glad we never played her at cards.

JAYNE & CHRIS:

Although our relationship changed after we became professional, we always stayed in touch with Betty, and when we approached her about joining us again for Lillehammer it was a happy reunion. The dynamic had changed somewhat – her role being a bit more 'advisory' this time around – but it was still the old team. She was like your favourite aunt, somebody you always looked forward to seeing. When we heard she'd died in July 2011 it felt like the end of an era; not just to us, but to everybody associated with ice skating. She was a wonderful, wonderful lady. We miss her.

COURTNEY JONES & BOBBY THOMPSON

Two people who have also been with us for a very long time – and are, we're pleased to say, still very much part of our lives – are Mr Courtney Jones and Mr Bobby Thompson.

Trying to categorise their mentorship is difficult because it's been so far-reaching. They designed costumes for us; chose music with us; advised us on performance, politics and people. But this has all been underpinned by companionship and friendship, the like of which we'd never experienced before – except perhaps with each other.

Although we already knew Courtney and Bobby to say hello to, we were first introduced to them formally back in 1978, shortly after teaming up with Betty. As well as performance, she was keen for us to improve our presentation at the time (such as it was) and had suggested a meeting with Courtney.

A four-time world ice dancing champion, Courtney was also a costume designer of some repute. He and Bobby – who, like Betty, was an extremely well-respected coach, mentoring the great John Curry, among others – had been partners for many years and lived in a flat in Bayswater. Our first meeting there was an auspicious occasion that will be etched on our memories for all time.

JAYNE:

We set off in my Mini in the morning and arrived around eleven. The flat itself was amazing, like nothing we'd ever seen before. Colour coordination, interior design, original paintings. Until then, sophistication had been something you tried to achieve on the ice. We had no idea you could do it indoors too. Both Courtney and Bobby were charm personified, and they made us feel completely at home.

JAYNE & CHRIS:

Although we were there to talk costumes, the conversation inevitably widened after a while. Hardly surprising given the wealth of experience we had sitting in front of us. Courtney and Bobby had an all-round vision of skating; we had lots of questions!

It ended up being more of an awakening than a meeting; an epiphany, even. Courtney was also a well-respected judge, not to mention president of the National Skating Association. You couldn't buy this kind of knowledge, so the fact that both were prepared to share it with us was a real thrill.

Eventually getting back to the subject, Courtney suggested two people who would be able to produce his designs for us: a Mr Bishop, based in Marlow, would make Chris's costumes; and a Mrs Parrish, based in Twickenham, would make Jayne's.

CHRIS:

They were both eccentrics. Mr Bishop lived in this huge old rectory which was packed to the rafters with what could only be described as bric-a-brac; there were old bottles of sherry and 78rpm records everywhere. It was like a twentieth-century version of *The Old Curiosity Shop*.

He was also obsessed with gussets. 'There's nothing quite as horrible as a baggy gusset, my boy – except perhaps a tight one that splits!' Sage advice.

JAYNE:

The thing I remember most about Mrs Parrish (apart from her being a wonderful dressmaker) was her talent for talking. She was absolutely world-class and would keep you there for hours if you let her. We used to travel down from Nottingham in a day: setting off at six, we'd pick up the designs from Courtney first, then go straight to Soho for the material, before going on to Mr Bishop's first and then to Mrs Parrish. It was always Mrs Parrish last, and as she started to talk you could feel your life slipping away from you. I'd be thinking to myself, If we set off now we might get back by eleven. Then it would be twelve, and so on. In the end I used to say, 'Sorry, Mrs Parrish, we have to get back home!' But she would still carry on talking. I could have been invisible. Once, she actually failed to finish a dress (her eyesight became poor at night) and asked me if I could pop back for it first thing ...

JAYNE & CHRIS:

Although Courtney designed every one of our costumes since 1981, including those for *Mack & Mabel*, *Barnum*, *Paso Doble* and *Face the Music*, the most famous costumes he ever created for us were those we wore for *Bolero* – a design, in our minds, of absolute genius and as memorable as the performance itself.

The reason we use the word genius isn't just because of their aesthetic qualities, although that alone would put them pretty close. It's the fact that they were designed with the music and the choreography in mind – a concept we hadn't appreciated until we met Courtney and Bobby. But instead of these costumes simply 'complementing' the routine, they actually enhanced it, such was the almost forensic knowledge and appreciation of the designer. The only input we had was colour, which we chose because of Chris's admiration for the iris.

JAYNE:

Like the dance itself, the costumes were a work in progress. They didn't just happen overnight. In fact, it was weeks before Courtney was happy with everything. He initially designed my costume with a slightly longer skirt so that he could see how it would move on the ice, but because it was made of pure silk chiffon it wasn't allowed to touch the ice. If it had, it would have become a mess. So what Courtney asked us to do was to run through the routine very slowly, while he followed on behind with a huge pair of shears. Then, each time the skirt touched the ice, he'd cut a bit off. That's why the hem of the dress is so uneven. It produced an excellent effect, though, even if it was accidental.

JAYNE & CHRIS:

Courtney and Bobby's influence pops up throughout this book, and by the end you'll probably appreciate exactly why we hold them both in such high esteem. But there is one piece of advice they gave us that stands out from all the others. It became the 'clincher' between us and our audiences – eye contact. Courtney summed up the conversation perfectly.

'Ice dancers never make eye contact with each other because they're too busy skating. The moment you get over that and begin to engage with one another, the mood changes. A reality takes hold; something which transcends technique. Then and only then will the audience become totally yours.'

That conversation took place in 1981 while we were rehearsing *Mack & Mabel* and *Summertime*, our original set pattern (OSP) for that season. Take away eye contact from either dance and you take away its heart.

Courtney and Bobby once told us we were like the children they never had, and that's exactly how they've always treated us – as their own. They always wanted to start a family, but were born in the wrong era; more's the pity, as they would undoubtedly have made marvellous parents. Had they been young people today, of course, things would probably be different.

It is such a touching sentiment, though. They're both extremely special to us.

GRAEME MURPHY & ANDRIS TOPPE

The nervousness we'd both felt standing on the ice that cool May morning in 1975 was nothing to how we felt when we turned professional nine years later, which really drives home the importance of having somebody you trust standing alongside you; the reassurance that if something goes wrong you won't be on your own.

Suddenly, though, all that was gone, and for the first time in nine years we were on our own, without a mentor at a time when we needed one most. Betty, Courtney and Bobby were still friends, of course, but we'd now left their world, flown the nest, if you like, and were no longer able to turn to them for support. Despite being professionals, we still thought and acted as amateurs, which would have to change very, very quickly if we were going to survive and progress.

Our first offer after turning pro came from an Australian impresario named Michael Edgley. He wanted us to go to Australia and perform in a number of shows for him. He must have been serious because he sent one of his directors over to meet us, which we found difficult to fathom at the time. 'This man's flying all the way over from Australia, just to meet us? That's absolute madness.'

The offer was a two-week engagement in Sydney comprising 12 shows with the Russian Olympic team. Michael Edgley had been sure that a Russian couple would take gold in 1984, so when we won instead it kind of messed things up a bit. According to Andrew, the chap he sent over to meet us, when Michael found out that an English couple had won he went ballistic. 'Get that bloody Pommie couple booked!' was his response.

After being in Australia for a week or so we were invited by our company manager to attend a ballet that was being staged at a cabaret club called Kinsella's. It was called *Seven Deadly Sins* and the troupe responsible for putting it on was called the Sydney Dance Company (SDC). We both loved ballet but this was like nothing we'd ever seen before, very avant-garde. Whereas classical ballet can be quite formal, this was the absolute polar opposite. What we saw really opened our eyes. It was passionate and beautifully danced, but above all had an infectious sense of freedom and humour to it – something which was almost palpable. We were used to having to perform things in a certain way, or in a certain time. This complete freedom of expression was ground-breaking! .

You could say that amateur skating is a bit like classical ballet, in that it is a discipline and is therefore bound by certain rules and traditions. Professional skating, on the other hand, is more akin to contemporary ballet; the only rule being that there are no rules. It's entirely up to you.

That performance was to transform our lives, and when the ballet finished we were taken backstage to meet the choreographer of the piece, who was also the company's artistic director, a man called Graeme Murphy. We were a little nervous about this, as we always assumed that 'ballet types' would be aloof and probably quite snobbish. Well, we certainly got that one wrong! Graeme was vibrant, humorous and extremely laid-back, which just goes to show that you should never pre-judge people.

CHRIS:

It turned out that Graeme had been dying to meet us ever since he'd heard we were in town. He had seen *Bolero* and said he appreciated its 'complete movement', using one piece of music that didn't present itself like something that had been created following a rule book (even though it had), the emphasis falling more on the *artistic* elements than the *ritualistic*. He completely understood what we were trying to achieve, which was to turn ice dancing into an art form. That's how we'd always looked at it.

Our one big ambition on turning professional was to put on our own show: our own choreography, our own dancers, the works. Something huge! It was actually more of a dream than an ambition, as at the time we had absolutely no idea whether it would ever be possible. We'd run the idea past Michael Linnitt, who had become our agent when we turned pro, and he was looking into it for us, but I think he was probably humouring us a bit.

After a couple of weeks we asked Graeme if he might be interested in working with us at some point. His influence must already have been rubbing off on us, as under normal circum-stances we'd never have dared ask such a question. We had to fly over to Oberstdorf in a few weeks to prepare for the World Professional Championships. Maybe he could work with us on a routine?

'Sure. I'll be over in Europe then. How about the week of the ...'

'Hang on. One week? We can't possibly choreograph an entire number in just a week. It's impossible.'

'That's all I've got, I'm afraid.'

'Oh, OK.'

We were disappointed but still asked if he'd come along. After all, who knows what we might pick up?

I remember that first session with Graeme as if it were yesterday. Talk about a eureka moment. Although we were now professional skaters, our creativity was still being stifled by the amateur rule book. This had been our bible for almost 15 years; our every thought, word and deed dedicated to doing its bid-ding, and as a consequence we were lacking a sense of freedom.

We'd been conditioned for so long and were now led as much by compliance as we were by creativity.

Fortunately Graeme had no such baggage. He saw the ice merely as a platform, a platform on which we could and should express ourselves – nothing more, nothing less. He'd been classically trained, but rather than live by what he'd learned he simply used it as a tool, together with dozens of other elements. This was the antithesis of what we had experienced previously. Amateur ice dancing is a sport that incorporates dance. Take away the 'amateur' and you're left with ice dancing, which, regardless of surface, is the embodiment of freedom and expression. Suddenly we viewed the ice in a totally different way, almost like seeing it for the very first time.

But the speed with which Graeme worked was astonishing, and within five days we had devised and choreographed an entire routine, something we'd genuinely considered to be impossible.

On the morning of the sixth day, Graeme said: 'OK guys, let's see the routine.'

Now, devising and choreographing a routine is one thing, but perfecting the performance on the ice is quite another.

'We can't. We're nowhere near ready.'

'Of course you are! Come on, off you go.'

'The whole thing?'

'Just as a mark through. Come on, you can do it!'

We were used to building things up a few steps at a time. We couldn't possibly perform the whole routine yet.

'But we'll make mistakes.'

'Of course you'll make mistakes. How are you going to learn if you don't make mistakes? I want to get an overall feel for it. Come on, give it a go.'

We did as we were told – and did indeed make mistakes. We got through it, however, from beginning to end, which meant we'd designed, choreographed *and* skated a four-and-a-half-minute routine in under one week. This method saved us months of time and our producers many thousands of pounds. Nothing would ever be the same again.

When we eventually did get to put on our own show – which turned into our first world tour – we approached Graeme to do the choreography. We had no experience of choreographing for large groups, so his expertise proved vital.

Off the ice, Graeme's influence on us was equally dramatic. He's quite an off-the-wall character, outrageous in everything he does, from the way he dresses to the way he choreographs, but he also has a wicked sense of humour and made us laugh like drains. We were very serious back then and still quite shy. Graeme could poke fun at himself, which was something we weren't used to.

JAYNE & CHRIS:

Graeme's assistant at this time was Andris Toppe, who was also the company's ballet master. Andris had danced with Graeme at the Australian Ballet Company and when Graeme had been appointed artistic director of the SDC, he had invited Andris to join him there.

When Graeme was choreographing our first world tour he drafted Andris in as rehearsal director. But when Graeme went back to Australia after that, Andris stayed with us for the next 13 years! He became indispensable and although we'd choreograph the majority of pieces he was like our third eye. Like Betty, he helped us refine what we were doing and that was invaluable. In that respect he was like a coach, but Andris became much more than that. He was our coach, friend, confidant and mentor. But, if anything, he mentored us through his knowledge as much as his instruction. He seemed to know so much about music. He went to see plays, musicals and ballets almost every day of the week. He lived, ate and breathed culture, but especially dance. This meant he could call on examples he'd seen at the drop of a hat and was always able to either explain or demonstrate them clearly. He also seemed to know which ballets or shows we might benefit from seeing for ourselves. It was like working with some kind of walking interactive reference library!

Another gift of his was timing. He could always sense the mood very accurately and knew exactly when he needed to back off and just let us sort ourselves out. He also has a great sense of humour but again knew when and when not to make light of things. He always knew exactly when to say something that would lighten the atmosphere if one of us was becoming frustrated, bringing us back down to earth a bit and helping us regain some perspective.

JAYNE:

Andris is a very good-looking man – quite striking. Although he's gay, he's often mistaken for being heterosexual.

I remember we were rehearsing in Russia once, and one evening he heard a knock on his hotel door. When he opened it a woman was standing there wearing a big fur coat and probably nothing underneath. She walked right up to him, held up an unlit cigarette and said, 'You have fire?' Apparently the hotel was full of 'ladies of the night' and if they saw anyone they thought might be a potential customer, they'd follow them up, make a note of their room number and wait for their time to pounce! I think it scared him to bits.

Andris also has an infectious lust for life. He seems to love every day. Being around somebody like that can create a really positive atmosphere. It's good for mind, body and spirit.

CHRIS:

I remember when we were doing our first world tour. After about six months things started to become a little bit monotonous. We were performing the same show every night, day after day; sometimes in the same venue for weeks on end.

Sensing we were becoming a little bored Andris began play-ing a game with us. It started during the run at Wembley, I think, where we were performing for six straight weeks. He came in before a show one evening: 'Guess who's in tonight?' he said.

'Go on, who?'

'Joan Collins!'

'Really? Are you sure?'

'Yes, I've just seen her arrive.'

So we'd go out there, and all the time we'd be looking for Joan Collins. It certainly spiced things up a bit. Then a couple of nights later he'd say, 'Guess what, Mel Gibson's in tonight', and we'd say, 'Wow, is he really?', and so the whole thing would start again.

After a few weeks of star-spotting we realised that some of the people he'd said were in, weren't, but we never knew which ones. This went on for the entire tour. Every night we'd be look-ing for a Bruce Willis or a Shirley Bassey, not knowing if they were actually there. I should ask him for a list of the genuine ones. Princess Margaret definitely did turn up, because we saw her afterwards. I'm not sure about Mel Gibson though . . .

Andris is back in Australia now, so unfortunately we don't see him very often. We do keep in touch by email, though. He's unique.

JAYNE:

One of the most eye-opening things we encountered because of Graeme Murphy was nudity. Despite all the travel and competitions, we'd led extraordinarily sheltered lives until then. Neither of us had been in a serious relationship and we certainly hadn't seen anybody naked before. Then, after being invited to a show in which Graeme was performing one evening, that all changed.

We were waiting for him in his dressing room after the show and, within a few minutes, in he came. But rather than just sitting down and having a chat, he started to get changed right there in front of us. There he was, chatting away merrily, quickly coming apart from his clothes! Just imagine it, Torvill & Dean, sitting on a sofa, in Sydney, with a naked Australian standing in front of them.

We soon realised that this was the norm in Graeme and Andris' contemporary ballet world, with the dancers sharing just one dressing room. They even showered together! Inhibitions didn't exist with this company of dancers. Once again this was the opposite of what we'd been used to. Everything about our lives and personalities had oozed modesty, but this was all starting to change.

It's a good job it was, because when we eventually set off on our first world tour we only usually had one dressing room, so there'd be boobs and bums everywhere. It was quite liberating!

JAYNE & CHRIS:

We grew up immeasurably during our time with Graeme and Andris. We went to Australia as kids (albeit fairly old ones) and came back as adults, with more mature and liberal attitudes. Until then we'd been living in a bubble, a life made up of practice and competition – nothing else. They brought us out of our shells, put smiles on our faces and opened up our eyes to the outside world – three wonderful gifts. We're grateful for all of them.

4

Learning How to Win

JAYNE & CHRIS:

If we were to write chapter and verse about every win we'd ever had, what music we'd used and how we chose the costumes, it would probably bore you silly. It's all there on Wikipedia, though.

What we believe you might find interesting is how we actually went from being just competitors to potential champions – something that certainly didn't happen overnight – as well as the stories behind some of our more memorable but perhaps lesser known triumphs.

Winning is both motivating and addictive. It becomes all-consuming. Once you get your first taste of success it pulls you in, like a huge magnet; and before you know it, it's taken over your entire life. But that's precisely what every sportsperson in the world strives for. You have to dedicate yourself to a sport if you want to be the best.

Even more demanding than *becoming* a champion is *remaining* a champion. When you're at the top there's only one place you can go, and that's down. We were always very conscious of that. You have to keep moving forward if you're going to keep ahead of the pack.

Although Janet Sawbridge made us believe we stood a chance, Betty Callaway was the person who taught us how to win. Prior to that it had all been about preparation – about learning our craft and getting ourselves into a position where we might be able to mount a challenge. When we first started training with Betty we were what you might call 'young pretenders'.

We knew how to skate and we even had a feeling for choreography. We were also well organised, motivated, had a good work ethic and knew the rule book inside out. But in most cases that still won't get you a win, especially if your rivals are more experienced than you. The magic ingredient that shifts you from being 'in the game' to top middle of the medal rostrum is confidence – the way you think about what you do and who you are. Once you're able to achieve that mindset and maintain it, you can take yourselves to the next level.

But just like skating itself, self-belief is not something that will necessarily come to you straight away. Some people are born with it – or the makings of it – but the vast majority aren't. The Russians were undoubtedly the masters. They all had it driven into them from an early age. Over there, attitude was taught *alongside* skating so they always appreciated its importance. They knew that it was an essential part of becoming a champion. This gave them a head-start of about ten years on the rest of us, especially if you also take into account the infrastructure they had in place. And did it pay dividends, as for years they turned out world-class skater after world-class skater.

When it came to the two of us, it's probably fair to say that Jayne had to work harder on attaining the right competitive attitude. Having said that, neither of us would naturally expect to win. We both needed guidance. One of the first things Betty did was make us believe that we were equal to the competition.

Until then we'd always looked at our fellow competitors almost as heroes, especially the Russians. She said we had to convert that sense of awe into nothing more than respect. 'Don't ever think you can't beat them. You're easily as good as they are.' She was right, but it took us quite some time before we actually started believing it. We had to develop a winning mentality.

The other lesson Betty taught us was how not to become complacent. She used to say, 'You might have won this time, but don't assume that you'll win the next. You never know what or who is around the corner. You always need to be humble, but act like a champion and maintain your inner confidence.'

This became our mantra, and it pushed us on to becoming ever more daring and creative. We could only ever be as good as our last routines, and so we had to keep on reinventing ourselves year after year. It was a snowball effect: in order to win we needed to have the best routine, and in order to have the best routine we needed to have new music and choreography. Then, if you also have the right people behind you, which we obviously did, you stand a very good chance of coming first. It was like building links on a chain and each one had to be as strong as the last.

JAYNE:

I remember in the late 1970s when the Russians completely dominated the sport. Some of their couples, if they'd had success with a routine the year before, would dance the same thing again the following year. Their mantra must have been something like: If it isn't broken, why fix it? But to us that was just being lazy. As Betty reminded us, you never knew who was waiting in the wings, and, as far as the Russians were concerned, that was us.

By performing the same routine and not trying to improve,

you're assuming that nobody else has improved, and that can be dangerous. We learned from things like this, and while we weren't necessarily always looking over our shoulders (we were too busy looking forward) it taught us the dangers of resting on your laurels.

Being creative also helps to keep things fresh, and if you introduce it into your daily routine it also helps stave off boredom. If all your days consist of nothing but practising, eating and sleeping, you're far more likely to lose interest, especially if you're doing it for months on end. So having the responsibility of choosing a new piece of music, or working on some new costumes or choreography, makes for a more stimulating existence, which means you're far more likely to remain committed.

There was a second catalyst for us with regard to becoming winners, and that was making the decision to skate full-time.

CHRIS:

That would happen after our first Olympic appearance back in 1980, but in order to be eligible to take part in any kind of major championships – the British included – we first had to complete a series of tests called the Inter Golds.

Getting through the Inter Golds was anything but a formality. How it works is that the skaters perform as a couple twice, but are assessed individually, as opposed to collectively – one during the first dance, and the other during the second. We were dancing the rumba and after the first dance I was told I'd failed. Then after the second dance Jayne was told she'd passed. We had to wait a month until we could take the test again, so for a while we were on the brink of being no more. It was an awful time. Fortunately, after a ridiculous amount of hard work, I passed the test and so we were free to progress.

I was still a policeman and, although I was sure I wanted to skate full-time, I still didn't see it as a career. I'd been taught that once you had a job that was what you did for life. Breaking free of that notion – and in effect giving up my vocation – was hard to come to terms with, especially as I couldn't yet reconcile the alternative with earning a living.

Until then my life had been lived to a strict schedule, and it only ever deviated when Jayne and I went away to compete. It had always been like that. First I had school, then the police cadets and now the police. I had a regular income, good friends and a bright future. Everything was in its place and I was happy. I like order in my life!

Up to that point we'd already had a certain amount of success on the ice, but that all changed in 1978 when we first won the British Championships. We were the number three couple at the time, and so weren't expected to win. Then, the number one couple, Warren Maxwell and Janet Thompson, had to drop out through injury, which meant we'd have a much better chance. And we took that chance, but because it was the number three couple who had won, the coverage from the press was more local than national. We were British champions yet only received coverage in the Nottingham area. Our status there improved immeasurably, but wider recognition would have to come gradually. We felt like champions, and that was the main thing. Even with Warren and Janet dropping out, it still didn't feel hollow at all. We were aware of all the British champions who had gone on to become European and world champions, so that victory just motivated us to improve. The following year things moved up a gear yet again: as well as winning the British Championships, we achieved our first score of six. That was an altogether different feeling to winning a medal. It was another huge confidence boost.

As current British champions we were then chosen to compete at the 1980 Winter Olympics at Lake Placid. At the time we just couldn't see how it could get any better. I remember putting on the team uniform for the first time and looking at myself in the mirror. It was a tremendous feeling.

Despite being under the radar at these Olympics we finished fifth, which made us ask the question: 'What might have we achieved had we been training full-time?' Finishing so close to a medal position had given us a taste for it, and we now wanted another Olympics. We knew of at least two couples who'd be retiring after Lake Placid, which meant we could well be in with a chance of a medal next time around. We came away with so much confidence and it made us realise that perhaps the only thing now separating us from an Olympic medal was our jobs.

When we arrived home, I made an appointment to see the Chief Constable of Nottinghamshire, Mr Charles McLachlan. I told him of my dilemma; that I wasn't sure what to do and was apprehensive about throwing everything away for something that could end at the drop of a hat. I also made clear my appreciation of how I'd been treated by the force, all the encouragement I'd received. In the end, though, I had to make a decision.

Fortunately, Mr McLachlan made things a lot easier for me. 'If I were you, Mr Dean, I'd seize the moment and skate. You're already a champion. Think what you might be in a few years' time. If it doesn't work out, you can always become a policeman again.'

What a relief! The support I'd received from the police thus far had been almost unconditional, but this was above and beyond. My dilemma was no more, and I was able to concetrate on skating one hundred per cent. Yet there was one problem. Although Jayne and I had some savings, it was only enough to get us through to the next European Championships. After that we'd have nothing, and with no money coming in, we wouldn't be able to live, let alone skate. I was potentially back to square one.

JAYNE:

The decision was a lot easier for me, both professionally and personally. I was still living with my parents, so didn't have to worry about where I was going to live, or even about bills and things. I paid rent, of course, but was still spared quite a bit of domestic responsibility.

For Chris, joining the police had been an ambition, a vocation. He'd been a part of it all since he was 15 and had a future mapped out. My job at the Norwich Union was a very different proposition. As much as I liked the people, I was there because I had to have a job. Handing in my notice was more a formality than a decision.

My final pay packet was minuscule. Because I'd borrowed so many hours over the years (which you had to pay back, of course), I was, shall we say, in the red when I handed in my notice. In the end I just left, owing about 20 hours. My mind had been elsewhere for months and I wanted to concentrate on the future.

Not long after leaving I too cottoned on to what lay ahead for us both. I had some savings, but pretty soon they'd run out. If we weren't going to make fools of ourselves and end up with nothing, we'd have to act fast.

JAYNE & CHRIS:

First stop was the DHSS. According to some skaters we knew, you could get some money if you signed on, and so off we went. The conversation that ensued was, in hindsight, quite amusing, but at the time it was anything but:

'We'd like to sign on, please.'

'All right then. First of all, what sort of jobs will you be looking for?'

'Oh, we won't be looking for jobs.'

'Pardon?'

'We're skaters. We want to skate full-time. We just need some money.'

The look on the woman's face was one of pure amazement.

'I'm sorry, but if you're not looking for work, I can't process your application.'

We couldn't lie and abuse the system. That just wasn't us. And, besides, Chris had just left the police! We'd have to think again.

Somebody suggested looking for sponsorship, so we sent off some letters to local businesses. We had a few interested parties, but once we'd explained to them that we wouldn't be allowed to carry advertising or mention them by name, they soon went off the idea.

In the end, Jayne's mother suggested we get in touch with Nottinghamshire City Council. She'd pleaded our case to a councillor who was a customer of theirs at their newsagent's, and they had suggested we write a letter. It was worth a try. So, we spent a whole day composing a letter, explaining our situation. It went something like this:

Dear Mr Carroll,

I don't know whether you have seen my partner, Christopher Dean, and I on television recently, but if you did, you will no doubt have heard that we have given up our jobs to concentrate entirely on our skating careers. Our aim is to 'Go for Gold'!

It was all pretty innocent, but definitely heartfelt. Anyway, we eventually received a response and were asked to submit a business plan, listing everything we thought we'd need to get by, including anything from travel expenses to rent. After totting it all up, we came to a figure of about £7,000 a year, each, which included renting a flat for Chris. We had absolutely no idea whether they'd take our request seriously and so had no expectation.

After about six months we'd heard nothing back, so assumed that the application had been rejected. Then, one day, while we were training, we received a call at the rink from BBC Radio Nottingham. We weren't used to anyone calling us there so at first we were slightly alarmed.

'Hello, can we help?'

'This is BBC Radio Nottingham. We wondered if you'd like to comment on the grant you've just been awarded?'

'Sorry, what grant is this?'

'The application you made to Nottinghamshire City Council – you've won a grant for forty-two thousand pounds.'

'FORTY-TWO THOUSAND POUNDS?! Are you sure? We haven't heard anything.'

'That's what we've been told by the council.'

'Really? Wow! Would you mind if we got back to you once we've spoken to them? Thanks!'

We hung up and immediately rang the council to ask if it was true.

'Yes. You'll be receiving full details by post in the next few days,' came the reply.

Apparently the council had put by a pot of money to fund some local athletes at the 1980 Moscow Olympics, but because of the boycott – which resulted in Great Britain sending a much smaller contingent – the athletes had all stayed at home, so the money was just sitting there.

This was an absolute life-saver for us: £7,000 each for the next three years, which would take us right up to the 1984 Olympics. If we were careful it should just be enough.

Our two key goals at the time were freedom from full-time employment and financial security, but they had to come as a pair. Having just one was no use whatsoever if we wanted to challenge for the Olympics. From then on there'd be no more obstacles, just challenges.

JAYNE:

Our first real challenge, competition-wise, came about a few years before, back in 1976 when we had to travel to Oberstdorf, in Germany, for our first ever international competition. What made it really daunting was the fact that we had to travel alone and unsupervised. Janet couldn't come, and our parents had to work, so it would just be us. We didn't mind, however; Chris had been to Czechoslovakia before and we both knew at least three words of German. What could possibly go wrong? It would be a real adventure.

So one morning, carrying three bags each full of skates, clothes and our fancy matching zip-up cardigans which Chris's stepmum had knitted for us, we jumped into my dad's car and made our way to Heathrow.

Oberstdorf is near the Austrian border, not far from Munich, but for some unknown reason our plane tickets – which had been provided by the National Skating Association – were taking us to Zurich, which was another two or three hours by train.

When we arrived in Zurich at about 11pm, the entire airport seemed to be empty. There were no taxis, nobody manning the information desk – the whole place was deserted. In the end we managed to catch a bus from the airport to the train station. We might not get any sleep, but at least we'd be able to catch the first train to Oberstdorf in the morning.

So, at around seven, after managing to grab no more than an hour's sleep, we bought our tickets to Oberstdorf. 'Change at Immenstadt,' we were told, so we piled our bags on to what we thought was the right train and tried to relax. It was the right train but, according to the guard, we were in the wrong section. It was scheduled to divide part-way through the journey so we'd have to move. So up we stood, picked up our bags and made our way through the train, probably inflicting minor injuries on several fellow passengers as we did so.

Immenstadt, we'd been told, was just a small station and would be one of many. Nod off for a moment and you might miss it. Nod off was all we wanted to do at the time, but we managed to keep ourselves awake somehow and when Immenstadt came into view, we got ready to disembark. After yet another round of standing up, sitting down and bashing fellow travellers with our bags, we eventually arrived in Oberstdorf, where we were greeted at the station by the organisers.

Situated on the edge of the Alps, and flanked by mountains, Oberstdorf is one of the most beautiful places you could ever visit. Not that we were aware of this at the time, because as soon as we arrived we were whisked straight off to our accommodation. Sightseeing would have to wait.

The accommodation – an out-of-term boarding school called an *Internat* – was basic and *almost* comfortable; and, by the time we arrived, absolutely full of skaters.

We didn't know anyone, other than one or two of our fellow Brits, but they weren't what you'd call close friends, just acquaintances really. This meant we were pretty isolated. We also had very little money with us, but had worked out a daily budget. As long as we stuck to that and had no surprise expenses we should be able to make it through the week. Fortunately, breakfast turned out to be included at the *Internat*, and so each morning we stuffed ourselves silly on things like pâté, ham and boiled eggs. It wasn't exactly ideal, taking to the ice on a full stomach, but it was the only way we could skip lunch and ensure that we'd have enough money to buy an evening meal. Being short on finances and occasionally hungry are probably the two dominant memories of our first visit to Oberstdorf – apart from the result itself, that is.

From a skating point of view we were organised and ready for what was to come, but other than that we definitely felt like outsiders. We were inexperienced, and there without a coach, so we tended to keep ourselves to ourselves. Better that than commit a faux pas of some kind, which could happen occasionally.

We had our practice times, when we'd run through our numbers, but when not on the ice we either sat in the stands watching the other couples or wandered around Oberstdorf, trying not to look inside all the fabulous bakeries.

We couldn't have been any more low-key. We also had no expectations about where we might finish in the competition, which meant that when we ended up in second place nobody was more surprised than we were. There must have been people asking, 'Torvill and who?'

The reaction to our coming second was subsequently quite subdued, just one or two pats on the back. We didn't have anyone with us, no family or coach, so had nobody to share in our elation but it kept us grounded.

When we arrived in St Gervais, which was the venue of our next competition, Chris discovered that he'd be sharing a room with Robin Cousins, who was already ice skating royalty to us. He explained that Oberstdorf was like a dress rehearsal for St Gervais, and predicted that we'd do quite well here. He was right, as we ended up doing very well; better than anybody could have predicted – especially us.

After the compulsories and the OSP we were in the lead, but only just. It would all be down to the free dance, which was due to take place the next day. Back at the hotel later that evening, there was a knock at the door. It was Chris.

'Jayne, I think I've got food poisoning. I've been sick about ten times.'

'OK, drink plenty of water and go to bed. Hopefully you'll feel better in the morning.'

He didn't. In fact, all through the next day he carried on being sick, although not quite as often. Goodness knows how (maybe it was adrenaline), but Chris managed to keep his stomach under control long enough for us to complete our free dance – and we won! Our first ever international victory.

CHRIS:

We should have felt absolutely elated, but the moment I got off the ice I started to feel sick again. I went straight back to the locker room and flaked out on a bench. Eventually one of the officials sent for an ambulance.

JAYNE:

I wanted to go with him but the official said I couldn't. 'Somebody has to go to the podium, the ceremony is about to start!' So off I went. The photographers all looked very confused when they saw me standing there on my own. I'd also changed out of my costume, thinking I'd be accompanying Chris to the hospital, so it must have looked very strange: two couples, left and right, in skates and costumes; and then me, top middle, on my own, wearing a skirt and blouse!

CHRIS:

While all this was going on I was arriving at the hospital, still sporting my navy blue cat suit with its silver lame collar! It was a horrible night and the doctor spoke no English, which made trying to explain my symptoms almost comical. I kept pretending to be sick (which I almost was again, several times) and eventually he got it. The next day when Jayne came to collect me, I realised I hadn't brought a change of clothes, which meant I had to travel all the way back in my cat suit. Some of the looks I received!

JAYNE & CHRIS:

What an adventure it had been. There may have been one or two mishaps along the way, but at least we'd come through them all. What's more, we'd won! We'd done this all by ourselves, too, and were taking our first steps towards becoming independent.

Winning was a huge boost for us, but not so as you'd notice by the reactions at home. Jayne's dad picked us up from Heathrow. Nobody back home knew how we'd got on as we hadn't the money to phone them, so we were itching to tell them our news. The reaction was typically under-stated. 'Really? Oh, that's nice.' It was the same with everyone else. Perhaps it's a northern trait: never knowingly overexcited!

In terms of our career, the win in St Gervais had laid a foundation. We were now senior competitors, no longer allowed to compete at junior level. It was our version of getting the 'key of the door'.

CHRIS:

The next two years were some of the best we ever experienced. Ask us for a highlight from that period and you'll be a long time waiting for an answer – there were so many of them.

After coming third in only our second British Championships, we were selected to represent Great Britain at the 1978 European Championships, which were due to take place in Strasbourg.

Being chosen was a truly amazing feeling. Our journey had started. It was one of those marvellous moments you only usually experience in childhood, before any of that awful expectation has landed on your shoulders. You can just enjoy it for what it is. There was also an awareness surrounding our selection, the understanding that we were somehow about to turn a corner now that we were no longer juniors.

When we first found out we'd been selected, Janet had said to us, 'Enjoy yourselves, you two. This will be your last chance to do so without the responsibility of having to improve on your previous result.'

She was right. Whatever happened after this, we would never feel the same sense of elation again, not without it being tainted by what we'd have to achieve the next time. The further up the ladder you climb, the more you're expected to accomplish, not just by you yourselves but by those around you.

In Strasbourg, we did everything we could to live up to what was now expected of us and finished ninth out of 16 couples. This was yet another coming of age – the start of our education in competing at major championships.

JAYNE & CHRIS:

Our last ever win as amateurs happened at the 1984 World Championships in Ottawa, which took place just a few weeks after Sarajevo. The competition was being held in the afternoon, because that meant it would be peak viewing time over in the UK, and it was being shown on both ITV and the BBC.

Shortly before the competition was due to begin at 4pm, a small fire broke out within the arena which caused the electricity to fail, and this meant the ice started to melt! The repair would take hours, and so they rescheduled the competition to begin at 8pm. We found out later that the mood back home was one of feverish anticipation; not unlike ours really! Millions of people had been sitting by their television sets willing us to win, exactly as they'd done a few weeks before at Sarajevo. *Bolero* had been so popular and this was to be our final amateur performance. It didn't matter how long they had to wait, they weren't going to miss this for the world. As it turned out, they'd have to wait a lot longer than first anticipated.

The damage had been worse than originally thought, and by the time we took to the ice it was almost three in the morning in the UK, several hours later than scheduled. The public stuck with us, though, and we finally rewarded them with another gold medal.

How do we know they stuck with us? Because when we arrived home we had literally thousands of letters from people, all telling us about their experiences. There was no way they were going to be beaten, regardless of how tired they were. We even remember a quote from one of the letters: 'I stayed up until 3am to watch you. I haven't done that for over thirty years!'

For years afterwards we still had people coming up to us and telling us their stories. It seemed to catch the public's imagination perfectly.

The win itself was the icing on the cake. It was our Triple Crown – holding the European, world and Olympic titles simultaneously. But it was also tinged with sadness. This wasn't just a conclusion to the past four years' hard work; it was a conclusion to the past nine – our entire amateur career. There was also a certain amount of trepidation about what had just happened. We no longer lived for competition – our whole world was about to be turned upside down.

Thirty years on, people still ask us if we miss competing. 'No!' we reply. We look back on this period with nostalgia but we don't miss it. We enjoyed it but don't need to go back.

5

Bolero

JAYNE & CHRIS:

Apart from the usual speculation regarding our relationship, the subject that people generally want to ask about when they meet us is *Bolero* – a conversation we're far happier having.

But when they talk to us about *Bolero*, they're not simply referring to an ice dance. They're referring to an occasion: to the Olympics and the significance of Sarajevo; to the costumes and, of course, the music, as well as Valentine's Day and all the rumours that surrounded our relationship. They're referring to the fact that they can remember exactly where they were when it was broadcast, not to mention who they were with.

That *Bolero* became a marker in people's lives fills us with an enormous amount of pride. Usually these instances are associated with death: JFK, John Lennon and Princess Diana, for example, so to have helped create a moment in time that people associate with happiness, like when England won the World Cup, is something very special. That – coupled with competing and winning the gold medal – is without doubt our proudest achievement to date.

The story of how *Bolero* came about is quite a tale, and covers a period of our lives that we have enjoyed recalling. But it doesn't, as you'd be forgiven for thinking, simply end with the medal ceremony in 1984. Far from it.

Since then we have skated the routine on no fewer than two thousand occasions, and in all four corners of the globe. But it doesn't matter when or where we perform *Bolero*, the reception it receives is always the same.

The audiences aren't simply applauding the performance, even though we always put our heart and soul into it. They're clapping because of the memories it evokes for them, and all its different associations. We feel we have a responsibility to do that justice. What's fascinating, though, is that *Bolero* seems to mean a lot of different things to a lot of different people – not least us.

On 13 February 2014 – almost 30 years to the day since we won gold – we went back to Sarajevo to do it all again, and what an emotional rollercoaster that was. It's all part of the story, though. *Bolero* seems to have a timeless quality; an event engrained in the minds of millions of people.

We could probably write an entire book about it but this is how it all happened. We hope you enjoy it.

Some may believe, perfectly naturally, that *Bolero* was put together a few months before the Olympics. In fact, it took us a year to devise, rehearse and perfect, and was a real adventure. An adventure, incidentally, that we very nearly didn't make the end of.

We first began talking about what music we'd use for the Olympics at the start of 1983. Choosing your pieces (especially for the free dance) can be difficult, and we'd been throwing ideas around for a while without really coming close to anything we felt was right. Although couples are free to choose what music they dance to, tradition suggests you probably work with three different pieces, starting off with something fast-paced, then slow in the middle and something fast again to finish with.

While we're respectful of tradition there's nothing to say it can't be challenged occasionally. So, when Jayne had the idea of turning things around and starting with something slow for a change, we jumped at the chance.

'You mean like *Bolero*?' Chris said.

'What, for the opening section?' replied Jayne.

'No, for the whole dance.'

The suggestion of *Bolero* wasn't quite as inspired as it sounds, because we'd actually already been using the music during our warm-ups. But it *was* revolutionary in that it meant we'd be using just one piece of music instead of the usual three, something that, as far as we know, had never been done before, and certainly not for a free dance. We had no routine in place, and to be honest the main reason we'd started using *Bolero* was because of its length: just over 17 minutes, and about the right length for warming up on ice.

We were with Courtney and Bobby in their flat when the suggestion was first made, and while they greeted the idea with an enthusiastic nod, our reaction was slightly more extreme: a mixture of excitement and foreboding. Excitement because we knew the piece inside out and could already see its potential, our imaginations running wild at doing something different; and foreboding because of one very obvious flaw. *Bolero* was 17 minutes long, and we had a maximum of 4 minutes 10 seconds. If it was going to work there'd have to be a serious edit.

But as the four of us began discussing the idea in earnest, our enthusiasm grew and Ravel's 17-minute epic quickly went from being an off-the-cuff suggestion to our chosen music for the free dance at the 1984 Winter Olympics. Dramatically it was perfect, going from pianissimo to fortissimo via a continuous crescendo, built around a simple rhythm played on a single snare drum. We've since found out that Ravel actually wrote the piece for a ballet, so it was meant to accompany movement. That had to be a good omen.

All we had to do now was find somebody who could cut it by 13 minutes (without losing any of its dramatic effect) and then record it for us using an orchestra. Not much to ask, was it? Especially as we had hardly any money.

But before all this could happen we first had to get the support of our coach Betty Callaway and the actor Michael Crawford, who had been so instrumental in helping create our *Barnum* routine the previous year.

On first hearing the news, neither he nor Betty was convinced *Bolero* was right for us and they both took some persuading. Michael in particular found it a little *too* dramatic for his taste, it was out of his comfort zone; whereas Betty thought we were taking too big a risk using just one piece of music and would have preferred us to run with tradition.

It was a huge gamble, we knew that. After the success we'd achieved with *Mack & Mabel* and *Barnum* most people would have gone with something similar. It would have been so simple just to go down the same road again. If it isn't broken, why change it? It might have been the easy option, but for us it was never *an* option. We've never been ones for standing still, and the confidence we had in our ability back then was strong. We also had a wonderful team of people around us. What was the point in having that if all you were going to do was perform variations on what we (and everyone else for that matter) had done a thousand times before? This was the Olympics – our ultimate ambition. If we were ever going to genuinely distance ourselves from the field we had to start pushing boundaries. 'Is the Winter Olympics the right place to start?' we were once asked. Maybe, maybe not, but our minds were made up. We would be using *Bolero*.

Once everyone had been convinced, we went about trying to have an edit done so we could begin work. We were due to start rehearsals in June over in Oberstdorf – our training venue of choice since the late 1970s – and so didn't have long. The person we approached for help was a friend of ours, the theatrical agent Michael Linnitt, who looked after Michael Crawford at the time, and who would later look after us. Michael Linnitt had been positive about *Bolero* from the start and always said that if we thought he could help, we only had to ask.

The reason we went to him in the first place was because he knew everyone in the entertainment industry, and sure enough he knew exactly who to call – a client of his called Richard Hartley. Richard was a composer and immediately agreed to produce the track. But, just as importantly, he also knew an arranger, the person whose job it would be to edit *Bolero* from 17 minutes down to just over four, probably the hardest job of all. His name was Bob Stewart and Richard arranged for us to meet him a few days later.

Bob, who is sadly no longer with us, lived in south London with his mother and was an amazing character, not to mention a very, very clever man. Standing about 5ft 5in tall he had, shall we say, a full figure, almost no hair, small round spectacles and was never without a lit cigarette and a glass of red wine. There was a genuine air of eccentricity about Bob, but also great warmth.

From a very early age his life had revolved around music. Not only was he organ scholar to Worcester College, Oxford at just 16 years of age, but he got a first in music at just 19 and was now a professional pianist, conductor, teacher and, of course, arranger. He lived, ate and breathed music.

After meeting Bob at his home and explaining exactly what we wanted – Ravel's *Bolero* edited down without losing any dramatic effect whatsoever and then recorded by a professional orchestra – he said he'd be delighted to help. We were in business.

Although *Bolero* may sound fairly straightforward, it's actually an extremely complex piece of music and has a structure that is not easily changed. In the end, the new arrangement took Bob four whole weeks to complete, during which time he worked on nothing else.

News that he'd finished the arrangement meant we were free to pack our bags and head off to Germany to begin training. We'd be there for six months in all, and we were offered the opportunity to borrow an estate car from a local Volvo dealership. Being amateurs we weren't allowed to accept cash, of course, but apparently we were allowed to borrow cars. We'd be in the front of the car, with all our worldly belongings in the back – which, in actual fact, didn't amount to very much at all.

But before we could set off anywhere we had to go to Bob's and make a recording of his new arrangement, which we could then take with us to Oberstdorf. It was going to be a while before the track was produced professionally and we had to have something to work with. These days you'd probably get a demo sent directly to your computer, which you could then take with you anywhere in the world and play through a PA system. But back then things were rather more primitive, and what we actually ended up doing would probably make anybody under 25 howl with derision.

Jayne had in her possession at the time a portable cassette recorder. It was about 25cm long by 10cm wide (10in by 4in) with a small speaker on top, and a space for the cassette and a few buttons. Although it wasn't what you might call cutting-edge technology – even back then – it was all we had. So we made our way over to Bob's house, put the recorder on top of his upright piano, pressed the record button and away he went.

When we played it back it sounded absolutely awful. This was nothing to do with Bob's playing, by the way. He had given a virtuoso performance. But even Bob's dexterity on the keyboard couldn't provide the punctuation we needed for the dance, especially when it was played back through Jayne's tinny tape recorder. Even so, it would have to do. We'd have to use our imaginations.

So, cassette in hand, we got up to leave, but as we did Bob stopped us. 'Hang on,' he said. 'I'm afraid there's a small snag.'

'Oh no, really?' we said, trepidation creeping into our voices. 'It's about the timing,' he said.

According to Bob, the closest he'd been able to get to our desired time of 4 minutes 10 seconds was 4 minutes 28. We were 18 seconds over. He'd done all the 'compressing' the score would allow and so we were stumped, thwarted at the last hurdle. It was an awful feeling. A real hammer blow.

In desperation we started coming up with all kinds of silly ideas, the daftest being to increase the tempo and skate faster. As if we hadn't done *Bolero* enough damage. Ravel would be turning in his grave!

After exhausting every option with Bob we set off to see Bobby and Courtney, to discuss costumes and have a bite to eat before setting off for Germany. When we arrived we sank into the sofa and explained our dilemma. We were about to move to Germany for six months to rehearse for the 1984 Winter Olympics, and had no definite music for the most important dance. It was an absolute disaster.

JAYNE:

As we sat there trying to reassure ourselves that everything was going to be OK, Chris suddenly sat bolt upright. 'Wait a minute,' he said. 'What's the rule about timing, exactly?' We asked him what he was getting at but he just told us to grab the rule book. Then, as we read the rules on timing it became obvious what he meant and what he was hoping we'd find. The rule book stated that the clock would only begin once a blade had touched the ice. If we didn't skate, the clock wouldn't start. It was obvious really. How many ice skaters start their routines exactly when the music starts? It doesn't happen. Or it didn't then. Most started a beat or two after.

JAYNE & CHRIS:

After we all calmed down a bit we talked about how best to approach the beginning of the routine. There was only one option: we'd have to start on our knees. Nothing else would work.

As with the music itself, the more we talked about the idea the more it made sense. In fact, the creative process for that first 18 seconds was enormously gratifying. And this time there was no sense of foreboding, just relief and excitement. Now, two elements of our routine would be completely new to the sport, and still within the rules.

After going over Courtney's ideas for the costumes, which we were thrilled with, we set off for Dover in our Volvo to begin the journey to Germany, rejuvenated and full of hope.

CHRIS:

A couple of hours after arriving in Calais something happened that I freely admit haunts me to this day. It was just after midnight when we got off the ferry. The crossing had been smooth and I was looking forward to getting behind the wheel and being back on the road again. By then I'd been awake for just over 24 hours but with all the excitement of the day's events, not to mention the prospect of moving to Germany for six months, it never once occurred to me that I actually might need to sleep at some point.

At around 2.30am, as things became quieter, Jayne eventually dropped off to sleep, leaving me alone with my thoughts and the road ahead. I still felt OK but, as my mind began to settle a bit, I suddenly started to feel extraordinarily tired, both physically and mentally. Even so, I still actually failed to equate these feelings of tiredness with any kind of potential danger. I was driving us to Oberstdorf and that was that. But the more

Wearing my special bridesmaid's dress, aged five, with my cousin Gillian (left) and her brother Geoff. I kept my arms out all day, so as not to crease it.

With my parents, Betty and George, on one of our regular summer holidays in Cornwall.

I'm the one second from the left in this picture taken at my primary school.

Mrs Fitzhugh, on the right, was the one who organised my first-ever skating trip. Little did she know what she was starting.

My parents on their wedding day, with my aunt Madge and uncle Jack.

The earliest picture I have of me.

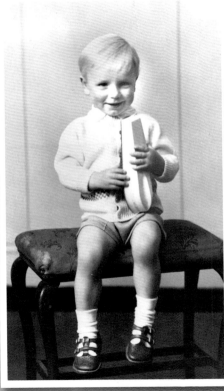

A few years on, and I am getting in some early practice for holding on to trophies.

It's hard to tell under all the face paint, but I think I'm the one second from left here, as the Ice Cubs put on a performance in the Nottingham Ice Stadium.

Proudly displaying my first skating trophies.

Aged 11, with Len Sayward, one of my first coaches.

With my first skating partner, Michael Hutchinson.

Janet Sawbridge at the European Championships in 1972. Having someone of her experience to coach us was wonderful, and she made sure she overcame our mutual shyness in our first session together. (Getty Images)

Andris Toppe became our coach , friend and confidant.

Betty Callaway took over as coach from Janet and, with the advice of Michael Crawford, helped us develop a greater theatricality on the ice. (Rex)

This picture shows us in the St Ivel competition in 1979, soon after we started working with Betty. (Rex)

Performing *Mack & Mabel* at the St Ivel Rink in Richmond in 1981. (PA)

With Betty in Oberstdorf, which became a regular base for us, preparing for the World Championships in 1983. (Getty Images)

The team ahead of the 1984 Olympics: Nicky Slater and Karen Barber, us, Stephen Williams and Wendy Sessions. (Getty Images)

Nottingham council gave us a huge amount of financial support so that we could focus on winning gold, and we were even given the freedom of the city in 1983. (PA)

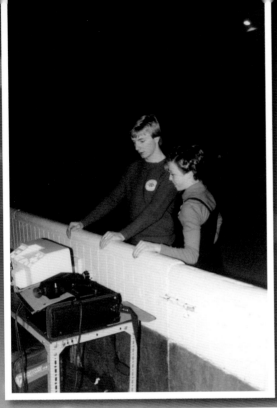

Our video recording equipment back in 1983 seemed extremely hi-tech at the time, but now it looks positively prehistoric.

Action from an exhibition in Nottingham, September 1983. The Olympics were now looming very large in our minds. (Getty Images)

I drove the more tired I became, and after a few more miles the inevitable happened. All I wanted more than anything else in the world was to close my eyes and go to sleep, and as my eyelids began to shut I could feel myself surrendering to the beckoning slumber.

I don't know how long I was asleep but it can't have been more than a few seconds. Then, all of a sudden, it hit me – where I was, who I was with, where we were going and, most importantly of all, what I was supposed to be doing at that moment. I have no idea where it came from but the realisation hit me like a freight train. I woke up with a jump, absolutely wide awake, and I tried to get my bearings. I could hear the engine straining. My foot was flat down on the accelerator and we were heading straight towards the central reservation barrier. We'd obviously veered across all three lanes and were now only a few feet away from it. It was a miracle we hadn't already been killed.

I then latched on to the wheel, taking my foot off the accelerator, and tried to pull hard to the left. As I did, the front of the car swerved back on to the road but the back of the car headed straight towards the barrier. There was then one almighty bang, at which point Jayne woke up screaming. The back of the car had hit the barrier and we were now swerving violently, left and right. All I could do was hold on to the wheel as tightly as I could and pray that it would eventually come under control. The alternative was certain death. We'd stopped off for fuel a bit earlier and had an almost full tank. If we'd crashed, the car would have become a fireball in seconds. After what seemed like forever – but was probably no more than a second or two – the car levelled off and I managed to regain control. Goodness knows how, as at one point it honestly felt that the car was about to roll. As soon as I knew it was safe and that there was nothing behind us, I pulled over on to the hard shoulder and stopped.

The first thing I did was make sure Jayne was all right.

Fortunately she was. Scarred for life mentally, perhaps, but physically in one piece. We were clearly in a state of shock and for quite some time afterwards just sat there staring into space, trying to take in the enormity of what had happened, not to mention what might have happened.

Finally coming to my senses, I vowed there and then that I would never do anything as stupid again as long as I lived. The thought of what we were striving to achieve versus what almost occurred on that motorway was a sobering one.

JAYNE & CHRIS:

Not long after settling into our dorms in Oberstdorf, which were basic to say the least, we had to return to the UK to sort out what would hopefully be our last hurdle (off the ice, at least) – obtaining a professional recording of *Bolero*. There was no way in the world we could afford to hire a 60-piece orchestra; in fact, we'd have struggled to find the money for a string quartet, so we had to look for alternatives. Once again, Michael Linnitt came to our aid, this time recommending another friend of Richard Hartley's, the composer Alan Hawkshaw. Not only is Alan one of the most respected TV composers in the UK (*Countdown*, *Grange Hill*, *Love Hurts*, to name but a few) but he's also a consummate musician and has worked with everyone from David Bowie to Cliff Richard and the Shadows.

Richard said that Alan had recently acquired a new synthesiser, something called a Fairlight, which could imitate with frightening accuracy just about any instrument imaginable. It also allowed you to combine the instruments and thus create and record your own orchestra. Perfect!

Watching Alan produce the arrangement was an experience in itself, and is all now part of the *Bolero* legend. He began by finding an appropriate snare drum sound before programming in the rhythm pattern and there it was, the spine of our piece.

After that, he went over it again and again, each time adding a new instrument, until eventually, after a few hours, we had 'our *Bolero*'.

We arrived back in Oberstdorf armed with our tape and ready to start work on the choreography. This was where the hard work really started.

JAYNE:

Nobody had ever started a routine on their knees before, so we were really breaking new ground. But it wasn't just our initial stance that challenged convention; it was our entire demeanour. Audiences and judges were used to bright, energetic starts, all smiles and engagement, whereas we would be in the centre of the rink, completely stationary, engaging only with each other. This, we were hoping, would help create an air of hush and expectation, with every spectator focused and eager for us to begin.

JAYNE & CHRIS:

There was something else unique about our routine that would prove to be absolutely pivotal. As we were dancing to just one piece of music, we decided to create our own original narrative, a storyline to run alongside the music. This would help us to generate the emotion needed as well as aid our concentration. You wouldn't normally do this when dancing to four pieces of music as it would be far too complicated. Once again it would be a first, but a very useful one.

The storyline itself isn't too dissimilar to *Romeo and Juliet*: a man and a woman, desperately in love, who ultimately cannot be together. At the start of the routine they're simply two young lovers courting, blissfully unaware of the fate that awaits them. Then, slowly, they begin to realise that their love for one another is doomed and that the only way they can be together is in death. They then search for the path leading to a volcano. When they find the path the woman beckons the man to follow her. As the path becomes difficult, the man helps her by lifting her higher, but eventually she becomes tired and collapses. The man picks her up and urges her to go on. Then, at last, they reach the summit and, as the music reaches its final fortissimo, they throw themselves into the volcano. Cue applause, flowers and success – we hoped!

It all sounds a bit over the top, and we fully admit that it's almost impossible for spectators to know precisely what's going on, but we hoped that people would still somehow catch on to the fact that we were playing out a story, even if they couldn't necessarily follow all of it. We wanted them to sense they were watching something intimate and honest, and engage with it.

But as important as the narrative was in helping us generate emotion, there was one final piece of the jigsaw that we hoped would bring everything together – and that was the audience itself.

On seeing the routine, which we first performed at an exhibition in Oberstdorf, Betty said, 'This could either be fantastic or a flop. It all depends on the emotion.' She obviously didn't realise it at the time, none of us did, but we later found out that *Bolero* only *really* worked when performed in front of an audience. They would be the linchpin, the energy, if you like.

At the time, though, we obviously weren't aware of this and the fate of *Bolero* – as well as our chances of winning a medal – were still very much in the balance. We'd rehearsed it hundreds of times, of course, but never in public, and we still had absolutely no idea how it would be received.

Our first opportunity to perform it in front of a live audience on a competitive level would be at the British Championships in November 1983. While this didn't necessarily provide us with an accurate measure of what it might be like performing in Sarajevo (the championships were being held in our home town of Nottingham – hardly an unbiased crowd!), it did provide us with our first inkling of what would happen when all the elements came together.

Our first competitive performance of *Bolero* was good enough to help us win the British Championships for the sixth year in a row. In fact, we were awarded six 6.0s for artistic impression.

Bolero was now in the public domain and was being talked about all over the skating world. Expectations were always going to be high, because of our previous achievements, but when you also start challenging conventions as we had – and with a dance that was created with a gold medal in mind – expectation can quickly turn into opinion. 'Have you heard about that new Torvill & Dean dance? Breaks every rule in the book,' or 'I saw that new dance of theirs. In my opinion they're trying too hard to be different.' The pressure was now starting to build and it was becoming increasingly difficult to remain unaffected by all the rumours circulating, not to mention the media attention.

Our next focus in the short term would be the European Championships, which were being held in Budapest. That would be the last time we were seen before the Olympics. This experience, however, would introduce us to a new form of exasperation – politics! We knew it existed in skating, of course we did, but we'd never really been directly involved before.

A judge, who was present at rehearsals but not part of the actual panel, began to criticise some of the new holds we'd been experimenting with during the compulsories and promptly started planting seeds of criticism and derision within the panel itself. We can only assume that this was all a result of us becoming, as one member of the press put it, 'maverick'. Some people just don't like change, and, when they are faced with it, they retaliate. In our opinion this is exactly what was happening.

This particular judge wanted to maintain the status quo and, despite the fact that we were not actually infringing any rules, still decided to take the law into their hands and broadcast their thoughts to the other judges.

What this judge wasn't aware of was our friendship with Courtney Jones, somebody who enjoyed far more respect within the sport than this person did. In a gesture for which we're grateful to this day, Courtney jumped on a plane to Budapest and made his own, far more valued opinions known to the panel, thus putting an immediate stop to the machinations.

The competition itself was going well for us and we went into the final day with a lead, but only a slim one. Last year's winners, the Russian couple Natalia Bestemianova and Andrei Bukin, were hot on our heels and everything would hinge on the free dance.

Given our rivals' experience, as well as their undoubted talent, we made sure we used every second available to us to iron out any creases – and it's a good job we did.

CHRIS:

In one run-through, a ring I was wearing caught on the hook of one of Jayne's boots. As we untangled ourselves we vowed there and then never to wear jewellery again on the ice. One more potential disaster averted!

JAYNE & CHRIS:

When we arrived back in our dressing room Betty was there waiting for us. She had news of a fresh problem.

'You know the move where you [Jayne] step briefly on to Chris's boot?' said Betty. 'Well, rumour has it that some of the judges were watching and are questioning the legitimacy of the move.'

While we were absolutely astounded by the speed and efficiency of the rumour mill, we were grateful too, because it afforded us the opportunity to change the move to something more innocuous. It was no easy task, though. This was just before our final practice session. To alter a move at this late stage – something we'd rehearsed every day for months – seemed like a very big deal indeed. We had to keep telling ourselves that it was just a 'change', as opposed to a problem.

Despite the late scare, *Bolero* went down wonderfully and we ended up scoring eight 6.0s for artistic impression, enough to ensure we were champions. It was exactly what we needed going into the Olympics. We were all absolutely thrilled!

Far more so, it has to be said, than Natalia Bestemianova and Andrei Bukin, or indeed their coach, Tatiana Tarasova.

Tatiana had also heard the talk about the potentially illegal move, but she had not been informed of the counter-rumour regarding our decision not to use it. The Russians have always been fantastic skaters, but they are also adept politicians, and once they see an opportunity, they grab it. There followed a rather ugly round of accusations in the press, all of which were completely untrue. We felt that we'd won fair and square.

When Betty was asked to respond to Tatiana's finger-pointing she simply said, 'Huh, I'm delighted they have finally found a rule book' – which was a reference to their (alleged) often flagrant disregard for it.

Winning in Budapest had been a marvellous experience, not least because it provided us with a reward for all our hard work, as well as vindication for the choices we'd made and all the risks we'd taken. Above all, winning the European Championships made us more confident going into the Olympics and helped us realise we could achieve our ultimate ambition – Olympic gold. However daunting the prospect and however difficult the task, we now had the level of confidence and experience needed to be successful.

But first we had to get there. We'd been training in Oberstdorf prior to going to Sarajevo and were due to travel with the German team, who had also been training there. It was a long journey, about 20 hours in all, and involved sharing compartments with a bunch of excitable German athletes.

This affected Chris more than it did Jayne, and he was becoming jittery about not getting enough sleep. In the end the German team doctor gave him some sleeping pills, which ended up making him feel drowsy for the next two days!

It was hard to get a feel for Sarajevo when we first arrived, as the moment we got off the train we were rounded up, put on a bus and then taken straight to the Olympic village. The organisers were very conscious of security too and if you wanted to go anywhere outside the village you had to get a pass. One look at the soldiers and security guards usually put you off trying. They were extremely stern-looking, all about 7ft tall and brandishing huge Kalashnikov rifles. It was all extremely frightening.

There was a genuine tension in the air, an all-pervading sense of nervousness. To be honest, that was the last thing we needed. We were nervous enough already! So, instead of venturing out we tended to just flit between the village and the practice rinks. Taking in the sights and sounds of a capital city would usually be a welcome break from the monotony of hanging around waiting for the next practice, but with security being as tight as it was, we thought it best to stay put and read a book.

The atmosphere inside the athletes' village was diametrically opposed to the atmosphere in the city. There was still an almost palpable nervousness in the air, but this was born from competition and anticipation rather than fear and paranoia. Hundreds of young people from all over the world, gathered together with one common goal: to compete to the best of their ability in one of the biggest sporting events on earth. It was enormously exciting, totally different to Lake Placid in 1980.

Back then, we hadn't yet won a major international championship and were certainly not expected to challenge. We came fifth and gained an enormous amount of experience, and we used that experience to grow. This time around we were champions elect, favourites for Olympic gold. It felt totally different.

Each sport had its own apartments in the village, and when it came to allocating the bedrooms Jayne and I were both given singles, which was a huge bonus. We didn't mind sharing under normal circumstances, but these were not normal circumstances. We were attracting an increasing amount of publicity at the time and were being followed absolutely everywhere. Knowing we both had an oasis – a place where we could get away from it all – was an absolute blessing. We later learned that it was partly because we were considered 'senior' members of the team that we were given our own rooms. It did make a big difference, though. Life was bearable.

CHRIS:

A couple of days before the Games began I was approached by the team manager and asked if I'd like to carry the flag during the opening ceremony. To say I was shocked would be a huge understatement.

'You want me to carry the flag?'

'Yes, Chris, we want you to carry the flag.'

'On my own?'

'Yes, on your own.'

'Couldn't I do it with Jayne?'

'Do it with Jayne? How? Now, would you still like to?'

'Yes, of course. Thank you!'

The team manager did actually enquire as to whether it would be possible for both of us to carry the flag, but the Olympic Committee refused.

When everything had died down I was left juggling a

maelstrom of thoughts and emotions. What an honour! I couldn't wait to tell my dad.

We'd had several days' practice after arriving, except that it wasn't really practice, because the judges were watching, weighing us all up and forming their opinions. This meant we treated every session like a performance.

The compulsories and the OSP, which took us into the second week, went well, and we picked up several 6.0s, including our first ever for a compulsory. Quite a reassurance.

But the thing that really inspired us was the last practice, which took place on the morning of the final: Tuesday 14 February 1984 – Valentine's Day.

We were due on the ice at 6am, so we got up at about 4.30 because we knew that the bus left at least an hour before the training session. The other skaters who were supposed to be on the same practice had decided not to come, but we wouldn't have missed it for anything. It was our big opportunity to run through the free dance on the main rink. We'd had plenty of time on the practice rink, of course, but it wasn't the same. A session on the main rink was a rarity and we were looking forward to it. The fact that everyone else had stayed in bed was in many ways the icing on the cake. We'd have complete privacy.

JAYNE:

As soon as we finished the run-through, which had gone well, we suddenly started to hear applause. Slightly taken aback, we looked round and there on the other side of the rink were 30 or so cleaning ladies, who'd obviously decided to down tools and watch. Why not? There they all stood, cigarettes in mouths, clapping like mad.

We greeted their applause with a selection of bows, curtsies and a few grateful waves before skating off to get changed, both of us grinning from ear to ear. It was a wonderful moment – a spontaneous boost and a good omen, we thought. With luck it would set the tone for what was to come.

JAYNE & CHRIS:

The rest of the day was spent relaxing in the village, somewhere the press weren't allowed to venture into. It was good to take a break from the usual 'When are you going to get married?' questions, although once the competition was over it would begin all over again.

That evening, as we waited to go on, we slowly sank into ourselves. This is a healthy kind of isolation, which allows you to prepare mentally for what lies ahead.

When the competition began in earnest, we made sure, as we always did, that we wouldn't be able to hear anybody else's marks: Chris standing in the corridor with his fingers in his ears, and Jayne sitting quietly in the dressing room, nicely out of earshot of any scores or announcements.

When we eventually skated on, we felt an expectant hush sweep across the arena. There were friends of ours in the audience, as well as relatives and VIPs – Princess Anne, who was president of the British Olympic Association, among them – but neither of us can remember a single thing about the performance itself. For those four and a half minutes or so, we were lost in concentration. These days people refer to it as being 'in the zone'. It was almost as if we'd been hypnotised. Even watching it back on TV doesn't help jog our memories. It's like watching two different people.

JAYNE:

I remember coming round a few seconds after the music stopped. I suddenly began to feel my heart beat again, which was going at about a hundred miles an hour, before feeling an enormous surge of relief.

CHRIS:

I came round a couple of seconds before Jayne as, believe it or not, I made a slight mistake at the very end of the routine. Instead of following Jayne and throwing myself on to the ice flat, I did a kind of 'overenthusiastic roll'. The only person who would have noticed it was me, and it wasn't going to lose us any marks; but it was enough to bring me round pretty quickly!

JAYNE & CHRIS:

And then came the noise. That bit we *do* remember.

It was like a wall of sound had just been dropped on us, and we could hear everything: clapping, screaming, foot stamping, people calling out our names, others shouting 'SIX!'

Then, as we started to look up, we were able to put some faces to the noise – hordes of them, in fact. What an unbelievable sight. Thousands upon thousands of people, all on their feet looking absolutely thrilled to bits. What better sight is there than that? It was like waking up from a dream.

As we skated around the ice, Chris waving and Jayne picking up a never-ending stream of flowers and bouquets, we started to be able to pick out a few familiar faces, such as our parents and one or two friends. Jayne even caught sight of some colleagues of hers from the Norwich Union – an entire block of them! Apparently they'd all decided to buy tickets and jump on a flight. Without wanting to sound too sentimental, at that very moment in time we felt like we knew every single person in that arena. They simply radiated affection.

Then came the marks, which suddenly reminded us why we

were there. Technical marks first: three 6.0s and six 5.9s. Not bad. Not bad at all. The crowd were happy, and if they were, we were. If we could get the same for artistic impression, we'd be home and dry. But that wasn't to be, of course, as the six judges who'd just scored us 5.9 for the technical marks surely had other ideas. And then, just as we were picking up yet more flowers, we heard a deafening scream. We looked round at the scoreboard:

'Torvill J, Dean C'
6.0 6.0 6.0 6.0 6.0 6.0 6.0 6.0 6.0

Nine perfect scores!

As we came off the ice and gave Betty a huge hug, we knew that we'd won. Nobody had ever got a straight-6.0 score at the Olympics before. Not for ice dancing. It was beyond anything we could have wished for.

When we looked at the crowd again we suddenly saw dozens of Union Jacks scattered about the place. There seemed to be hundreds of them. They must have been there before but for some reason we hadn't seen them. Despite being over a thousand miles away, we felt like we were on home ground.

JAYNE:

Everything that happened directly after the medal ceremony, with the dope-testing and the press conference, meant that we'd been first into the arena that morning and were the last to leave – save for the cleaners. In fact, I don't think we got back to the village until almost midnight.

Unbeknown to Chris and me, the team had thrown a cele-bratory party for us, which had started an hour or so earlier. I remember seeing Princess Anne holding a plastic cup of cham-pagne. She could and probably should have left ages ago, but had very kindly said she wanted to stay until she'd seen us. Hers were some of the warmest congratulations we received.

The following day I took my parents to the airport. As I went to say goodbye to my father, who is normally a very measured man, he suddenly burst into tears.

My mother, being her usual self, just dismissed it. 'Take no notice of him. He's just sad to be leaving. Look after yourself, dear. Bye-bye.'

I've never asked my dad why he broke down, but I don't think I need to. As we said at the start, *Bolero* means different things to different people.

GOING BACK

JAYNE & CHRIS:

The invitation to go back to Sarajevo came about through the mayor of the city. They're going to be hosting the 2017 Youth Olympics and that gave them an excuse to completely renovate the Zetra stadium, which had been badly bombed during the Bosnian War of the 1990s. As the 30th anniversary of the Sarajevo Olympics approached, they got in touch and said that they'd like to mark the opening of the new ice rink by commemorating *Bolero*.

Our first thought was, Wow, has it really been 30 years? We hadn't been counting really, so at the time had no idea it was almost upon us. Then we thought what an absolutely brilliant idea – to recreate *Bolero*, 30 years to the day after it happened in the same city, on the same site even. It was an amazing yet frightening idea.

Logistically it was going to be a nightmare. We were right in the middle of filming *Dancing on Ice* and were soon to go out on tour. Rehearsals were going well but that was because we were sticking to the schedule. A detour to Eastern Europe would throw all that into chaos. There were also rehearsals to consider for the event. The *Bolero* that we performed on the *Dancing on Ice* series took place on a smaller rink and so had to be choreographed differently. It was also slightly shorter than the original – musical edits being far easier to achieve with digital technology – so we'd have to rehearse the original from scratch. Just to round things off this would all have to be done on a full-size ice rink, which meant yet more planning and logistics.

We didn't *have* to go to Sarajevo. As we were told, it was just an invitation. But to us it was more than that: it was an opportunity to give something back to the city; a city which today experiences problems of a different kind, swapping civil war and unrest for poverty and mass corruption. It's a beautiful but desperate place.

But the closer we got to the event the more daunting it all became. Not least the question of whether we'd be in a fit state to perform the full routine.

We ended up rehearsing for an hour and a half at Alexandra Palace every morning – which was the closest full-size rink – followed by a full day at Elstree where we filmed *Dancing on Ice*. All in all it added about four hours on to our day. But once we became used to training on the full surface again it actually became quite liberating, as it was so much bigger than the one we used at Elstree. It was like being amateurs again.

Going back to Sarajevo was an extremely emotional experience, for all kinds of reasons, and not all to do with gold medals and perfect scores; not by any means. For instance, the area where the opening ceremony had taken place, which was still there, had later been used as a kind of outdoor morgue during the war, often housing thousands of dead bodies. We were just as aware of the other side of the coin. Definitely a bittersweet experience.

Aesthetically, the city was almost unrecognisable. The grey concrete Soviet buildings which had marred every horizon had been replaced by newer, more welcoming structures. Sarajevo is a city of contrasts, of extremes. We remember going into the Old Town while we were last there, which has an almost medieval feel to it, with beautiful buildings, all perfectly preserved. Then, just a street away, you'll see some horrible throwback to the Soviet era, fortunately now a dying breed in the city.

Despite its troubles you can tell that it's doing its best to drag itself fully into the twenty-first century. It's almost there.

But it was the reception we received from the people that brought a lump to our throats. They seemed genuinely thrilled to see us again, as we were them, and it turned out to be a very happy few days. Somebody who lived in the city said to us that it reminded them all that good things happen, and heaven knows they needed reminding. What better way to celebrate the 30th anniversary of *Bolero* than to be part of something positive again? Suddenly those four hours that had been added to our days seemed very, very worthwhile.

The most emotional part of that visit was meeting the flower girl again. Anybody who was watching *Bolero* on TV, or has since seen it on DVD or YouTube, will probably remember that just before we took to the ice, a small girl had to skate on to clear the ice of some bouquets that had been thrown on. We were standing there, waiting to be announced.

She's 36 now, so would obviously have been about six at the time, and has a daughter of her own who also skates. She was so overcome; in floods of tears. Much of what has gone on in Sarajevo since 1984 has given little cause for celebration, save for the end of the war, of course. She, like everyone else, had had a difficult life. For her, she said, that memory from 1984 was by far her happiest.

When a 36-year-old woman with a young family has to go back 30 years for her happiest memory, it makes you realise just how lucky you are.

It was only after this trip that we began to appreciate the

ripple effect that something like *Bolero* can have, and how important these events are.

Look at London 2012. We could all lift our heads a little higher after that. It created the most enormous buzz, and you could almost touch it. You didn't have to be interested in the sport; you simply fed off the excitement. It's impossible to put a price on something like that.

During our final tour of *Dancing on Ice* there was some talk of us retiring *Bolero*. 'Maybe this is it?' 'Will they ever perform it again?' But that would be unthinkable. One day we obviously will perform *Bolero* for the last time, but I doubt we'll know it at the time. For as long as we think we're able to do it justice we'll carry on performing it. Retire *Bolero*? That'd be like retiring us. Not yet.

6

Fame

JAYNE & CHRIS:

There was never a point when we woke up and realised we were famous. It was a gradual thing. And because it was gradual we were able to acclimatise and adapt. It was the same with signing autographs. We don't remember signing our first autograph for the simple reason that we were just doing what was expected of us. Fame, or perceived admiration, didn't come into it. When we first got into ice skating we would ask for the autograph of anyone entering the British Championships, which were then held in Nottingham every year. It was what you did.

CHRIS:

I remember one of the first times I actually *felt* famous. It was in 1981, when we were training in Oberstdorf. I was in my dorm, reading in bed one evening, when there was a knock at the door and in walked a young man who must have been in his early twenties. At first I thought one of my ears must have been hanging off or something, as when he saw me his eyes opened and he just stood there staring at me, open-mouthed. Eventually he spoke: 'I think I'm sharing with you,' he said.

'Oh, OK. I'm Chris. Pleased to meet you.'

I held out my hand but before it even got halfway he threw down his bags and left. Actually, he didn't just leave, he fled, and at great speed.

It turned out that the man in question was Paul Duchesnay, one half of an up-and-coming brother-sister partnership from Canada. As Jayne and I were the current world champions, Paul recognised me and had run off to tell his sister, Isabelle – who, unbeknown to me at the time of course, would later become my wife.

I must have been fast asleep when he went to bed, and in the morning I left him still fast asleep. At least that's what I thought. He later admitted that he'd actually been wide awake, but didn't dare move in case he had to speak to me!

But despite not always appreciating how well-known we might have been, we have always appreciated the kindness and dedication shown to us by our fans. Dennis McCarthy, a presenter at Radio Nottingham, once said to us, 'Always look after your fans. Reply to everything, sign everything', which was and still is one of the best pieces of advice we've ever been given. Not just because it's polite and the right thing to do, but because our fans are a fantastic group of people. Dedicated, supportive and, above all, appreciative. They come from all over the world when we're on tour – Australia and New Zealand, America and South Africa. Some of them have been following us since the early 1980s, and of course we've got a whole new group of fans since *Dancing on Ice* took off.

JAYNE:

I used to be a real collector. Not so much now, but in the 1980s I wouldn't let anything go. This started to get out of hand when at some point word got round that I liked cuddly toys. After that people began throwing them on to the ice after competitions, and I'd pick them all up and take them home.

Once, during our first trip to Australia, not long after we'd turned professional, I ended up sending back an enormous steamer trunk full of cuddly kangaroos and koalas, which had been thrown on to the ice after a performance. My mum and dad used to have an entire room at home that was totally dedicated to housing these creatures. At one point there were literally thousands of them. In the end I had to rehome them via a children's charity, as my parents wanted to reclaim the room!

It was also in Australia that I mentioned during an interview that I rather liked a brand of sweet they have out there called Violet Crumble. Sure enough, after the next show there was a sea of confectionery covering the ice. I didn't ship the chocolate, of course. That went straight to the dressing room with me!

But I would always keep all of our fan mail; every single letter. During the aftermath of *Bolero* we were receiving at least a sackful a day. There must have been tens of thousands and from all over the world, some just addressed to *Torvill & Dean, England,* but they got to us somehow. I used to archive them, put them into folders in date order, something I'd been trained to do at Norwich Union. Nobody could put things into folders like me! Looking back, I was very fastidious. And if I ever saw one without a date on it, I'd be absolutely beside myself.

As with the cuddly toys it all got a bit much in the end. It was impossible to find space for each and every one of them so I could only keep a select few. Choosing the ones I wanted to hold on to took well over a week.

The majority of letters we receive are supportive and congratulatory, but we have had our fair share of strange ones over the years. In the 1990s, not long after our second Olympics, I began receiving letters from a prisoner. At first they were friendly enough, but after a while he began to get abusive; his final letter declaring that as soon as he was released he'd come and find me and kill me. The police were called and nothing happened, but I remember being very scared for a while. We even had a bomb threat while playing our first run at Wembley, during our inaugural world tour. That was quite bizarre, and for some time afterwards we were surrounded by security guards.

CHRIS:

The closest we came to being shocked by our fame was after the Olympics in 1984. We didn't arrive back in the UK until six weeks later, and when we landed it was just pandemonium. We had no idea what was waiting for us. In our minds the world had probably moved on, and we were following suit; whereas in actual fact it seemed like the whole of the UK had been waiting patiently to celebrate, and in particular our home town of Nottingham.

We'd read about the viewing figures – half the population tuned in to watch us that day – but it didn't really sink in. We were just thrilled that we'd achieved our goal. We'd ticked a box. We weren't being blasé or arrogant; it was more a case of being conditioned to behave and think like athletes. 'You've done that, great. What's next?'

But when we eventually did arrive back home we were spellbound. It was like the whole nation was in the throes of holding an enormous party. Everywhere we went – everywhere – people just seemed to want to congratulate us. The generosity of spirit we felt was truly moving, but what made the experience even more special was that everyone seemed to be genuinely proud of us. Proud of what we'd accomplished and proud that we hailed from the same country. It was a tremendous feeling. Something that I knew could never be bettered.

JAYNE:

When we went to Australia as professionals a few months later, we were treated pretty much the same – like rock stars – except that this time some of the adulation would be conditional.

The first big surprise was the plane journey. The producer, Michael Edgley, had sent us first-class tickets, which meant we turned left when we got to the top of the aeroplane steps, something we'd never, ever experienced before. It was a jumbo jet, and I remember walking up the spiral staircase into the bubble at the top, before reclining in these enormous bed-like seats. We'd never known luxury like it.

When we landed we were met by a lady called Diana. She was very sophisticated and introduced herself as our PA.

'But what's a PA?' I asked

'It stands for personal assistant. I'm your personal assistant and I'll be looking after you while you're here.'

'What? You're here just to assist us?'

'Yes, that's right. Now, let's see about getting you out of here.'

This just amazed us. We thought that the only difference between amateur and professional skating was that you got paid for doing it. But they were actually two completely different worlds. What astonished us even more was that, rather than trying to force a way through the waiting crowd, Diana managed to get us out through the back door. We skipped passport control, customs – everything.

There must have been hundreds of people waiting for us, as well as dozens of journalists and TV crews. Heaven knows how she arranged it. When we emerged into the car park, there was a huge black limousine waiting for us.

Not long after setting off, we suddenly became aware of a helicopter overhead. 'Who's that?' I asked. 'That belongs to Channel 7, one of the big news channels,' replied Diana. 'They're covering your arrival live on air.'

'They're covering our arrival, with a helicopter!?'

This was rather more than we could cope with. It was proper 'rock star' stuff, like nothing we'd ever experienced before.

It didn't stop there, though. In fact, every day brought new surprises. Having our own PA was pretty cool, although Diana was more like a nanny, really. We needed somebody to look after us!

Then the next day when we were all out shopping, she handed us each some money.

'Here you go. This is your daily allowance.'

'What do we need this for?

'Everyday expenses?'

It was about $250, which was about £100 at the time. It was a huge amount of money. Diana made some suggestions about things we might need, such as clothes and some luggage. After that, we were free to spend it as we wished.

I'm afraid I took that a little too literally and ended up trying to spend every penny that was given to me – mainly on clothes. This went on until Chris pulled me up and asked what I was doing.

'I'm spending my allowance. It's my money. Diana said so.'

'Yes, but you don't *have* to spend all of it on a daily basis.'

'Really? I thought that if you didn't you'd have to give it back.'

'No, that's not how it works, Jayne.'

It didn't take us long to realise that anything you receive as a professional, whether it be a first-class plane ticket or a handful of Australian dollars, you ultimately pay for. So, as tempting as it is to be extravagant, we've always managed to stop our-selves. These days, if we don't need it, we won't ask for it.

The money Diana gave us was an advance on our wages and the plane tickets and limousines would be paid for out of the profits from the shows. In other words, it all had to be accounted for. This was a good lesson learned, as when it came to putting on our own tours we'd be receiving a share of the profits. Nothing was for free.

CHRIS:

This should have been a completely enjoyable experience, but from the moment we got into the back of that limousine we were hit by the enormity of what becoming professional skaters meant. As amateurs we had skated for ourselves and our coun-try. There'd been no pot of gold to aim for and no contract of employment. It was all about perfecting the performance and, apart from having to do a few interviews, we were kind of left to get on with it.

Now, all of a sudden, we were sitting in the back of a lim-ousine with our new PA, being chased by a helicopter! We also had a contract with us that listed everything expected of us, from the minimum amount of time we were required to spend on the ice during each show, through to how many interviews we'd have to do. The list seemed endless.

It was definitely a rude awakening for us. Fame and fortune are all well and good, but when there are contracts involved, you have to work hard for it.

JAYNE:

We were never very comfortable in interviews. We were so shy back then and must have been an interviewer's nightmare!

Later we did have media training in New York, just before we began a tour there. It was based mainly around how to handle interviews, making sure you made the most of your airtime and deflecting difficult questions. It's an important skill these days, especially in America where you might only be given a few seconds. That time has to be totally dedicated to promoting your show, and promoters expect you to do a good job. Dry up or say the wrong thing and you potentially jeopardise sales.

The course we went on lasted two days and ended up being a strange experience. The chap who was teaching us would be deathly quiet prior to the clock striking nine, hardly even acknowledging we were there, and then the moment the day began he turned into this kind of media-training whirling dervish, all high-fives and enthusiasm. Then as soon as lunch was called his face would drop and he'd run off into the corner, eating his sandwich while staring into space. He either didn't like his job or he didn't like ice skating. We couldn't figure out which. Although we felt a bit uncomfortable, the course was actually extremely useful, as before that we'd been inexperienced in front of the camera and found interviews hard.

JAYNE & CHRIS:

A slightly quirkier side to our fame is that we've always had a lot of things named after us – anything from household pets such as dogs and cats through to farm animals. Then there are the more official tributes, such as the Torvill & Dean rose and the T&D Café in the National Ice Centre, not to mention several roads. In fact, in the Wollaton area of Nottingham there's a housing estate called the Torvill & Dean estate. If you put it into Google Maps you'll see names such as Dean Close, Christopher Close, Callaway Close, Bolero Close and Courtney Close. There's also a Bolero Square, just in front of the National Ice Centre.

Over in Sarajevo, when they set up a semi-permanent camp at the Zetra stadium during the Bosnian War, they named it

Camp Bolero. There's also a working tram named after us. According to Jayne, she's the front half and Chris is the back!

But the most surprising tribute of all came when we were told that two gigantic Russian cargo ships had been named after us – one christened the *Jayne Torvill* and the other, of course, the *Christopher Dean*. We were even presented with two huge models of them. Jayne still has them in her attic. We've since been told that Chris's ship has been refurbished and is currently operating out of Panama, but that Jayne's was scrapped about three years ago!

CHRIS:

One of the more unusual things to emerge from the Sarajevo Olympics was a request by Madame Tussauds to make models of us for their wax museum. It was literally just after *Bolero*, so they made exact copies of our costumes and set us up in a pose from the routine. Jayne's looked fairly lifelike but I'm afraid mine just looked different to how I saw myself.

The strangest part of the process came when it was time to choose the eyes. Suddenly they pulled out this huge tray of eye-balls, hundreds of them, all different colours and sizes, and we had to decide which ones were closest to ours. The models are still on exhibition in Blackpool and have aged far better than we have.

But by far the most embarrassing thing that ever happened to us as a result of being famous was when Noel Edmonds caught us with one of his 'Gotcha' awards. These mock honours were handed out to unsuspecting celebrities on his Saturday night TV show, *Noel's House Party*, usually after setting them up with some kind of elaborate hoax.

Once he got you, you were then invited on to the show to watch it all back, in front of a live studio audience and around ten million people at home. It was car-crash television *par excellence* and we fell for it hook, line and sinker.

The ruse was based around a TV show Noel was (apparently) presenting called *A Time of Your Life*, on which celebrities were invited to reminisce about past successes, and at the same time be introduced to people who'd also been making the headlines at the time. Think *Surprise Surprise* meets *This Is Your Life* – except that none of the people invited on to our show were for real. First on was an ice sculptor, who was asked to create something specially for us there and then, making an enormous racket in the process. He was followed by a pop band called the Noisy Boys, who'd supposedly had a hit in the charts at the time ... When Noel asked us if we remembered the song we apologetically said that we didn't – one of us even claiming that we were probably out of the country at the time!

Straight after this the director stopped the cameras and asked us if we'd be willing to do a retake. 'Would you mind pretending that you actually do remember the song? It's for the sake of continuity, really.'

We were too confused to refuse and so went along with it. In fact, I think I even claimed that I bought Jayne a copy of it. Fancy asking Torvill & Dean to lie, though – and live on TV!!

But the show's *pièce de résistance* came when Noel invited on Lionel Blair, who was introduced as a close personal friend of ours. After hugging us both, Lionel went on to tell some made-up anecdote about him secretly dressing up as a waiter while we were all having a meal in Nottingham. Apparently we'd all had a great laugh.

The fact was we'd never met Lionel before in our lives, and so had been thrown into a state of embarrassment and mild panic.

They even made us wear some horribly garish 1980s clothing – Jayne like a reject from *Dynasty* and me like Rick Astley.

JAYNE:

There have been plenty of times when we've been affected by other people's fame, of course. One memorable occasion happened when we were working with Michael Crawford on *Barnum*. He called us up one day. 'Are you two busy tomorrow?'

'No, I don't think so. Why?'

'I'm going to take you on a little trip. There's a friend of mine who'd like to talk to you about music.'

We were intrigued. The next day Michael arrived in his car and off we set. We eventually pulled up outside this enormous Edwardian house in Mayfair. We followed Michael up the steps and he rang the bell. After a few seconds the door opened and standing there was Sarah Brightman.

'Hello, Michael! Hello, you two, nice to meet you. Come on in.'

This wasn't what we were expecting at all. Sarah Brightman! But that was just the start of it. We were then led into this huge room, only to find Andrew Lloyd Webber, Trevor Nunn and the actress, Finola Hughes, all chatting away about what they were working on at the time. As fans of musical theatre, it was like hobnobbing with royalty.

It turned out that the reason Michael had invited us was specifically to meet Andrew Lloyd Webber. We were choosing our music for the 1984 season (we hadn't yet considered *Bolero*) and he wanted to ask Andrew if he'd consider writing something original for us. 'I'd be delighted to help if I can. What sort of thing are you looking for?'

'I'm looking for something which explores emotions, all the different aspects of love,' said Chris.

Andrew laughed. 'Really? Aspects of love, you say?'

'That's right.'

We were a little bit perplexed at the time. Chris hadn't said anything amusing. He'd just told him what he was thinking. What was so funny? It was a good five or six years before we

realised the significance of what he'd said. Andrew had just finished reading a book called *Aspects of Love* and was considering
turning it into a musical.

As is often the way, nothing came of our little chat. He was
obviously a very busy man and had other things occupying his
time – including a new musical called *Aspects of Love*, of course.

CHRIS:

Our next brush with celebrities en masse happened when we
were asked to appear at a Royal Variety Performance in 1985,
not long after we'd turned pro. We'd just arrived back from
Australia and had been approached about doing something.
We obviously couldn't skate on stage so the producers suggested something more creative.

David Jacobs was the host, and he would announce that we
were in Australia at the time and so were unable to appear in
person, but that we would like to skate something for the audience via satellite link-up. They would then play a video of us
performing *Song of India*, one of our professional routines, after
which we'd walk on and surprise the audience. It was a very
special moment.

The last time we'd been at the Palladium was when we'd first
met Michael Crawford, back in 1982. He was our first celebrity
encounter. Now the place was absolutely teeming with them. It
was our first ever showbiz event – an unfamiliar situation as
we'd never really been part of mainstream showbusiness.

So we were horrified when we saw a rather large Australian
man in his mid to late fifties looking rather worse for wear,
lurking around backstage. He had stains all over his suit and
tie, and his demeanour suggested he'd been drinking. We
moved away as far as we could from him, and eventually
became quite indignant.

'He looks drunk. Why haven't they thrown him out? The

Queen Mother and Prince Charles are just beyond those curtains.' We were very wary of him.

In fact, the 'inebriated' Australian was none other than Barry Humphries' alter ego, Sir Les Patterson, the Australian cultural attaché.

'Thank goodness we never reported him,' said Jayne. 'It would have been so embarrassing.'

JAYNE:

After we did our bit with David Jacobs, we thought that would be that, and were about to walk off stage when the actor and singer Howard Keel was introduced, which stopped us in our tracks.

Howard had been the star of many a musical film, not least *Kiss Me Kate*, which was one of my favourites. To suddenly have him there, standing in front of me, was a huge thrill. I was star-struck. What happened next, though, was beyond a dream.

After being introduced, he handed me a rose and began singing the love song from *Mack & Mabel*, which is called 'I Won't Send Roses'. I was almost in tears. It was such a beautiful moment, and he had such an amazing voice. Apparently it had all been David Jacobs' idea. He'd been responsible for breaking *Mack & Mabel* in the UK, and had been a big fan of our routine. He was such a lovely man.

CHRIS:

There was a time when I had aspirations of becoming a musical theatre actor.

After I broke my wrist at the end of 1986 I honestly thought for a time that I'd never skate again. So, with my wrist in a cast and a seemingly bleak future ahead of me, I decided one day that the time had come for me to consider a change of career –

and, after much deliberation, I settled on becoming a song and dance man.

I could dance on ice well enough, and surely it couldn't be all that different? I was also reasonably musical and had an amazing singing voice – or at least I did in the shower.

When it came to the dancing I'd have some support, which would come in the shape of Karen Barber. I'd known Karen since the mid-1970s, and when she and Nicky Slater stopped skating together she'd joined our company. We were great friends and she too was at a loose end. 'Why don't you come down to London with me, stay at my flat, and we'll take some lessons together,' I said. 'It'll be fun.'

I knew Karen could dance, so together we embarked on our musical theatre career.

With perhaps a little too much optimism, I rented a flat in London, got somebody to help me pack my belongings into my car, and headed off to the big city. I should point out that I fully intended to stay in London. This was certainly no pipe dream; I was going to give it a serious shot.

The flat (which I later found out used to belong to Maggie Smith) was about three floors up, and so I had to figure out how to get the contents of my car into my new flat using only one arm. Thank goodness for Karen. I was able to fit a lot of luggage in my car, and as a result there were at least a dozen trips. By the end of it we were both exhausted.

A few days after moving in I went to meet my new voice coach. He was a very eminent gentleman and had been recommended as one of the best in the business. I'm afraid that I blocked out his name years ago, as I'm pretty sure he did mine.

'I'm going to play a scale, Chris, and I'd like you to follow it. OK?'

'Of course.'

So he began, and I tried to follow. But I'm afraid that as hard as I tried, I never even came close to finding the same notes. After about a minute of this he stopped.

'Let's try a single note, shall we?'

So he played a note on his piano and I tried again, but I still couldn't find it. To be honest, I wasn't sure I'd know even if I did actually manage to find the right note.

It was quite a revelation. All these years of what I thought were quite passable impersonations of Freddie Mercury were in actual fact the work of a tone-deaf ice dancer. I've always been prepared to acknowledge my weaknesses, however, so decided to retire from singing there and then. Never mind, I thought, there's still tap-dancing. I might not be able to sing but I was adamant I could dance.

The lessons took place at the world-famous Pineapple Dance Studios in Covent Garden. To say I found it intimidating would be an understatement. The room was absolutely heaving with people, all of whom were clearly dedicated to tap-dancing. Only one person looked out of place – me.

Although it wasn't quite as bad as trying to sing, I still found myself edging to the back of the class. Partly because I felt self-conscious, but also because I wanted to see what everyone else was doing. This didn't work, as roughly halfway through the class the teacher said, 'OK, everyone turn round', which meant I was then at the front of the class, with everyone looking at me.

The main problem was that I felt I should be good at it. I was a dancer, and I was fit, strong and had coordination. I was also a choreographer. It was just going to take time and a lot of practice. I wasn't exactly a natural.

The difference was that my ankles had been strapped into skating boots for 15 years and, compared with all the loose limbs around me, I was positively arthritic. Even simply loosening up was going to take me a lifetime.

But it was my fellow classmates who really suffered. I was

still wearing my plaster cast at the time, and as soon as I started to sweat, it started to smell. It was impossible to clean inside the cast, so they just had to put up with it. It was appalling, though, and became so bad that I ended up dancing by myself in the corner. Paranoia followed me everywhere. Even at the cinema I'd move seats if anyone sat within five metres.

When the cast eventually came off I was told that my arm had healed perfectly, which meant I was OK to tour again. That was a relief for everybody, I think.

JAYNE & CHRIS:

We've been asked to do some strange things over the years, but there's one that stands out as being perhaps the most unsuited to our talents: we were invited to make an album together.

We had already had one record released under our name – a recording of our arrangement of *Bolero*. It went under the title of *The Music of Torvill & Dean* and reached an impressive number nine in the charts. We even received a gold disc each.

The beauty of that record, apart from the music, of course, was that it didn't feature either of our voices. If it had, it might not have been such a hit.

But who were we to argue? Chris said he was a strong singer; in fact, in his mind we were going to be the new Kylie and Jason! Anyway, it might be fun and it would help pass the time while Chris was recovering from an ankle injury and couldn't go anywhere.

No such luck. The entire experience was a nightmare from start to finish. It's a good story though . . .

We were in Australia at the time, and had been contacted by a man called Kevin Stanton. He had a studio in Sydney and approached us to make the album.

'We're not experienced singers,' said Jayne.

'Aww, don't worry about that, we have the technology,' said Kevin. 'Just you see!'

We were staying in Palm Beach, which is a suburb of Sydney, so he suggested that he come over to our place so we could choose some songs together.

'OK,' we said, 'that sounds fine.'

'Thing is, guys, I'm banned from driving at the moment. Any chance you could come and pick me up?'

'But you're over an hour away! Oh, all right then.'

We have to admit we weren't exactly used to being asked to pick potential employers up, but we didn't really mind. Once we were all back at ours Kevin got out his guitar and we began trying out a few songs. What a din that must have been! But six hours later we were still at it, and this went on into the following day, and then the day after. We knew it was all part of the process, choosing songs and rehearsing them, but it was tedious beyond belief. In the end Jayne got bored, and waited for an opportunity to escape.

'I'm just going out to buy some coffee, we've run out,' she said, while Kevin and Chris were rehearsing one of his lines. 'I won't be long.' And off she went shopping for the afternoon. Four hours later she reappeared.

One evening, after a particularly gruelling rehearsal, we were all sitting around chatting when Kevin mentioned that he used to be into yoga, back in the 1970s. 'Have you ever tried the lotus position?' he asked.

'No,' we replied

'It's easy, watch this.'

So he sat on the floor and began to rearrange himself. Then, as he began to shove his knees sideways we heard a nasty cracking sound.

'Bloody hell! What have I done? Guys, you've gotta help me, I'm in agony!'

We're ashamed to say that our immediate response was to

laugh. Jayne even had to go to her room. After five minutes or so we composed ourselves and went back to help Kevin to his feet. By this time his knee was the size of a football.

'That looks serious,' said Chris. 'Looks like you might have torn a ligament. I'll tell you what, let's take you to my doctor. He treated my ankle and he's very good.'

Sure enough Kevin had torn a ligament, and required surgery. By now we were just a few days from recording, after which we had to fly straight back to England. Even with Kevin's injury there was no way we could move things. We'd have to carry on regardless.

Things were about to get even worse for poor Kevin, however. The day before recording was due to begin he had a huge row with his engineer, who decided to shut up shop and leave. This meant there was nobody to run the studio, so when we arrived the next morning, Chris and our then assistant, Debbie, had to open up while Jayne fetched Kevin from hospital.

Kevin, who was now in a wheelchair, which Jayne had had to pack up into the car, had been put on some extremely strong painkillers and so was all over the place. He could hardly speak, let alone record an album.

In the end it was decided that Debbie would operate the multi-track, under Kevin's groggy guidance, while we did what we were being paid to do, which was sing.

As we watched him through the glass partition, we could see his eyelids start to droop.

'Kevin, wake up,' said Debbie. 'What do I do now?'

'Hey? Erm, press that one.'

'What, this one here?'

'Yes, that's the ... Zzzzzzz.'

He was off again.

We had less than a week to record 14 songs. Two a day! If we were actually going to do it we'd have to get cracking. Then, when Kevin started to perk up a bit, we discovered a new delay.

'Aww, sorry, guys. I need to go to the toilet. Could somebody give me a hand?'

'Sure, no problem,' replied Chris.

But Chris was wrong, this *was* a problem. Kevin had his whole leg in plaster, so negotiating him into the loo was no easy task. In the end it took the best part of half an hour, and because he'd been told to drink plenty of fluids he needed to go again, and then again. Chris became quite proficient after a while and managed to get there and back in about 15 minutes.

Recording so many songs in such a short space of time eventually began to affect our voices. They weren't especially strong to begin with (or tuneful, for that matter) and after a while began to disappear. Then Kevin had an idea.

'Port's good for the voice. Yeah, that's what we need – port!'

So off Debbie went and before long came back with a bottle. We have no idea, or indeed memory, as to whether the port helped bring back our faltering voices, but it did help quell Kevin's pain. Sure, he wasn't singing, but he did like port.

On the final day of recording, we found out that it was Kevin's birthday. Despite the Whitehall farce we liked Kevin and felt sorry for him (he'd spent almost all his remaining money on the operation, and was pretty short of funds by now), so decided to give him a party.

Jayne bought him a cake, but as she carried it through to the studio she tripped and dumped the entire thing on the floor. We managed to salvage enough for us all to have a slice (or a dollop), but it was final proof that Kevin Stanton was, at that time, Australia's unluckiest man.

The album, called *Here We Stand*, eventually came out, but was never released in the UK – only in Australia – and so is probably a collector's item. It's still available on iTunes, though!

7

Accidents & Injuries

JAYNE & CHRIS:

Accidents and injuries are an occupational hazard for ice skaters.
It doesn't matter how good you are or how experienced, when
you're working on a surface as unpredictable and fast as ice,
absolutely anything can happen – and probably will. We've seen
some real horrors in our time, and have even been involved in
one or two ourselves. But unlike, for instance, footballers or
actors – who can be replaced by either a substitute or an under-
study – we have to carry on regardless. If we can, that is.

This means that the lengths we sometimes go to in order to
perform probably appear quite extreme to some people, but
when it's your name on the posters, it's your vital duty to
deliver the best show you can on the night. If you don't, you're
not just letting the audience down, you're letting all your colleagues down: the cast and the crew and the promoter, not to
mention all the local businesses. The responsibility feels
immense.

Jayne has had asthma for a long time, which is now under

control, but there have been times over the years when she's become so breathless during a performance that she's had to be given oxygen backstage. But it's not something that she would ever question or consider. It's just part and parcel. You can let it affect you or you can just get on with it. All ice skaters are the same.

But there are times when something so bad happens that there's just nothing you can do about it. Fortunately for us, that's only happened on a couple of occasions in our shows, and only once during our amateur career, so we've been lucky. But that statistic would be far less impressive (over the last 20-odd years) if it wasn't for our physio, Sharon Morrison.

Sharon has been working with us now since the early 1990s and has, since then, attended every show we've ever performed, as well as every television rehearsal and recording. And thank goodness she has, because without her we'd have been forced into retirement years ago, like a couple of old racehorses!

During our first world tour, we'd be on the ice for much of the show's two-and-a-half-hour duration. We'd perform *Mack & Mabel*, *Barnum* and *Bolero*, plus all the big company numbers. Some of those would last for up to 25 minutes each. It was very physically demanding and is definitely a job for the young.

Because of the sheer physicality of what we do, it takes more than just a quick stretch to get us ready for the ice, especially these days. We have to let Sharon work her magic before we're ready to go, and then she has to do the same again when we come off. Even after we finish a tour, there's a strict regime we have to follow in order to let our bodies wind down.

During our second world tour, which was called *Face the Music*, we'd probably have likened ourselves to a Formula 1 team: two highly tuned performance machines with Sharon as the mechanic. These days, however (and Sharon agrees with us), it's like keeping a couple of classic cars on the road.

Don't get us wrong, we're doing pretty well for people of

our age, and we can still hold our own on the ice, but keeping fit and staying in good condition has become more and more important. Again, if it wasn't for Sharon, who also works with us on our general fitness, we'd probably have suffered more over the years.

But, as we've already suggested, you can only take so much preventative medicine. Accidents happen, and if you can't go on, you can't go on. In those circumstances you have to submit and let nature take its course. Not always easy, we have to admit, and it's always tempting to come back before you're ready. We've both been guilty of that on occasion.

JAYNE:

I've been very, very lucky when it comes to accidents and injuries. In fact, the only thing I could ever class as being serious would be the time I fell from a lift when skating pairs with my first partner, Michael Hutchinson. I fell from the lift and suffered concussion after landing on the side of my head. Apparently I started saying all kinds of strange things!

That was pre-Chris, and since then I've been blessed. In fact, he seems to have had my share of mishaps. I've had a couple of near-misses, though.

Towards the end of one of the early *Dancing on Ice* tours, I remember everyone being extremely tired. We'd been performing two shows a day for what seemed like forever and we were all starting to become a tiny bit weary. Then one day at Wembley Arena, towards the end of one of the big group numbers, a disaster was averted that would probably have spelled the end of my career.

Roughly halfway through the routine I had to run on to a large ramp situated in the corner of the rink, before diving forwards and being caught by a group of male professionals. As I reached the top of the ramp and turned my back on the rink, the skaters began to move into position, except that this time they didn't quite make it. One of them fell as they were skating towards the ramp and took the rest with him. The whole group were on their backsides! The only person in the arena who wasn't aware of this was me. I knew there must have been something amiss by the reaction of the audience, but as I hadn't heard anybody shout 'Don't jump!' I committed myself and went ahead. So there I was, flying through the air, about to hit the ice headfirst. Fortunately, but only by a hair's breadth, the boys managed to get up in time to catch me, but probably with less than an inch to spare before I hit the ice. Ice can be so, so dangerous.

One of the more light-hearted moments at Wembley Arena, where we've performed a record 133 times over the years, did actually involve an accident – although a very minor one.

We were just starting a matinee performance of *Dancing on Ice*. The judges were being presented to the audience, and last on to the stage was the wonderful actress, Ruthie Henshall – who, when introduced, promptly curtsied, tripped and fell flat on her bum. Being a true professional, Ruthie got straight back up on her feet, curtsied again, and this time managed to take her seat. Once she'd sat down, Ruthie reclined slightly, looked at her fellow judges and said, 'Bloody hell! Did you see that?' The judges were in hysterics, as were the 10,000 members of the audience, all of whom heard every word. Ruthie had obviously forgotten for a moment that she was wearing a microphone. Andi Peters, who was the presenter on that tour, covered it up beautifully.

This next story is more about illness than accident or injury, but it did involve us having to cancel a show once.

We were in Glasgow, again on one of the early *Dancing on Ice* tours, and somebody in the company contracted norovirus. For those of you who don't know what norovirus is, its other name is the winter vomiting bug, which should tell you all you need to know. It spreads like wildfire and so can wipe out an entire company in a matter of hours – and that's exactly what happened to us.

Chris had been the first to come down with it. It was a Friday night and we were mid-show. He suddenly came off the ice and just vomited quite violently.

'Chris, are you OK?'

'I think it's just something I've eaten. At least I hope it is. I'll be fine.'

But he wasn't. He kept going on and having to come off again, each time vomiting more and more. He obviously wasn't well at all.

That night after the show we got a doctor in and he said that if anyone else vomited we should let him know. About 6.30 the next morning I felt unwell. This was a Saturday and we were due to have two shows that day, arriving for warm-ups at about 10am. I managed to get myself to the rink, but no sooner had I arrived there than two of our professional skaters started being sick, at which point we were down to a company of about seven. Chris was feeling better by this point, and I, despite feeling dreadful, was still OK to perform. Some of us had been injected with an anti-sickness drug, which seemed to work.

With the number of skaters still standing, we worked out that with some changing round and a little bit of luck, we could just about put a show together. Then, literally a few minutes after we opened the house, Dan Whiston, one of the only professional skaters who hadn't been sick, suddenly ran to the side of backstage and started vomiting. And that, as they say, was that. Dan was integral to so many numbers, including an excellent solo routine, so after he went we realised that it simply couldn't be done.

We were due to fly out to Belfast the next morning, but were all told to stay in our rooms and not open the door to anyone. Naturally we had to cancel our flights and in the end had to charter a plane to get us there on time. Years earlier, on the *Face the Music* tour, we had again had to cancel our flights and were stuck on Vancouver Island. Tony Harpur, our extremely resourceful tour manager, managed to charter an enormous ferry, which was used during the day to carry thousands of people. I shudder to think how much it cost but at around 2am we all got on board and set sail for mainland America, all 35 of us! We each had a go at steering, too, which was great fun.

CHRIS:

I'm afraid I haven't been quite as lucky as Jayne. In fact, you could say I have a genius for accidents and injuries.

My first accident on the ice happened just a few weeks after I began skating, at just ten years old. Dad and Betty had dropped me off at the rink one afternoon and before I took to the ice I went to get my skates sharpened. After that I joined the other kids and grown-ups and started doing what I did best – which, at the time, was skating very quickly. I've always been a bit of a speed freak, and used to love nothing more than tearing around the rink, weaving in and out of the other skaters.

What I didn't really appreciate then was that sharp skates meant more speed, and I underestimated just how fast I was now going. So when I zoomed up to the barrier to do one of my skid stops, I didn't stop at all. I ended up in a heap on the ice with a searing pain running through my leg.

Before I knew it, Fred, the chap who ran the skate-hire stall, was kneeling next to me. He felt my leg for a moment. 'You might have broken it, Chris. We'll have to get you to hospital.'

When my dad and Betty came to pick me up they were sent straight to the hospital, where I was waiting for them with my leg in plaster. Things didn't stop there, though, as the first time I tried to negotiate stairs using my crutches I toppled forward and went flying, ending up, once again, in a heap on the floor!

Since then it feels like I've broken most bones in my body.

In the mid-1990s, during the *Face the Music* tour, there was one number in which I had to arch my back and pass under a huge desk. The day before the show, I'd pulled my back and Sharon had advised me to leave it a few days. I can be quite stubborn at times, especially when it comes to performing, so I said, 'No, I'll be fine.' I went on to do the number, couldn't arch my back, and five minutes later she was trying to patch up my chin in the dressing room. I'd hit the desk so hard that I now had a hole about an inch wide below my bottom lip. I could actually stick my tongue through it, so every time I tried to have a drink, I leaked! The stitches were agony.

Probably my worst injury as an amateur was when Jayne broke my nose. Not intentionally, I should add! We were practising a lift during training one day, when her elbow made contact with my face. All of a sudden I felt my nose crack, and before I knew it there was blood everywhere. 'Do you think it's broken?' I asked. 'No,' she said, 'it looks fine to me.'

We carried on skating for a bit, until the pain became so unbearable that I had to stop. When I went back to the dressing room and looked in the mirror my nose was pointing to my right ear! We were in Oberstdorf, and I took myself off to a doctor who said, 'Right, there are two things we can do. We can either set it now while you're in pain, which will obviously hurt a lot, or you can come back tomorrow and we can set it under anaesthetic.' I said, 'Do it now! I just want to get it over and done with.' So he sat me down, put straps over my wrists, which kind of alarmed me slightly, and set about resetting my nose. The pain was excruciating! A few days later it still didn't look or feel right so I went back. 'Oh, it hasn't worked, I'm afraid. Let's put you under anaesthetic.'

Another painful episode that springs to mind happened one day when we were rehearsing a lift. We both fell – me landing first, then Jayne – and my hand got in the way of one of her skates. The blade went straight into the side of my hand, resulting in yet another hole and missing my tendons by millimetres. Once again there was blood absolutely everywhere. I remember looking at the wound and being able to see part of the muscle in my hand. I quickly held it up in the air and rushed off to get it seen to. Cue more stitches and agony!

On top of these mishaps I've had a broken wrist as a result of a fall backstage (which I'll come to later), ruptured my cruciate ligament after falling on the ice, had surgery on both shoulders following injuries during *Dancing on Ice*, broken a bone in my foot after falling off a pavement and herniated a disc while on tour in Australia. That was unbelievably painful; one of the most excruciating sensations I've ever experienced. I remember hobbling round to see Michael Edgley, the producer, straight after I'd done it.

When I found him I told him what I'd done. 'I'm in agony, Michael. I'm afraid I can't go on the ice like this.'

'Aw, you've gotta go on, mate, you've gotta go on!'

'But I can hardly walk!'

'Can't you do *Bolero*? You must be able to do *Bolero*?'

'Not like this I can't! I can hardly even *say Bolero*.'

Faced with a possible cancellation Michael rushed in a string of chiropractors, none of whom did me any good. Then, out of sheer desperation, he brought in a faith healer . . .

Before he led her into the dressing room, where I was lying face up, Michael came in and said: 'For heaven's sake, Chris, don't laugh. She looks a bit weird, but whatever you do, DON'T LAUGH!'

So in walked this faith healer. And precisely because Michael had told me *not* to laugh, that's exactly what I wanted to do. As she stood over me, doing something that resembled a kind of 'laying on of hands' exercise, I had tears running down my cheeks. When she asked me if I was all right I just blamed it on the pain. After about ten funny, but ultimately ineffectual minutes, she decided it might be a good idea to hypnotise me instead. I actually fell asleep after a couple of minutes of her trying, and when I woke up the pain was just as bad. If anything it had got worse through the strain of trying not to laugh. In the end I took all the painkillers I could, just to get through.

You have to try and make light of these setbacks. If you didn't, you'd go mad. But when something befalls you that eventually results in the cancellation of an entire tour, it suddenly becomes very hard to see the funny side.

This happened to me in America, about ten shows into a 60-date, coast-to-coast tour. We were due to perform in some iconic venues, such as Madison Square Garden, and had been really looking forward to it.

During the warm-up one afternoon one of our professional skaters came on to the ice and told me he wouldn't be able to perform that evening. He'd hurt his back earlier that day and would need a few days to recuperate. This was a huge blow and meant we'd have to make all kinds of changes to the forthcoming show. As I was leaving the ice – my mind frantically searching for solutions – I lost my footing and fell on to the matting. I'm not sure exactly how it happened; all I remember was feeling an agonising pain in my left wrist.

The pain was so excruciating that tears were running down my cheeks. I put my forearm in a bucket of ice for 15 minutes, hoping it was just a sprain, and then got myself ready for the opening number. It was no good. I couldn't grip, which meant I couldn't pull, and if I couldn't pull I'd be no use whatsoever. How on earth would I get through *Barnum* with only one arm?! It was a hopeless state of affairs.

The company managed to finish the first half without us, but in the interval it was decided that we'd have to cancel the second half. So the management made an announcement, explaining that I'd injured myself earlier on and was unable to continue. Listening to that announcement was one of the worst points of my professional career.

Misfortune still wasn't quite finished with me yet. I hoped it would be nothing more than a sprain, which would mean about five days' rest. That would be bad news, but not a disaster. Even so, I had a horrible feeling that this was something worse. It felt different from a sprain.

Unfortunately, I was right. When I went for an x-ray later that evening it was confirmed there and then that I'd broken my wrist. It would take a minimum of two months to heal.

Out of sheer desperation I sought a second opinion, but the doctor said exactly the same. 'It's a bad break and you'll need at least eight weeks' rest, maybe twelve.' I was devastated; overcome with sadness.

The following day our producers, Michael Edgley and Michael Linnitt, called a company meeting. Only they, myself and Jayne knew the full extent of my injury, and so when the news was broken to the company there were gasps of shock from all around the room. By the time the producers had finished speaking every single person was in tears. The 50 remaining shows, which included Madison Square Garden, would have to be cancelled and the company abandoned.

People asked whether we might be able to start again once my wrist had healed, but unfortunately that wouldn't be possible. I knew that my wrist would eventually heal, but I'd been told that it might never be strong enough for me to skate with Jayne again. This was another cloud hanging over me.

The sense of responsibility I felt was overwhelming. It wasn't just the two of us, as it had been in our amateur days; we were part of a company now. But as we've already said, when it's your name on the poster the responsibility falls far and wide. As well as our fellow skaters there were also the technicians, the staff at the arenas where we were booked to appear, the truck drivers, the riggers, the administrators. Scores of people would be affected by the cancellations.

Then there was the financial aspect. Tens of thousands of

dollars had already been spent on advertising, and millions of dollars had been taken in advance ticket sales. An entire mini-economy had just crashed. Insurance would cover any outright losses, but it wouldn't cover our loss of earnings.

My wrist healed quite quickly in the end, far quicker than my feelings of responsibility.

JAYNE:

Fortunately, situations like this don't arise very often. More often than not, accidents on the ice result in embarrassment rather than injury. We've both had our fair share of those over the years.

The first piece of choreography we worked on with Graeme Murphy was for a number called *Song of India*, which was created specially for the 1984 World Professional Championships. It was a technically demanding piece and won us straight 10.0s at the Worlds. When we went out on tour the following year we decided to create an extended version featuring the entire company.

I remember watching one of the early rehearsals. We were in Australia and before the company went out on to the ice Chris lined everyone up and gave them a talk on what was expected, finishing with the line, 'OK, then, I want everybody concentrating. No falling over!'

So, off they all went to get into position and during the very first step Chris got tangled up in his trousers (which were huge baggy things) and fell flat on his face – bang! That was my fault, of course.

CHRIS:

Although accidents on the ice can be painful, they're rarely scary. Those kinds of misfortunes usually happen off the ice, and I've had two in my lifetime. One that happened at sea, and the other on four wheels.

While on tour in Australia in the late 1980s, a bunch of us took off for a few days to a beach house in a place called Terrigal, which is north of Sydney. We had a break between venues so decided to treat ourselves. The beach itself was fantastic. It seemed to stretch for miles and had fantastic waves. Great for surfing.

Courtney Jones was over at the time to discuss costumes, and while he and Jayne had a stroll on the beach I decided to go off and have a swim.

I'd been in the sea for around 20 minutes when I suddenly got caught on a rip, which is like an undertow. I tried to swim back towards the shallows, realised I wasn't getting anywhere, so started doing a racing crawl. But the harder I swam, the further out I seemed to go. What I should have done in this situation was just stay afloat and let myself drift until the current died, but instead I kept on swimming – pushing harder and harder.

Eventually I started to feel tired; exhausted, in fact. It got to the point where I could hardly move my arms and legs. Waves began to slosh into my face and I began taking in mouthfuls of seawater. This made me heave violently and that was when panic really started to set in. I could see Jayne away in the distance, so began waving at her frantically. She eventually saw me, but simply started waving back. She obviously had no idea what was happening and just thought I was being friendly. Looking back, it reminds me of that old public information film from the 1970s, where Petunia and Joe are on a beach and see a man in the sea waving at them, but instead of calling the coastguard they wave back!

When you think you're about to die your life really does begin to flash before your eyes. I knew I was drowning and was starting to feel like I couldn't hang on. Everything went into slow motion, so much so that it was like having a montage playing before me – pictures of people I knew and places I'd been, a whole trail of events popping up before me. I remember wishing I was back home in England, doing something humdrum.

Then all of a sudden I heard somebody calling my name. 'Chris! Chris, mate, are you OK?'

I looked round and there in front of me was Wayne Deweyert, one of our company members. I didn't have to say anything, nor could I. Wayne could see I was in trouble and started swimming straight towards me. On seeing him approach I suddenly felt a surge of energy and began flapping my arms and legs for all I was worth, determined to try and keep myself afloat.

When Wayne reached me he pushed his boogie board in front of me and I managed drag myself on to it. I lay there for what seemed like an age, trying to get my breath back and come to terms with what had nearly happened.

I'm sorry to say I was rather rude to Jayne when I eventually made it back to the beach. I may even have used one or two expletives. I think it was shock more than anything.

Our next trip to Australia was no less eventful. Again during a break in the schedule, I got the chance to fulfil a dream of mine when I was invited to take part in a celebrity NASCAR race.

As a self-confessed speed freak, I even at one point had my own racing car – a Formula Ford 1600cc. I'd read in a magazine once that you could take lessons at Silverstone and so I enrolled on a five-week course there. Being an impatient so-and-so I didn't last the full five weeks, and ended up taking part in my first race after just two, with four or five more directly afterwards.

Wanting to take things up a level, I decided to hire the Formula Ford for a few months and see how I got on. All the other drivers had sponsors, but not me. I was the only one stupid enough to sponsor me! And, boy, did it become expensive. You don't realise what's involved until you actually run one. There's maintenance, fuel, transport to and from the circuit, fees to enter races; I could go on.

I had one or two bangs in my first couple of races; nothing serious, though. Or, as the mechanics would put it, 'nothing money couldn't fix', before sending me another astronomical bill. In the end I decided to hang up my driving gloves before I flushed more money down the toilet.

So the invitation in Australia was perfect. We were between tours and free at the time, so the insurers were OK about it. I didn't have to hire a car or pay any bills. All I had to do was turn up and drive. Easy!

The race was taking place at Melbourne's Calder Park Raceway and it promised to be a fun day. I was lent a car by one of the drivers and would be racing against some professionals, which suited me just fine. Exactly the kind of challenge I thrived on.

Jayne, our assistant Debbie, and a few members of the company came to support me, all wearing specially designed t-shirts with 'Dean Speed' printed on them.

Once in my overalls and helmet, I felt a sudden surge of excitement. I'd wanted to do something like this for years but had always been discouraged. 'What if you crash?' You have to take chances in life and just because I was a skater didn't mean I wasn't allowed to enjoy myself occasionally. It'd be fine!

As the doors on these cars are welded shut you have to climb in through the window. I tried my best to do this without looking like an idiot but I'm afraid I failed miserably. It took me about a minute! Once strapped in I began to psych myself up. 'Come on, Chris. You can do it!'

As it turned out I was the only celebrity taking part in the race. The rest were all professional racing drivers.

Jayne had been asked to start the race, and I remember watching her like a hawk, desperate for her to wave her chequered flag. When she eventually did (from a very safe distance) I slammed down my foot and we were off.

The sound of the engines alone was enough to scare the living daylights out of you. But I was in my element; the controlled slides into the corners, the acceleration down the straights. We were getting up to around 150mph in places. It was madness! After four laps I was lying fourth, with one driver sitting right behind me.

Coming round the bend into the straight, I hit a ridge that ran at a right angle across the track and, as I did, I felt the back begin to slide. I tried to turn into the skid, but knew as soon as it happened that I'd lost control. I hit the brakes as hard as I could and slid off over some grass, still travelling at least 70mph. Then I saw the wall.

Any one of the other six drivers would have taken their feet off the pedals before crashing and let the harness take the impact, but I'm afraid that everything I'd been taught previously had gone out of the window. Literally.

It was quite a stop. For a few seconds afterwards I didn't move. I couldn't. I just sat there, semi-conscious. Then, the pain started; first my neck, then my shoulders, followed by my left foot. At least I'm still alive, I thought. Then I heard a voice at my side, asking me if I was all right. 'Yes, I think so. I don't really know.' 'OK, just sit tight and we'll get you stretchered off to the emergency room.' What worried them most was any possible spinal damage from the whiplash, so the first thing they did was fit me with a collar.

JAYNE:

I'd lost track of which car Chris was in. There were so many distractions, not least the noise! I'd never heard anything like it in my life. Then I suddenly heard somebody shouting.

'One's off!'

'Who is it?'

'I think it's Chris.'

I prayed they'd got the wrong car, but they hadn't. I suddenly felt sick. It was one of the worst moments of my entire life.

They stopped the race and I saw the ambulance tearing up towards the crash. I asked the organiser if he was OK.

'We're not sure.'

'Is he alive? I have to know. Is he alive?'

'They're finding out, Jayne. Try and stay calm.'

'I can't. I need to know!'

'Yes, apparently he's alive. He's talking, too. They're taking him over to the emergency room.'

Only when I saw him with my own eyes could I breathe a sigh of relief. I didn't care if he couldn't skate again, just so long as he was still alive. The first thing he said to me when I saw him was, 'What about the poor guy who lent me the car? He was supposed to drive it in the next race. He's going to kill me!'

As the rest of the 'Dean Speed' team went off to a restaurant, which had been booked to celebrate the race, Chris was taken to the local hospital for a proper examination. Besides the bruising on his chest from the straps – which resembled some kind of weird crucifix – and a little bit of stiffness from the whiplash, the worst injury Chris had suffered was to his ankle, which had been hit very hard by the brake pedal.

They wouldn't be able to find out the extent of the damage until the swelling had gone down, which would probably take about four days. In the meantime he was free to go home.

CHRIS:

Those four days seemed more like 40. I'm a nightmare when I'm bored, but when I'm bored *and* immobile, I'm horrendous! Worse still, my ankle didn't seem to be healing, and was still quite swollen. Then I found out the extent of the injury.

The ligament to the ankle had been torn apart, leaving two separate, frayed ends. They would rejoin, but only if they were stitched together, and any delay would result in further damage to the ends. 'Do I have to make a decision now?' I asked. We were due to fly home in a couple of days, and if I had to have it done immediately, I'd be stuck in Australia for weeks.

'If you want to skate again, then yes,' was the reply.

It was settled then. The next day Debbie and Jayne delivered me to the hospital and I had the operation. They didn't know how long it would take to heal, but it was going to be a matter of weeks. Fortunately both Jayne and Debbie stayed to look after me and keep me company. Not that I gave them much in return. I was back to being bored in no time.

I tried going to the gym a few times, but couldn't do it on my own. In the end Debbie offered to come with me.

JAYNE:

The first couple of weeks were OK. He had plenty of video games and books, and we kept him company when we weren't out doing our own thing. We couldn't be with him all the time. If we had, there'd probably have been more injuries!

Inevitably, his frustration came to a head one day. We were all in the living room of the house we were staying in. Chris was sitting in his armchair and Debbie and I were reading. Suddenly he started to tap the arm of his chair with his fingers. This was never a good sign and was usually an early warning that he was about to either say or do something inflammatory.

Suddenly, he sat up in his chair. 'Watch this!' he said, before grabbing his crutches and launching himself across the room. 'I bet I can do a handstand against the wall on my crutches.'

Without waiting for an answer he pushed off with his good leg, swung hard and then stood upside down against the wall. We were impressed – for about a second – as what Chris hadn't reckoned on was the polished wooden floor that was then supporting him. Upside down and facing Debbie and me, he suddenly realised what was happening, and a look of panic came over him. 'Oh no!' he said, before his crutches did the splits, sending him straight down the wall and on to the floor – headfirst. BANG!

Debbie was the first to break the silence.

'I can't stand this any more. He's like a flipping time bomb!'

'Oh, take no notice of him,' I said.

He eventually picked himself up and got himself back in his chair.

'Are you OK?' I asked.

'Yep, fine,' he said.

He wasn't fine, though. Apart from his pride, which now had an enormous dent in it, he'd also scraped his back on the stone wall and had a great big bump on his head. But it had relieved his boredom, for a few minutes.

CHRIS:

My injuries have gone full circle now, as in recent years I've taken to falling off my bike again, just as I did when I was a child.

There's a hill running by my house in Colorado which is quite steep, and sometimes I charge down it at about 40mph. One day my front tyre burst and I ended up leaving almost all of the skin from my left side on the road, while I continued rolling. That took about six weeks before it even started to heal. Having a shower was agony. If I hadn't had the helmet on I'd have been down to my skull. These days I never go above 30mph!

8
Love & Marriage

JAYNE & CHRIS:

As you now know, we were both quite late starters when it came to love. Skating was all-consuming and, until our late twenties, we were happy being consumed by it. We didn't take holidays and we didn't have hobbies; neither did we have many friends outside of the skating world. It was to all intents and purposes a monastic existence; just the two of us. But then it had to be. Introduce romance into the mix and you're no longer in a position to give it your all. That was our mindset.

You're about to read an amalgamation of two very different stories: one of which tells of a happy, solid alliance. Not without its problems, of course, but ultimately steadfast. And another that is, shall we say, slightly more eventful.

CHRIS:

I'd initially met my first wife, Isabelle Duchesnay, in 1981, when she and her brother Paul were competing at Oberstdorf. I'd been attracted to her then, but had taken it no further. She was only 18 at the time, and I was still lacking in confidence.

Since then I'd followed their career with interest. They never managed to break through internationally in Canada, so had made use of their dual French-Canadian nationality and were now competing for France.

Then, in 1987, Betty Callaway asked me if I'd be interested in helping them with their choreography. It had been a long time since I'd choreographed for amateur competition, so the prospect was quite an exciting one.

We met up and started to workshop a few ideas, in the end choosing a piece called *Savage Rite*, which featured African drums – an instrument that had never been used for ice dancing before.

The fact that Paul and Isabelle were brother and sister made it impossible to introduce a romantic theme into the choreography, and this particular piece had no romantic connotations whatsoever.

After spending a couple of days talking through how the routine might go, we then took the ideas on to the ice and began choreographing. Not long after that Paul hurt his back, which left me to work one-to-one with Isabelle. It was during this time that I realised the attraction I'd first felt towards her hadn't gone away. Moreover, I was increasingly sure it was mutual.

On the ice, Paul and Isabelle were happy with the new choreography and it really seemed to work. So much so that it helped them win a bronze medal at the 1988 European Championships, and finish a very respectable eighth at the 1988 Olympics in Calgary.

It was a good showing, and although they hadn't quite made it this time around, I was sure they would make progress.

A few months after the Olympics they approached me again. This time they were preparing for the forthcoming round of competitions. Time was of the essence, though, and they only had a few weeks, so I suggested they use *Eleanor's Dream*, an old Paul McCartney number that Jayne and I had danced to. It wasn't a romantic dance, once more allowing them to play to their strengths as brother and sister, and I thought it would suit them. Again it worked for them, and by this time we were starting to become a team.

The following year they had more success, winning bronze medals at both the European and World Championships. Then, that same summer, both Jayne and I coached them together on a number called *Missing*, which we danced in our professional shows. We expanded it and turned it into a competitive programme for Paul and Isabelle. More medals followed at the Europeans and Worlds, by which time Isabelle and I were romantically involved.

It wasn't what you'd call a conventional relationship, in that we were apart for the majority of the time. It's so often the way in our line of work. But on top of this, our agent at the time, Michael Linnitt, had advised and suggested that we try to keep any romances we might be involved in under wraps, as they could damage our public image.

This made us feel slightly uncomfortable. It was all very well Jayne and I remaining silent about our own relationship. That was all very innocent and had been running for years. This was different, though. Keeping the press and public guessing is one thing, but this seemed to be taking it a step further.

JAYNE:

Just as it had with almost everything else, it was turning professional that brought me more in line with 'normal' people.

Until then I'd never had a serious relationship; just one or two boyfriends in my late teens. Skating was always my main focus.

My first two 'relationships' happened while we were rehearsing in Australia. Often in skating, as in the music business, people marry within the industry. It's all quite incestuous. That was never going to work for me, though. After all, if you have an argument with that person during the day, would you really want to spend the evening with them too?

That's another reason why a relationship with Chris would probably not have worked. He's somebody who likes to take his work home with him and carry on into the evening. He's so dedicated. Whereas I like to switch off, clear my head and not talk about it.

The only boyfriend I was ever keen to get Chris's approval of was Phil, my future husband. It was important to me that they liked each other. He and Chris were already friends, though, which helped.

I first met Phil in 1989. We were rehearsingwith the All-Stars tour of the USA. Sacramento was the first show and one evening we all went out with the crew: some Australian and some American. The Russian All-Stars we were touring with spoke little English, and we even less Russian, so we rarely socialised. I remember they used to like cooking their own food, and would often attempt to do so in their rooms, causing all kinds of fire alarm mayhem!

Anyway, while we were out that night I happened to notice a rather good-looking American chap. He was a member of our crew; our sound engineer apparently. His name was Phil Christensen.

By this time I wasn't quite as shy and demure as I used to be, so decided to go up and introduce myself. But having plucked up the courage to do that, I didn't have much else to say, so we started chatting about the show.

The last tour Phil had worked on was with Phil Collins, and so this was something quite different. We got to know each other well over the next 35 performances, and when he had to leave to prepare for the next Phil Collins tour, we were together. We, too, had been constrained by the need for discretion and secrecy, but it had still been a wonderful start to a relationship.

At the end of the US leg of our tour, Phil and I spent Christmas together at his house in Dallas, while Chris was finishing off some routines with Isabelle and Paul.

Phil and I returned to the UK in January. We were about to start the UK leg of our tour and he was expected in Bray, where he was due to start rehearsals with Phil Collins. We'd already arranged to spend a couple of days together. The plan was that after I'd visited my parents I would drive down to central London where I had a house, drop off my things and then head straight off to Bray, in Berkshire.

Under normal circumstances this would have been a fairly straightforward exercise: Nottingham to central London, central London to Bray – simple. In fact, it turned into an absolute nightmare that ended up lasting the best part of 12 hours.

I didn't know it at the time but, as I got on to the motorway, gales were beginning to hit the South-east. My car was fairly low to the ground, so I didn't really notice anything until I saw a lorry on its side a few miles north of London. Then I saw another, and another. Then some trees that had come down, too. It was carnage.

Needless to say, by the time I got into London there was pandemonium. The roads were blocked and, in all the hoo-ha, I managed to get myself lost. I ended up in Barnet, somewhere I've heard of now, but back then it was new to me. Eventually I hailed a cab.

'Can you take me to Knightsbridge?'

So that I didn't have to leave my car and pick it up the next day, I did as the taxi driver suggested and followed him in my car. We got as far as King's Cross when the traffic stopped us. The taxi driver pulled over, walked back to me and said:

'It's not going to get any better from here. If I were you I'd find yourself a hotel. I'd hurry up, though – there'll be thousands of people doing the same, I should have thought.'

'OK, thanks very much.'

I paid the driver, parked my car and set off in search of a room. It didn't take me long to find one; cash in advance, of course. Goodness knows what the chap behind the counter thought I was there for – it wasn't a particularly reputable part of town. I took my bag to my room, which was, it has to be said, like something out of a horror movie, and called my mum to let her know I was all right.

When I put on the news the weather man said the gale was dying down and everything should be back to normal soon. Right then, I'm off, I thought. I got on the phone to Phil and told him I'd be there as quickly as I could. I left my salubrious hotel – without asking for a refund – jumped in my car and finally reached him at around 10.30pm, exhausted but ultimately elated. It had been an interesting day; fortunately, though, not the kind that comes round too often.

After Phil had finished rehearsals, they all took off to Japan where they were due to begin the tour. I flew out too for the first ten days, stopping off in Chicago where I met Phil's family for the first time. When Phil's tour eventually moved on to Australia, I came back to the UK and joined the UK leg of the All-Stars tour. Phil was due to join me there on 10 April and when I met him at Glasgow airport he asked if we could go straight out and get something to eat. 'OK,' I said, 'I know this little Italian place not far from here.'

After we'd finished eating Phil reached over, took hold of my hands and asked me to marry him. There in front of me was the most beautiful ring I had ever seen.

'Yes!'

Until then I never really had Phil down as a romantic. How wrong was I?

Apparently he'd been planning the proposal for weeks. He'd spoken to his family about it and he and his dad had gone shopping for the ring in Chicago. After that he'd flown to England with it and planned to ask me as soon as he possibly could – which he did.

I wanted to tell everybody, but I couldn't; only my family and Chris. Chris congratulated me, although he did seem quite surprised at the time. Concerned, even. I knew it was only because he was worried about me. Although he knew Phil, he wasn't yet sure if he was right for me; he'd said as much just a few weeks before. Even though I knew he was, I didn't want to get into an argument about it. After all, Chris was only trying to protect me.

It was a few weeks later that the story about Phil and me eventually broke. It was only a matter of time. We were nearing the end of our UK leg and Phil was about to leave for the European leg of the Phil Collins tour. It would be a while before I saw him again so I decided to take him to the airport and wave him goodbye.

Chris told us to be cautious. 'You want to be very, very careful. They've got a journalist *and* a photographer at Heathrow full-time these days.'

'Really? There are thousands of people there, though. We'll be fine.'

'OK. Just be careful,' said Chris.

Because of Chris's tip-off, we were both on our guard, and it's a good job we were because as we walked towards the check-in desk I saw both a photographer and a journalist jogging towards us. 'Quick, split up,' I said. So Phil went one way and I another. Unluckily for Phil, both men decided to follow him and ended up cornering him by security.

'Who are you then?'

'I'm her cousin.'

'Of course you are! Pull the other one. Come on, who are you? Are you two an item then?'

'I told you, I'm her cousin.'

'All right then, what's your name?'

'Fred Smith.'

'Fred Smith? Of course you are . . .'

Needless to say that didn't help deter them much.

'All right then, where are you from, *Fred*?'

I think Phil was getting desperate by this point. 'I'm from Barcelona,' he said, before pushing his way past until he was safely through security.

Sure enough, the next morning one of the tabloids carried a photo of Phil with the headline: 'WHO IS THIS "FRED SMITH FROM BARCELONA"? IF YOU KNOW, CALL THIS NUMBER NOW . . .'

The only people in the UK who knew Phil were myself, members of the company and perhaps some of his colleagues from the Phil Collins tour, if they hadn't already left. This meant he was safe. Nobody called the paper and the story soon died down.

The memory of Fred Smith lived on for a while. When we moved to the Sussex countryside in 1992 we got ourselves a dog, and we decided to name him Fred. This one was from Sussex, though. He's never been near Barcelona.

After the Heathrow fiasco my mind was made up. There would be no more playing games. Phil and I were engaged and everyone would have to get used to the idea: the press, our management, everyone. So, when the tour reached Whitley Bay, which was the most out-of-the-way venue on the tour, I made my announcement. Phil was in Germany at the time, and I was miles away from London, so I figured it was the best time.

The first time we unveiled the *Bolero* was at the British Championships in Nottingham in November 1983. We won the title for the sixth year in a row. (PA)

It was a huge honour for Chris to be asked to carry the flag during the Sarajevo Games opening ceremony on 8 February 1984. (PA)

Two days before we got to perform the *Bolero*, we had to complete our set routine. (Getty Images)

We got a wonderful reception for it, with Princess Anne joining in the celebrations. (PA)

Skating on to the ice ahead of the biggest 4 minutes 28 seconds of our lives. (Colorsport/Rex)

Because the rules allowed us to skate for only 4 minutes 10 seconds, we spent the first 18 seconds on our knees. (Colorsport/Rex)

Our routine continued with Jayne skating round Chris, who initially remained on his knees. (Colorsport/Rex)

Then we were soon into the main routine. Bob Stewart was the man who edited *Bolero* down for us, with the music produced by Richard Hartley. (Colorsport/Rex)

The romantic nature of the music merely added to the questions we always had to face about the true nature of our relationship. (PA)

The music by Ravel was originally written for a ballet, so it was a natural to transform it for ice dancing. (Getty Images)

Building up to the emotional climax of *Bolero*. (Colorsport/Rex)

It wasn't until a few seconds after the music had finished that we came round. Even now, we can hardly remember our performance, as we were completely 'in the zone' at the time. (Getty Images)

When we recovered, there was a wall of sound and thousands of people on their feet cheering. Jayne was inundated with flowers. (Colorsport/Rex)

The scoreboard told the story: nine perfect 6.0s for artistic merit. We had won the gold medal! (Getty Images)

Enjoying the moment as Olympic champions. (Getty Images)

There was still a huge amount of interest, which puzzled me. What on earth could they find so intriguing? The headlines were many, but not especially varied; the majority going for something like: 'PHIL COLLINS' SOUND ENGINEER TO MARRY MILLIONAIRE ICE QUEEN.'

While all this was going on I never suspected for one moment that Chris was getting serious with Isabelle. He went off to Germany every so often to choreograph her and Paul, and I knew there was something there, but I never believed for one moment that marriage might be on the cards.

When the All-Stars tour reached the UK he invited Isabelle over. When he told me, my heart sank.

'I've invited Isabelle over for a few days. She's going to stay with me.'

'Oh, that'll be nice.'

It wasn't my place to say anything. I just had to let it happen.

CHRIS:

To be honest, Jayne's engagement came as quite a shock. We'd spent almost every day together since 1975 and so it felt as if a change was coming; a change in the atmosphere. I also had no idea what effect it would have on our partnership, let alone our friendship. It was all pretty daunting.

I also felt very protective towards Jayne, so I suppose was slightly wary of Phil right at the beginning, as I would have been with anyone.

It also got me thinking about my own future. What if Jayne moved to America? It was a possibility. Phil was an American, after all, and had a close family. And what if she had children? She'd have to give up skating then, and if that happened, what would I do?

The old team of just Jayne and me had changed. From now

on, any decisions regarding our future would involve a three-way discussion. It was going to be very different.

But there was a positive. I was also in a relationship and until that moment probably hadn't appreciated what it meant to me. Jayne getting engaged to Phil gave me the independence I needed to explore what I had with Isabelle, and allow the relationship to develop. And it did develop, which led me to make a decision.

At the end of July 1990, when we were with the All-Stars in Brighton, I booked a flight to Germany, so that I could see Isabelle.

Debbie heard me make the booking and gave me a look. 'Don't do anything stupid, Mr Dean,' she said. I didn't reply.

The next day I flew to Oberstdorf and proposed to Isabelle. She said yes.

JAYNE:

When Chris got back we were all in the lounge of the Grand Hotel in Brighton. There was a strange atmosphere when he walked in; almost as if he knew that we knew, if you see what I mean. Debbie had voiced her concerns about what he might be about to do and we were on tenterhooks. 'Do you think he's asked her?'

'I don't know.'

My biggest concern about Isabelle and Chris's relationship was that, in my eyes, they wanted different things from life. Isabelle wanted somebody who would be there for *her*. Not a househusband, but certainly not somebody with Chris's drive and determination. He's a creator, an innovator. He needs to have a constant flow of challenges. Isabelle wanted to settle down, and I didn't think Chris was ready for that. I could have been wrong, of course. It was just a feeling.

Phil, Debbie and I were sitting together when he walked in.

'Good weekend?' I asked.

'Yes, thanks, it was great. In fact, I've got something to tell you all.'

Before he broke the news Chris ordered a bottle of champagne from the bar. We already knew by then. I looked at Debbie and she just stared back, trying not to give anything away.

We made small talk until the champagne arrived. Then, as he filled the glasses, Chris made his announcement.

'Well, I've got engaged.'

'Really?' we all said. 'Congratulations! Who to?'

'Isabelle. I'm engaged to Isabelle.'

'That's wonderful, Chris, many congratulations.'

We did our best to look as happy as possible, but all I wanted to do was take him to one side and plead with him not to do it. I couldn't, though.

Phil and I were still engaged at this point, but were hoping to get married as soon as possible. If we had our way, we'd just slope off and do something quiet and with as little fuss as possible; but I thought that my mum and dad would want a more traditional ceremony. When I first asked them about it I was in for a surprise.

'You don't want any fuss, Jayne. Why don't you and Phil go off somewhere nice and have a quiet wedding, just the two of you. We can all have a party when you get back; maybe a church blessing?'

I was over the moon. It was a conversation I'd been dreading, as I was sure they'd want something formal, so when they told us to go off and do our own thing it was a huge weight off our shoulders. They both knew that anything in England would attract a lot of attention, and were always conscious of trying to avoid that.

Our chance to tie the knot would come at the end of the UK tour, while Phil was in Sacramento with Phil Collins. It was like fate, really. Sacramento was where we had first met, so getting married there would be absolutely perfect.

We only had one day, however, as the Phil Collins tour was due to move on to Los Angeles. Luckily, Phil had planned it down to the hour, with almost military precision. He'd booked us into the Sacramento registry office – the date was 21 September 1990. Until the night before we thought it was going to be just us and two of Phil's friends from the tour, who would act as witnesses, but at the concert the previous night the rest of the crew had asked if they were invited and Phil didn't have the heart to say no.

That same night, they were all given black shorts and t-shirts, all bearing the Phil Collins tour logo. And that's what they turned up in the following day, like some kind of uniform. It was better than a morning suit!

By the time the ceremony got underway, a certain amount of celebrating had already begun, and when the registrar walked in there was a barrage of wolf whistles and cheering. She happened to be rather attractive and got a great reception! Fortunately, she took everything in good spirits and our guests behaved themselves for the rest of the ceremony.

Afterwards, we went back to our hotel where we all had champagne and strawberries. Everyone who couldn't be there – Chris, Debbie and our families – had sent flowers and cakes. We had five in all, not to mention a gardenful of flowers.

Later that evening Phil and I flew to LA where I was due to catch a flight to Oberstdorf the following day. Being separated after 24 hours wasn't ideal, but it was something we'd have to get used to – for a while, at least.

CHRIS:

We were due in Oberstdorf to start rehearsing for an episode of the BBC programme *Omnibus*. They wanted to make a documentary about how we choreographed for the ice and had commissioned a new piece of music specially for it. First they'd film us choreographing, and then follow that with a full performance.

I was also choreographing for Paul and Isabelle at the time, also at Oberstdorf, which meant that noses were being put out of joint on an almost daily basis. I was spreading myself far too thin.

What made matters worse was that Isabelle and Jayne didn't see eye to eye. There was nothing underlying; it was just a clash of personalities. Yet the balancing act for me was delicate to say the least.

JAYNE:

I was in a state of shock when I reached Oberstdorf. Not only had I just got married, but I'd then been separated from my new husband after just a day. It had been an eventful couple of days, very bittersweet.

When we started rehearsing for the *Omnibus* documentary, I found it difficult to relate to the music. It was quite modern and seemed to me to be very stark. Not my cup of tea at all. I was also finding it difficult to interpret Chris's ideas. Everything seemed very alien to me and I couldn't see a light at the end of the tunnel.

Chris was under enormous pressure, too, which meant I felt uneasy talking to him. He looked like he could explode at any moment.

In the end everything came to a head during rehearsal one day.

'Chris, I can't do this. I don't understand what you want me to do.'

'You can do it, Jayne. Of course you can. Now let's just get on with it!'

But I couldn't. I got off the ice, went back to my dressing room and broke down. Andris, Graeme Murphy's assistant who had been working with us for a number of years, was the first to come and see me. 'What's wrong, darling? What's it all about?'

Then it all came out: 'I'm finding it hard to relate to the music and I know Chris is getting frustrated with me, and having just got married it's all a bit of a shock to the system.'

By this time Chris had joined us. 'Right then, you. What do you want to do?' he asked.

I have to say that Chris was absolutely wonderful when I said I wanted to take a break, especially given how much pressure he was under. He went off and booked my ticket, and arranged for everything to begin again in two weeks' time. I was so, so grateful.

When I landed back in England, Phil was there to meet me at the airport. I was delighted to see him. Fortunately there was not a photographer in sight!

In all, our wedding celebrations actually lasted about five months. First we had the ceremony in Sacramento, which was in September, followed by a big party in December with Phil's family at a golf club near Chicago. That took place just after we finished rehearsing for *Omnibus*, which in the end went very well indeed.

Then in February we had a church blessing and another party in the UK, followed by a four-week honeymoon. That's the way to do it, though. Why have one wedding lasting just a day when you can have three spread over a few months? The one thing that was consistent on each occasion was that I wore the same dress – a pink Versace number.

It's funny the way you keep learning new things about each other when you get married. The first surprise for me happened when we were rehearsing for our church blessing. After the vicar had told us how the ceremony would unfold, he asked us to come forward and kneel.

'Ooh, I'm afraid I can't do that,' said Phil.

'Why not?' asked the vicar, visibly puzzled.

'I've got bad knees. It'd be far too painful.'

After the rehearsal I said, 'Have you really got bad knees?'

'No. I just felt too embarrassed to kneel!'

It made me laugh.

CHRIS:

After a Christmas spent with Isabelle's family in Canada, I started working again with Isabelle and Paul on their routines for the forthcoming World Championships. The message we'd received last time had been 'Too avant-garde – you have to tone things down a bit', so we'd decided to play it safe. The new number, *Missing*, would be a sequel to the dance of the same name that Jayne and I had taught them the previous year. Nobody had ever done a sequel before, so we hoped it would arouse some interest. And it worked, because in March 1991 Paul and Isabelle became world champions.

They were as ecstatic as I was. This was a new experience for me; watching your own creation being performed with such passion and energy. The appreciation shown by audiences and judges was also hugely gratifying.

It was an odd and unusual experience, however, as, although the dance was my own creation, I felt almost peripheral to its success.

After the medal ceremony I wandered down from the press box, where I'd been commentating for the BBC, to Paul and Isabelle's dressing room. When I opened the door the room was full of people: Paul and Isabelle, their official coach and his wife (who was also an advisor), their manager and their ballet master. They'd all been a team for years and I felt kind of separated from that. It was strange.

Isabelle and I were due to get married in May 1991, just a

couple of months after the World Championships. The wedding would take place in her home town of Aylmer, which is near Quebec. She and Paul were like royalty locally, even more so now that they were world champions.

The pressures they were under at that point must have rivalled even mine and Jayne's, but there was one major difference in play now: Paul and Isabelle were allowed to accept sponsorship, and had some extremely big companies working with them.

This meant there was also a huge amount of commercial interest in the wedding, something I discovered when I arrived in Aylmer a few days before the ceremony. Isabelle, her agent and her mother were in the middle of negotiations with *Paris Match* magazine, as well as with one of the French TV channels. Only once did I try and put my foot down. 'Please,' I said, 'no cameras in church!' But when I made my way in there it was like a TV set.

The venue was a small Catholic church situated by the river. In total 270 guests had been invited, ten of whom – Jayne and Phil, my mother, Betty Callaway, Debbie and a few others – were from my side. It's a good job we didn't have the bride's family on one side and the groom's on the other as it would have looked very uneven.

As we walked out of the church after the ceremony, we were greeted by a sea of people. Hundreds had lined the streets, and there were almost as many photographers and cameramen. I even saw a satellite van! It took about five minutes for the white Rolls-Royce to force its way through the mêlée and take us off to the reception.

Looking back, I should never have allowed the wedding to become so commercialised. It wasn't what I wanted; in fact, it was the exact opposite. I would have preferred something much simpler.

JAYNE:

Throughout this time, Phil had been coming to terms with the huge undertaking he'd made in marrying me. It was also a very steep learning curve for him, and at times it wasn't easy. Not long after we got married he moved lock, stock and barrel over to the UK, leaving behind his friends and family – a big step for anyone. Then, about a week later, I told him I was going to have to go to Germany for a month.

'A month? Why?'

'Chris and I need to rehearse.'

'Why Germany? Don't they have ice rinks in England?'

'Yes, of course, but we can't get the hours we need here, and the facilities are far better over there.'

As solid as I knew my argument was, I could see how ridiculous it must have sounded to Phil. I think he was horrified initially, but instead of making a fuss he decided to come to Germany with us, which again was a big move. If you can't beat them join them, I guess he thought.

That lasted about a week. As beautiful as Oberstdorf undoubtedly is, there isn't a great deal to do there; especially for an American sound engineer who can't speak the language. I was on the ice most of the day.

It was one long process of eliminations really. Some things would work, and some wouldn't. For the first few months at least, I think he would have been thrilled if I'd told him I was going to hang up my skates. But Phil too had led a pretty unconventional existence, and so knew exactly what this kind of life entailed. I just don't think he'd ever figured on marrying somebody who was in the same boat.

Over the next few months, Phil slowly began to realise what needed to be done if our marriage was going to succeed. It was no use just being in the same building as me while I was working. If things were going to work out long-term he'd have to find a way of working *with* me. Not on the ice, of course. He can't skate!

Soon after we first moved in together Phil noticed that the only letters I ever received were from either friends or fans.

'Why don't you ever receive any bills?' he asked.

'Michael Linnitt's office does all that. I don't have the time to sort it out.'

'You mean they have your cheque book?'

'Yes, that's right.'

To Phil this was crazy. I think he also found it a little strange.

'Would you mind if we brought them back in-house?'

'No, sure.'

Shortly after this we had to fly to Australia for a tour. Luckily, Michael Edgley, the producer, needed a sound engineer, and so it was suggested Phil take the job.

On paper you'd have thought this might be the perfect long-term solution. We'd be working with the same people, in the same building at the same time. Unfortunately, it turned out not to be so.

Phil found it odd being the husband of the star, which was how he was perceived. Plus, all I do when I'm on tour is eat, sleep and skate, so I wasn't able to offer him any kind of attention. By this point he was resolved to find a way in which we could spend more time together.

After the tour Phil sat Chris and me down and began going through our accounts with us. This was a real eye-opener; the first time we'd ever seen the financial details of our professional lives. That in itself was ridiculous. Phil just looked at us and said: 'I can't *believe* you guys!'

Chris and I could only sit there, looking embarrassed. It was a rude awakening.

After just a few minutes it became obvious that if we started to take responsibility for our own affairs, we'd be much better off. Michael Linnitt had done a great job for us, and had helped us realise a lot of ambitions, but it was time we stood on our own two feet.

'You don't need Michael Linnitt to organise a tour,' Phil said. 'You know the business inside out. You can sort out the ice, the skaters, the choreography and the costumes. And Debbie and I can sort out everything else.'

It didn't occur to Chris or me that we might be able to utilise Phil's contacts. He knew all the promoters; all the lighting and sound companies. Between the four of us we had just about every base covered.

In the end we all decided that Phil should become our business manager, an arrangement that has worked well on a professional and personal basis for over 20 years.

Michael Linnitt was naturally disappointed we were leaving him, but we knew it was the right thing to do. When Phil started looking after us things began to change very quickly. It was like bringing everything in-house – our own enterprise. Suddenly, for the first time in our careers, we felt like we were in control.

It was nevertheless a transitional period, and first of all trust had to be established. For me it was easy; after all, Phil was the man I loved, and I trusted him implicitly. But for Chris it was different. He didn't know Phil that well and there was an element of caution on his part. I had to reassure him that if Phil cheated on him, he would also be cheating on me, and there's no way he'd ever do that. I think that made him feel a bit better about things, and after that we all started to bond a bit.

Phil has drawn strict lines between business manager and husband, boundaries that are never crossed. In fact, sometimes he goes to ridiculous lengths. We could be at a party somewhere, and if he has to ask me a question regarding work, he'll send me an email from his phone. Then, as we're leaving, he'll say, 'Did you get that email?' At the end of *Dancing on Ice*, he said,

'OK guys, ten years' hard work, I think you deserve a break for a while.'

CHRIS:

My marriage to Isabelle lasted just under two years and was fraught with problems, the majority of which were circumstantial. It wasn't an especially amicable split, and many things were said that I'm sure we both now regret. We were so inexperienced when it came to relationships, and both had very busy lives. This led to a great deal of separation anxiety, which resulted in paranoia and a whole heap of other emotions. We did try to fix things, but in the end went our separate ways.

Time's a great healer, though, and many of the emotions and memories that were quite raw in the past have since softened, leaving me with a clarity I didn't have before.

If I saw Isabelle walking down the street tomorrow I'm sure we'd be fine with each other. Life's too short for recriminations.

I've been married again since splitting with Isabelle. This time to a wonderful woman named Jill Trenary, who was also a world champion singles skater and is the mother of my two boys, Jack and Sam. This time round things were a lot different, and even though we're no longer together, I'm pleased to say that we're still very close, very much part of the same family.

Jill had been with us on the Tom Collins tour in the USA in 1993, prior to our second Olympics. She and Jayne had become friends and, as a consequence, I got to know her too. I already knew *of* her, as in 1990 she'd won the World Figure Skating Championships in Halifax, Nova Scotia, where I'd been commentating for the BBC. She had shown prodigious talent as a child, becoming the US junior champion, and her career had gone from strength to strength.

After touring together for a few weeks, our friendship had grown into something much deeper. In fact, we became very close. Not to the detriment of my partnership with Jayne, however. Jill had no problem stepping back when she needed to. I hadn't long split up with Isabelle at the time, so people naturally thought I was on the rebound, but I knew differently. We were kindred spirits, but had also had the benefit of starting our relationship 'together', without having to suffer too many early separations.

Jill has great generosity of spirit, not to mention sensitivity, two qualities that seemed to balance my impulsive and sometimes volatile nature. We seemed to understand each other implicitly, and from the end of the tour we became inseparable.

We got married on 15 October 1994 and in 1998, when Jayne and I retired from skating, Jill and I moved to Colorado where we started a family.

It wasn't until *Dancing on Ice* started that things began to go wrong. In the end we just couldn't deal with being apart for so long, something that happens a lot with people in the entertainment industry.

This was very different from what had happened with Isabelle, though. For a start, Jill and I had a family. There was absolutely no possibility of moving everyone over to the UK for five months of the year.

Yes, Jill had given up her career to look after our boys, but at the same time I was making a living for everyone; and, if I wasn't doing this, I don't know what my options would be. I'm a bit long in the tooth for the police. My popularity isn't in the USA, it's in the UK. That's my place of work.

Questions obviously arose: what's more important, your career or your marriage? But they were questions I was asking myself as much as Jill was. I just couldn't reconcile these two parts of my life, not without a) giving up everything I'd worked for over the past 40 years, and b) causing a huge amount of resentment. That would probably have had a hugely damaging effect, not just on us but on our boys.

Ending our marriage was actually something that we arrived at, rather than just decided. It wasn't always easy, but the decision was almost made for us, and without there ever being any blame thrown around.

Our biggest support through all this – and probably the reason why we didn't really fall out – was Jill's father. He made sure we kept everything amicable and helped us to come out the other side. I will always look after my family, and even though we're now divorced, Jill will always be part of my life. She's the mother of my children, and a great one too. We have dual responsibility for the kids but she's dedicated her life to looking after them.

For us, it's all about the children. They're what matters most and they're the reason we're still such good friends. That, some grown-up thinking and Jill's dad.

In some funny way I think we have a greater understanding of one another. The elephant in the room, if you like, was a combination of our circumstances and commitments, and the fact that they no longer enabled us to be a married couple. Take them away and you're suddenly able to see clearly, concentrate on the important things. Now, we only look at each other as friends and parents to our children; we appreciate each other far more.

Jill's now engaged again and I'm genuinely happy for her. She's also happy for me, now that I'm with Karen Barber.

Since Karen and I got together, people are always intrigued to know if anything went on before. After all, we've known each other for about 40 years, since we were kids, and have during that time spent quite a bit of time together. 'Surely something must have happened?' they ask.

We simply never looked at each other like that. Then, about three years ago, it just happened – we found each other. And I'm pleased to say we're both very happy.

We have lived similar lives, come from similar backgrounds and have similar sensibilities, all of which makes up the foundation of our relationship. But one of the many things that actually draws us together is laughter. Nobody makes me laugh like Karen, and hers is infectious.

Who knows what the future will bring. I'm happy just to let it unfold.

9
The Russians

CHRIS:

If you were to evaluate our relationship with the Russians so far you'd probably say something along the lines of mutual respect and frustration at the same time – and you'd be about right.

In the past we've made no secret of our admiration for their ice dancers and choreographers, who, back in the 1970s, completely dominated the sport. But we've certainly had our battles with them over the years, not to mention the odd adventure.

In the 1960s and 70s I was actually rather afraid of Russia, or the USSR, as it was then. This was during the Cold War and every time you turned on the TV there were reports about the number of missiles or tanks they had over there, and I remember as a child being quite worried about it all. But there was a real mystique about the place, and especially the people, not least the skaters. You'd see them compete on TV and then you wouldn't hear from them again until the following year. No TV interviews or press reports, nothing. They just seemed to disappear.

Watching them on television was always an event for me. I loved to see their fantastic abilities and the marks they received. When the Russians were on the ice it was all about the movement. I was transfixed.

They made skating look artistic. They made it look complete. Not just in the way they danced but in the way they were dressed. Their costumes were made by the Kirov and always looked magnificent. Even the manner in which they skated on to the ice prior to a performance could be commanding – all confidence and nobility. They were the leaders and they dominated.

Moiseeva and Minenkov in particular were the ones Jayne and I both really admired. They were the most artistic couple, not simply relying on high-energy routines, which the majority of skaters did at the time. They were the ones who began turning ice dancing into more of an art form, which – later on – was precisely what we strived to do. They were the pioneers, though; the ones who first dared to be overtly expressive.

Their look was also amazing, like nothing we'd ever seen before. They were both tall and elegant, with a majestic air about them. More classical ballet dancers than ice skaters. To us they seemed almost exotic.

When we eventually became their competitors, the mystique that had surrounded them previously multiplied tenfold. They were impossible to actually befriend. The best you could ever realistically hope for was a quick nod as you passed them in the locker room during a competition. Minders, too, were a permanent fixture in the Russian camp, and they took their roles very seriously indeed. It was their job to make sure the skaters didn't try to defect! At least that was our impression.

When we first began competing internationally it always felt like it was the Russians versus the rest of the world – a kind of 'Cold War' on ice – and in many ways it was just that. They thrived on it.

Then, when we won our first European Championships in 1981, it became Russia versus Torvill & Dean. The balance had started to shift.

The 1970s may have belonged to Russia, just as the 1960s had belonged to the UK – but come the early 1980s, we were ready to change places again.

JAYNE & CHRIS:

Earlier we told you about a run-in we had with the great Tatiana Tarasova, who, in spite of what we may have thought of her in 1984, is one of the most successful ice dancing coaches of all time.

She, perhaps more than anyone else in the Russian camp, was both surprised and challenged by the emergence of these two upstarts from the UK. Yet all we were ever trying to do was carry on the work that she and her compatriots had started, and invigorate ice dancing even further, making it even more innovative.

But of course we never got a chance to tell them how much we admired them because there were never any lines of communication – not between competitors. We'd never dream of knocking on their door and saying, 'We just wanted to let you know how wonderful we think you are.' Not only was there the language barrier, but we were also quite shy.

So, you can imagine our surprise when, in 1987, we were asked if we'd like to go on tour with the Russian All-Stars, a Moscow-based professional company made up of former Olympic ice dancers – in other words, our former rivals. Actually, surprise is probably too weak a description. Shock or astonishment would work better!

It was the producer, Michael Edgley, who first posed the question.

'You mean like we did in 1985 after we turned pro?' we asked.

'No, that was just a few dates in Australia after the Olympics. This would be well over a hundred dates covering several countries – like your world tour. You'd also be partly responsible for the content, but would be working alongside somebody else.'

'You mean we'd be working with another choreographer?'

'That's right.'

On the face of it, it seemed like an exciting proposition, so we accepted. We'd have six months to prepare the numbers and rehearse; some of which would take place in Oberstdorf but most of it in Moscow, as this was home to the majority of the company.

After accepting it was suggested that we make a five-day preliminary trip to Moscow, where we could meet the company and discuss some ideas.

'By the way, Michael, who's going to be our principal colleague on the tour?' we asked.

'Tatiana Tarasova,' he replied.

'What . . . ? Well, that's going to be interesting – especially after what happened in nineteen eighty-four.'

We knew there and then that there might be one or two creases that would need to be ironed out, but it had the makings of a revolutionary and exciting project. Skaters from the East and the West had performed on the same bill before – our first Australian dates after turning professional had been with Russian Olympians – but they had never collaborated with anyone to put on a show together before.

With the advent of perestroika, the Communist ideal that had administrated the sport as well as the country was no more, and Tatiana – the doyenne of Soviet ice dancing – was now looking to make a living for herself with a new company, the Russian All-Stars. But in order to make this work in post-Communist Russia she would need a lot of foreign currency, which meant touring abroad as often as possible. To do this she'd need Michael Edgley.

And we all needed Tatiana, of course. The management needed her because the only way to keep costs down was to rehearse in Moscow, and we needed her because we were now committed to combining our two skating cultures. She had been integral to Russian skating for many years and we couldn't wait to begin working with her. It was our equivalent of performing with the Kirov or the Bolshoi.

But with Russian society on the verge of change at the time, it wasn't going to be easy, as we realised very soon after arriving in Moscow. We were met at the airport by Andrew Guild, Michael Edgley's director who had travelled over to meet us before our first visit to Australia, just after we turned pro. He was married to a Russian ballet dancer and spoke the language fluently, which meant he was always instrumental in Edgley's productions over there.

From our hotel, Andrew took us to meet Tatiana, who was waiting on the pavement outside.

'Why is she waiting outside, Andrew? Why doesn't she come in?'

'It's a "foreigners only" hotel, no Russians allowed.'

We were more than a little embarrassed about this, because although we didn't know Tatiana well, we were aware of her standing both within ice skating and Russia itself. She was a very big name in the country and had won a raft of medals and awards. Furthermore, her father, Anatoli, had been the country's top ice hockey coach, and was still a living legend. Then there was her husband, Vladimir, who was one of Russia's most respected concert pianists. That she had to wait outside felt very wrong.

Everything about Tatiana Tarasova – who is still coaching

and producing shows – is larger than life. Always fully made-up, she wears huge dangly earrings and enormous fur coats, or at least she did then. We were almost overwhelmed by her flamboyance – her grand gestures and her beaming smiles. And as for her hugs – she could suffocate a bear with one of them.

'Chreees! Jaynichka! Good to seeing you both. We go back to my apartment. I having food for you.'

Her English was difficult to understand at times, but still much better than our Russian.

When we arrived at her apartment we realised how much trouble she'd gone to in preparing a welcome for us. For a start you could hardly see the table for food. There was every kind of Russian delicacy imaginable: caviar, dressed herring and heaven knows how many salads. There were also several bottles of champagne. Tatiana obviously had some good contacts, and so life was easier for her than for some, but regardless of what country we were in it was an astonishing sight.

After introducing us to everyone present Tatiana told us how much she was looking forward to working with us and said she was determined to make a go of it. We echoed the sentiment, and were all getting along famously – until Andrew Guild broached the subject of billing.

'Tatiana, you do know we're going to have to rearrange the billing when we're abroad.'

'Whaaat? No no no! We are very famous name. It have to be the Russian All-Stars with Chreees and Jaynichka.'

'But nobody's heard of you abroad, Tatiana. The All-Stars sounds like a football team.'

This probably wasn't the best thing to say, especially as Tatiana had designs on aligning her All-Stars with the likes of the Bolshoi.

'No no no. I can't believe you insult me like this. The billing have no change!'

So that was that; it would have to be 'The Russian All-Stars and Torvill & Dean' – for the time being, at least.

Andrew was keen to show us the better side of Moscow, but there was no hiding the fact that the country was experiencing some massive problems. In the market on our second day there, we saw some disturbing and truly moving sights: women wearing nothing but rags, trying to sell pieces of string or single buttons. One woman, who had a particularly weather-beaten face, was obviously suffering from rickets. The sight of her, all alone, looking on the brink of death, reduced Jayne to tears. We hadn't seen poverty like this ever before. These were desperate people.

We didn't have time to see much more, and with heavy hearts moved on to Leningrad – not yet renamed St Petersburg – where the All-Stars would be performing next.

The train journey was yet another reminder that the transition from Communism to capitalism was going to be gradual. The train was old, noisy and painfully slow, and had two different kinds of sleeping compartment – ones that slept two to a room and ones that slept about 12 – and at the end of each of these sat a large lady who would serve tea. That was all there was.

We arrived in Leningrad on 1 May, and as we emerged from the train station we realised very quickly that the May Day parade had begun. This, we were told, was an annual event that saw millions of factory workers from all over the country converge on the major cities. Once there they would then march through the streets carrying banners and singing workers' songs, the pavements lined with soldiers and spectators. The problem for us was that the street down which this particular parade was going was blocking the path from the station to our hotel. If we sat and waited for it to pass, we'd be there for hours.

'No matter,' said Tatiana. 'You come.' And so she proceeded to lead us first under a parked lorry, and then straight through the crowds of marching workers. She was like a mother bear – totally in control. Some of those marching began to recognise Tatiana, and as she beckoned us to follow, the scene gradually began to resemble the story of Moses and the parting of the Red Sea.

Suddenly Chris had a thought. 'What if a cameraman sees us? Imagine the headline: "TORVILL & DEAN DEFECT!"'

Eventually making our way through the throng, we ducked into our hotel. The rooms were enormous. Jayne's had a grand piano in it, but the shower didn't work and there were no towels. 'Why don't they sell the grand piano, fix the shower and buy some towels?' asked Jayne, a little sarcastically. 'Give them time,' said Andrew.

It had only been a short visit – we were due to fly back home the following morning – but it had been interesting, a genuine eye-opener. We'd been disturbed by what we'd seen in Moscow, but we couldn't let it affect us. Companies like the All-Stars were part of the cultural fabric of the country, and responsible for a certain amount of its economy. Being there meant we'd be helping out the All-Stars in some small way.

Rehearsals started a few weeks later in Moscow with a two-week trial workshop.

The first piece Tatiana wanted to do was based on the life of the Italian violin virtuoso, Niccolo Paganini, a troubled genius who was devoured by depression. Yuri Ovchinnikov – the former Olympic figure skater and Tatiana's business partner – would be dancing Paganini's depressed persona, Chris his creative persona, and Jayne his muse. Neither of us really took to the number, but decided to take a back seat in the spirit of collaboration.

Chris's idea for the workshop was a version of the German play, *La Ronde*, which tells the story of a necklace that is passed from husband to wife to lover to mistress, and so on, until it finally arrives back with the husband. It deals with subjects that, it has to be said, were until then pretty alien to ice dancing: prostitution, class ideology and adultery to name but three. The choreography was complex and depended on group patterns and intertwining couples – not at all what the Russians were used to. But again, in the spirit of collaboration, they did it and performed it well.

Rehearsing two very different numbers with two very different choreographers would be the first test in our cultural artistic experiment, but before we could begin work we'd have to do something about the language barrier. Clearly, we needed an interpreter.

At first, Tatiana decided to use a friend of hers. Now, this friend spoke perfectly good English, but only conversational English – 'Hello, how are you? I'm fine, thank you' – which meant she had to improvise any skating terms. Consequently, our ideas were incomprehensible to each other, so a search began for somebody more suitable.

Once we actually got to work we soon realised that Tatiana was no democrat. She did things very differently to Betty and Bobby, whose approach was always calm and consultative; never becoming flustered, thus never flustering you.

Tatiana's pupils were completely obedient, and for good reason. Vocally, she had only one volume setting – loud! Even when she was praising her skaters, it would be shouted and never spoken. She was used to being in control, and if you were ever stupid enough to answer back, she would shoot you down with the kind of verbal barrage that could floor a man at 20 paces – or, in her case, absolutely anywhere on an ice rink. Conversely, Tatiana was actually a very warm person and despite the volume she obviously cared deeply for her All-Stars. She was like a rather strict mother figure.

CHRIS:

We separated the working time into two periods – hers and ours – rehearsing alternately in the mornings and the afternoons. But when the time came for Tatiana to relinquish control and hand over the reins to me, she found it difficult to let go.

I'd be standing on the edge of the rink, giving out instructions, when I'd suddenly hear a '*Nyet!*' or a '*Da!*' To be fair to Tatiana, she'd also let us know if she was impressed by something. This would result in her yelling '*Horosho!!*' – usually in my right ear.

It was a frustrating time, but we could also see her good side: her commitment to the company, as well as her fighting spirit. We also saw the conditions she was working under. There was little money and good food was scarce. Even some of the most basic things were only available by barter. She was a survivor, though, and we admired her for it. It also meant that I was happy to keep my mouth shut, even when she was trying to monopolise my rehearsal.

One day I was on the ice trying to demonstrate a move to one of the skaters, when suddenly there was a cry of, 'CHREE-EEEEES!'

'What on earth does she want now, Jayne?' I asked.

'I'm not sure but she looks like she's about to explode!'

'*She's* about to explode? She's not the only one!'

'Just behave yourself.'

Those two weeks were the beginning of what was going to become a long, hard struggle; for the management as well as us. We had always known that the rehearsal period would be unpaid – any cash raised had to go to the All-Stars to cover costs. So, as a trial, and to help recoup some of these costs, they asked us if we'd put on some special performances after the two-week workshop. Not the finished show, of course, that was months away, just the two dances we'd been working on and perhaps some other more established routines.

Everyone seemed happy to give it a go, and so a venue was arranged and some dates booked.

JAYNE:

I have to say that the reception for the first show was amazing. We'd mainly lived apart from the Russian public since arriving in the country – spending most of our time either in the hotel or at the rink – so had no idea if anyone had heard of us. In fact, as Olympic champions, we were heroes out there.

Their only access to the outside world was watching Russian television, and they were very big on sports – especially winter sports – so anyone who'd won a gold medal in a winter sport was big news. It didn't matter where you came from. Skating was on a different plane, though, and the public seemed to understand and appreciate the combination of sport and art.

The first performance took place at the Luzhniki ice stadium, which was packed to the rafters – all 10,000 seats sold. And, afterwards, it was like Beatlemania. There were hundreds of people mobbing the stage door. We eventually made it to our car, with the crowd in hot pursuit. They began surrounding it – we were literally covered by a blanket of humans! In the end the driver said, 'I'm going to drive,' but we pleaded, 'No, you can't, somebody will get hurt!' He set off anyway and started to plough – very slowly, thank goodness – through the crowd. Once again this was a new experience for us. No other country had been quite so manic.

CHRIS:

When the time came to divulge what other numbers I had planned for the show, the Russians were left scratching their heads. First of all I wanted to do something based around the pharaohs of Egypt – in particular the love story between King Akhenaten and Queen Nefertiti. I've always been absolutely fascinated by Egyptology, and used to spend many an hour in the Egyptian rooms at the British Museum, soaking up whatever they had on the period. And, from a creative point of view, there was so much to fire up the imagination.

The only difficulty I really had was choosing the music. The soundtrack to the Burton/Taylor epic, *Cleopatra*, was a bit *too* Hollywood, so in the end I decided to use some music from the Philip Glass opera, *Akhnaten*. This in itself was a risk, as Philip Glass's music can be quite minimalistic and repetitive. In fact, I've even heard of orchestras who've refused to play his music.

In hindsight, it was perhaps a bit too long – around 30 minutes in all. I think I got a little carried away with that one. It was quite stunning visually, though. When the lights came on, the first thing you saw was a huge pyramid made out of silk – 25 foot square at its base – which is being admired by modern-day tourists. Suddenly, a wire attached to the top of the pyramid lifts it up to reveal a host of ordinary Egyptians from the fourteenth century BC.

I played the pharaoh and entered the rink on a huge throne, which was being carried by several servants. It was all pretty epic stuff.

The Russian skaters didn't know what to make of it; so much so that when I first tried to explain it to them I think they thought I was joking. But if you think that was difficult to explain, imagine the trouble I had telling them they were going to be a pack of dancing cards during a Scott Joplin-inspired routine, *Ragtime Poker*.

Perhaps the funniest was our version of Fred Astaire's *Puttin' on the Ritz* from the film, *Blue Skies*. This formed part of a tribute to Irving Berlin and featured black ties, top hats and lots of debonair charm. Can you imagine anything more un-Russian? It would be less so today, of course, but at the beginning of perestroika? It was all totally unfamiliar to them.

One of the skaters was about 6ft 6in tall, with shoulders like breezeblocks. In evening dress, he looked like the monster from *Young Frankenstein*, complete with top hat and tails. It took weeks to get him to loosen up, but he was committed to his performance.

JAYNE & CHRIS:

That entire period was as much a struggle with day-to-day life as it was with Tatiana. The bureaucracy we had to deal with was so frustrating. For instance, we could only ever get from the hotel to the ice rink by taxi, but you never knew if there were ever going to be any taxis available, let alone how much they might cost. Then, if you managed to find one, it wasn't simply a case of them taking you to the rink and you ordering one back later. Heavens no! If you wanted a return journey you had to hire that taxi for the whole time you were there, which in our case was usually about eight hours a day. For that whole time the taxi driver would just sit outside and wait. It was madness! Also, if you were ever more than a few seconds late they'd be off.

Then there was the problem of obtaining food, something we tend to take for granted in the West. That was the job of our company manager, a wonderful lady named Jeannie McPherson. She would arrive at work each morning with just two tasks to fulfil: what we were going to eat for lunch, and what we were going to eat for dinner. It could often take her most of the day just to find a few pieces of fruit, and on some occasions she could only find bread and jam. After that she'd have to try and negotiate some dinner for us. Every day Jeannie would say, 'What do you fancy then?', and we'd reply by rolling off a huge list of culinary delights. 'Beef Wellington, please.' 'I'll have a chicken dinner.' 'Chilli con carne for me, please.' But we always got the same reply: 'Potato salad and gherkins it is!'

During that period, when capitalism was starting to ease its way in, a van began parking outside the hotel selling pizza for a dollar a slice. That first taste was bliss. We stood there like children at a party, happily stuffing our faces.

Once we'd finished rehearsing we all set off to Australia, where the tour was scheduled to begin. The opening show would be in Newcastle, which is just north of Sydney, in a huge blue circus tent we'd used for our six-week stint at the Nottingham Goose Fair during our first world tour.

In Moscow, Tatiana had taken a bow with us at the end of the performances. Fair enough, we thought, as she was on home ground, but in Newcastle the producers said it had to be different. We had been to Australia before and were still fairly well known there. According to Michael Edgley, we were the ones people were coming to see – which had been made obvious by the billing on the posters. As far as they were concerned the end had to reflect that, so Tatiana was asked to take a back seat.

The new ending, which we rehearsed shortly before the first show, had the company making a couple of circuits of the ice before skating off, leaving us to take our final bows – without Tatiana. At the first performance in Newcastle, the company made their two circuits as planned, but instead of then coming off and leaving us to take our final bows, they continued for a third circuit. This meant that we were first to leave the ice.

CHRIS:

I was really annoyed at the time! We'd rehearsed one thing, which had been agreed by the producers, and Tatiana had told them to do something else. Still wearing my skates, I went backstage to my caravan. A few minutes later, there she was.

'That was a terrible thing to do, Tatiana!'

She looked at me, astonished. Understandably so, as in Russia we'd always kept our heads down and said nothing.

'Chreees, what you mean by this?'

'That ending! What's happening?'

She just stood there, open-mouthed.

A few minutes later, still angry, I told Andrew Guild that he'd have to explain to Tatiana that she had no right to change things without consultation. He did so, and by the following performance things were as they should be.

Tatiana knew that if she continued to incur the wrath of the producers, there was every chance they might break up the tour and that would leave her All-Stars with no foreign earnings. To be fair, though, it must have been very, very difficult for her. She'd had to fight tooth and nail to get the All-Stars off the ground and had shown an unbelievable amount of ingenuity getting them this far. The company was her life and she was quite rightly proud of what they were achieving.

Fortunately – for all concerned, I think – as the tour progressed Tatiana began spending more and more time back in Moscow and, when she wasn't there, we all got along famously. But whenever she came back she brought tension with her, as she once again shouldered the responsibility of her All-Stars.

There were regular eruptions. Once, towards the end of the tour, there was a row over a costume she wanted altering. Kim Bishop – a gentle and highly professional character who was responsible for the wardrobe – didn't know how to handle Tatiana and so called in Bob Murphy, the show's designer. 'Well, Tatiana,' said Bob, 'I don't think it's a good idea to start altering . . .'

'OK!' she shouted. 'I fix myself.' And, with that, she grabbed a pair of scissors and set to it.

'Tatiana, STOP!' screamed Bob. 'Somebody get that bitch away from my costumes!'

Bob's yell cut straight through Tatiana's tantrum. She looked at him, saw that he was on the brink of committing murder – and fled.

Histrionics aside, Tatiana did have some pretty serious problems to deal with on the tour. On departure from the USA to Moscow, five of her company failed to show up at the airport; in fact, we never saw any of them again, as it turned out they'd defected. This was a big embarrassment for Tatiana, but there was more to follow.

In Moscow a few days later, when the company were leaving for England, she discovered that two of her skaters were trying to smuggle dollars out of the country. They were fired on the spot, but that left an even bigger hole – seven pairs of skates, to be exact. Fill them she did, though, and what began as a tour of just five months ultimately turned into one lasting almost eight, including an immensely successful 14-week run in the UK.

Travelling over to Russia at such a historically significant time and being involved in something so ground-breaking was a truly life-changing experience, and I think that the push and pull of artistic differences brought out the best in all of us.

Like everything we'd done before, and have gone on to do since, going on tour with Tatiana and her All-Stars was a challenge. We found her frustrating at times, and I'm sure there were spells when she found us equally so. The difference between our two cultures – not forgetting the way we thought and acted – was vast, especially then. So the fact that we managed to establish and maintain a professional working relationship, and at the same time make a success of the tour, should be a source of enormous pride to all concerned.

10

Bronze Medals

CHRIS:

In June 1992 we were invited to Davos, Switzerland, to celebrate the 100th anniversary of the International Skating Union. It promised to be a grand occasion, culminating in a gala dinner where they'd show a specially commissioned film about the history of skating.

The film itself was wonderful; a joyous montage featuring the greatest moments the sport had ever produced. But what made it really special to us was that, rather than including just a small clip of our work – as they'd done with the majority of the other skaters – the director had used the whole of our *Mack & Mabel* routine, which received a great ovation from our fellow guests, which surprised and humbled us.

During the dinner that evening, a mass of people associated with the sport – past and present champions, not to mention judges – kept coming up and congratulating us; letting us know that we hadn't been forgotten by the amateur world, and that the work we'd done as amateurs was still appreciated. It was such a convivial occasion and we felt proud to have been part of the sport.

Towards the end of the evening, I overheard a conversation about a forthcoming change in the Olympic rules that would allow professional skaters to regain their amateur status – if they wanted to, of course. But it's important not to take the words 'amateur' and 'professional' too literally here. Professional skaters are remunerated for their efforts, and that's the only difference. Competence doesn't come in to it.

This planted a seed in my head, and a short while later I disclosed my idea to Jayne.

'Jayne, do you realise, if we wanted to, we could enter the Olympics again?'

'What? What do you mean?'

'This new rule that's coming in. They're opening it up to professionals. It's a one-time deal, though. Only applicable for the next Winter Olympics.'

'Really? I never heard that. It's about time, though. A lot of other sports have done it.'

I could tell she was already warming to the idea.

'Also, just think about it,' I said, 'we'd only have to prepare ten minutes' worth of dancing: a four-minute free dance, two minutes of set patterns, and four compulsories at a minute each. We have to choreograph and rehearse two and a half hours' worth of material for a tour, and we're on the ice for ten numbers per show, eight shows a week. We can do this.'

'You've got a point there,' said Jayne. 'This could really work, couldn't it?'

'Yes, of course it could.'

We were actually in a similar position now, as professionals, as we had been as amateurs back in 1984. When we won the World Championships after Sarajevo, we held all three major titles. There was nowhere else for us to go, no competitions left.

Now, as professionals, we'd reached a similar impasse. We'd won the World Professional Championships and had toured the world, playing to millions of people. We were ready for a new challenge. The biggest thing we could do at the time – the greatest test – was to go back to amateur competition and compete at the Olympics again. Nobody had ever done that before, just as nobody had ever used a single piece of music for a free dance. Granted, a return to amateur skating hadn't been possible until now, but somebody still needed to be the first to do it. If we were to compete, though, it would probably be the biggest task we'd ever undertaken.

The following morning we made our way to the train station, where we were due to catch a train from Davos to Zurich. The train itself was like something out of an Agatha Christie novel, with the old 1940s first- and second-class carriages, as well as a bar and a dining coach.

As we made our way slowly through the stunning scenery of the Swiss Alps, the subject came up again. 'We really could do this, you know,' I said.

'We could, couldn't we?' said Jayne.

Making absolutely no attempt to hide our excitement, we began discussing routines and music, even rehearsal times and costumes. We were like two children. As much as we enjoyed the creative freedom and financial security that professional skating brought, the thought of competing again was a proposition difficult to resist. It was in our blood.

Timing-wise, it was perfect. The Winter Games had been rescheduled so that their four-year cycle was two years apart from the Summer Games, and this meant we wouldn't have to wait till 1996 – the next Winter Olympics were now in 1994. And the practical demands would be minimal, compared to what we were used to dealing with as professionals. There'd be no company to worry about, and we could concentrate wholly on the competition.

The more we talked about it the more we took to the idea. We needed a challenge and this would be the ultimate. We were going back to compete in the Olympic arena.

JAYNE & CHRIS:

It was only when we began looking into the detail that we appreciated the amount of work that would be involved, and there was no point even applying unless we thought we had a chance of winning. But we also had to accept the fact that we might not. We'd be testing ourselves again against the best in the world, ten years after leaving. Pitfalls aside, this was an opportunity we just couldn't pass up.

There was so much to think about: months of training, choosing and recording music, designing and making costumes. This would be no small undertaking. In fact, once we'd added everything up, we realised it was going to cost at least £100,000 just to take part.

But the real risk here would be our reputation as former Olympic champions. This was something we couldn't actually put a price on, but that was part of the excitement. It's what drove us on. Win or lose, we wanted to do it.

First of all we had to familiarise ourselves with the rule book again, and consider how we could come up with the right strategy in order to impress the judges. But not just at the Olympics; we also had to think about the British, European and World Championships. In order to do this we would need advice from certain people we trusted.

To start with, we went to see Courtney Jones and Bobby Thompson, as well as Lawrence Demmy, who was vice-president of the International Skating Union at the time. How would they react to our idea? Fortunately, all three were in agreement: 'You're still good enough. Why not? Go for it!'

It was also something they said they'd like us to do for the sport itself. British ice dancing had slipped in popularity since 1984, and was in need of a boost. Anything at all they could do to help, they would.

The application was easy enough. As long as we had it in by 1 April 1993, and committed ourselves not to appear in any professional events not sanctioned by the ISU, we'd be OK. We'd also have to establish a trust fund that would administer any income from professional sources.

Having Courtney and Bobby working with us meant they could advise us on what the judges would be looking for ten years on, and show us how to strike that magic balance between innovation and tradition. 'You need to figure out how to impress them, without challenging the rules,' was how Courtney put it.

We had to be aware of the different interpretations of the rules, some of which would be new to us. In Courtney, Bobby and Lawrence, we had the best advice there was in the sport.

We went public with our plans on 30 March, just after we'd handed in our application. Now all we had to do was put together our game plan.

Advisors we had covered, but what about coaching? First of all we approached Betty Callaway. Although she'd slowed down a bit since Sarajevo, she was still coaching part-time and said she'd be delighted to help. Next we asked Bobby. He was the national coach at the time and completely up to date with everything. And then there was Andris, of course, with whom we had worked since turning professional. We thought it was a great team.

CHRIS:

I already had an idea for the music. I used to watch lots of Fred Astaire and Ginger Rogers films and my favourite routine of theirs was *Let's Face the Music and Dance*. Why not use that? A tribute to Fred and Ginger. The title of the routine also summed up exactly what we were trying to achieve.

The main piece of advice we'd received from Courtney, Bobby and Lawrence so far was: 'Back to basics. Get yourselves into that comfort zone and let's not challenge rules.' Well, the origins of ice dancing came from the ballroom, and so, in our opinion, who better to emulate than Fred and Ginger?

The music wouldn't work as it was. For a start, it had a vocal, which still wasn't allowed in ice dancing. Also, we needed to accentuate the ballroom rhythms more. Another rearrangement would be in order, as well as a recording. This was a big cost.

Luckily, Phil had a friend who came up with an idea that could mitigate this particular problem. Graham Pullen, who was Phil Collins' booking agent in the UK, pointed out that whatever happened at the Olympics, the music we danced to would receive a huge amount of exposure and, if an arrangement had been made, there might be a demand for it. Why not approach a record company to help pay for the recording, on the proviso that they get to release the record after the Olympics? What a great idea. The same thing had happened with *Bolero*. That had reached number nine in the charts. After a couple of phone calls, our recording was sorted.

JAYNE & CHRIS:

Next we had to find somewhere to train. But where would we go? Oberstdorf was being used by the German national team and, besides, that was a public rink. We needed privacy.

'I know,' said Chris. 'Let's use the new Olympic skating arena in Norway.'

'What, the one being built for the actual Olympics? The Olympics we'll be competing at?'

'Yes. Why not? The arena's finished but the village isn't, which means nobody else will be using it.'

'What a great idea. It'll be perfect.'

Chris was right: the arena had been finished and, although the athletes' village was still under construction, the neighbouring media village was complete and had within it two flats we could rent. These turned out to be more like prefabs, but they'd have to do. So we booked it all for six months and off we went.

Not long after we started training, it became apparent that things were far from perfect. It was too secluded, even for us. Phil and Jill would join us occasionally, but apart from that all we'd have to look forward to when we weren't skating was Norwegian language TV. There was just nothing there. If you wanted to eat out you had to hire a car, and hiring a car cost an absolute fortune. It was also summertime, and summertime in Norway means about three hours of darkness. The curtains in our bedrooms were flimsy, which meant we were waking up at about four every morning.

We managed to stick it for around three weeks, but even that was a struggle. We were very different people now and were a lot more sociable. We were no longer used to being quite so secluded.

So, we were back at square one. Debbie, our PA, started to research possibilities within the UK, but there wasn't a great deal to choose from. Even the ones that were available had priced themselves out of the market. We may have been comfortable at the time, but we weren't going to be exploited. Not by anybody.

Then Debbie came up with an idea. 'Here's one – Milton Keynes. It's Olympic size. Looks quite good.'

It was perfect; quite reasonable, too: £20,000 for four hours a day, six days a week for six months. Now, that may sound like an awful lot of money, but when you break it down, it works out at just £30 an hour. Not bad for an entire ice skating arena, complete with dressing rooms.

The travelling to Milton Keynes was a bit of a trek – about 90 minutes there and back for both of us – and then on top of that we had to warm up, get changed and then practise. It would be a long day. The ice rink itself was perfect, though, exactly what we needed, so we went ahead and booked it.

Working with two coaches at the same time proved to be a challenge, but in the end was easily remedied. Although Betty and Bobby were often saying the same things, it rarely came across as such, and there was still the occasional clash of opinions. Who were we supposed to listen to? It soon became obvious that they'd work better separately than together. They knew each other well and were good friends, so agreed to alternate. They also agreed to concentrate on separate elements: Betty more on the technical side of things and Bobby on the artistic side.

Even so, the sheer amount of advice we were now receiving was at times overwhelming, not to mention confusing. Under normal circumstances it would just have been us and Andris, who was more of an advisor than a coach. That had worked for ten years without a problem, but only as professionals. We were so paranoid about getting it wrong in the competitions that we overcompensated. It wasn't much of a problem at that particular time, but we could feel that it might be later on, especially when we had to begin making important decisions. At the end of the day, though, Bobby and Betty were friends of ours, and were as passionate about our success as we were. We decided to leave things be and try to filter the advice as best we could.

Going back to rehearsing the same prescribed steps to the same pieces of music time and time again meant we had to try and reset our minds and learn to work in a very specific way once again. Everything was methodical. But as we worked, both Betty and Bobby encouraged us to look ever more critically at ourselves, until we got to the point where we felt there was no way to improve further. In the end we had to strip everything back – our skating and our emotions – and start again with a blank canvas.

In the original dance – the rumba – there was at least some flexibility; but it was the free dance that would matter most. This would count for 50 per cent of the mark.

We choreographed the basic outline within a couple of weeks. It was all 'back-to-basics ballroom' – that was the mantra – and *Let's Face the Music* was exactly that. Our aim was to base the routine on flowing, intricate footwork and seamless transitions that would accelerate naturally, and in as technically interesting a way as possible, building speed by varying edges. We were also using only three out of the five lifts we were allowed, so that the footwork would become the highlight: real back-to-basics stuff.

Not long afterwards we were told that we may have taken this too far. Apparently the judges would expect us to use all five lifts allocated, so in the end we acquiesced and put in two more. It was against our instinct at the time, but we had to run with the advice we were given.

It was a difficult juxtaposition. For the last ten years we'd been our own judges, performing for an audience. Now we'd be performing for real judges again, which was a very different proposition.

Once training was well underway, we turned our attention to the costumes. This was Courtney's department, of course, and as well as finding us a new company who'd be willing to produce the outfits, he managed to persuade them to help us by doing it free of charge. This would be a huge saving; many thousands of pounds, in fact.

Back at Milton Keynes, we came up with an idea – an idea that would eventually become our nemesis.

Our only regret from our time working on *Bolero* was that we never had any of it filmed: rehearsing, choreographing, making the costumes and choosing the music. This time around, we wanted it to be different, and so Phil and Graham Pullen, who was our tour promoter, got on to the BBC and asked if anyone might be interested.

The first person to put their hand up at the Corporation was a director called Eddie Mirzoeff – a BAFTA award-winning film-maker who specialised in fly-on-the-wall documentaries, usually for the BBC's *Omnibus* series. He'd recently made a film about the Queen that we'd all seen and been very impressed by. He was willing to do it, but there would be conditions to him filming us, conditions that we took far too lightly.

We arranged a meeting with Eddie and once we were seated he got straight down to business. 'Are you sure you understand what's involved here? Once you say yes, that's it, it's a real commitment,' he told us. 'You're giving up your right of refusal. I just want to make sure the two of you understand.'

We understood. Or at least we thought we did. We'd done an episode of *Omnibus* before and the team then had been excellent to work with: technically brilliant and very, very patient. We assumed it would be a similar experience this time around. Maybe even with some of the same crew?

We soon found out that this wasn't the case. *Omnibus* was simply an umbrella title and each film was made by a different group of people. The only common denominator was that each one concentrated on the arts.

This had all gone completely over our heads. In fact, we were so sure everything would be fine that we even had one or two words of advice of our own for Eddie. 'Things happen very fast in the skating world, Eddie,' we said. 'Once it's gone, it's gone. We can't repeat or recreate things. They're spur-of-the-moment happenings.'

'Don't worry, that's fabulous,' he replied. 'That's exactly the way I work. I'm like a fly on the wall.'

And therein lay the warning – those four words 'fly on the wall'. It was all in the name, but this particular fly would become more like an albatross.

In hindsight, instead of replying with a rather nonchalant 'yes' to Eddie's initial questions, what we should have done was say 'no', and kept repeating that until we'd left the room. To be fair to Eddie, he did give us plenty of chances to do so.

'Are you sure you know what it's going to be like being the subject of a fly-on-the-wall documentary?' he'd asked.

'Do you understand the pain involved in making one of these? Having to lay yourself open, twenty-four hours a day if necessary, no matter how you're feeling. Are you sure you'll be able to cope being under constant scrutiny for months on end, never, ever getting any peace, because that's what it's like. I need total commitment.'

We knew all about commitment and, as for pain, we'd both had our fair share of that over the years. We had our director and we were happy. Not for long, though.

That September, Eddie began filming. He started off coming to training. No imposition there; he was cheery enough and we enjoyed having him around.

But then, as the British Championships approached, all his many warnings started to become a reality. Big Brother had arrived and was about to take over our lives. What's more, there was absolutely nothing we could do about it.

Everywhere we looked, whatever we were doing, there was a camera there. It didn't matter how we felt at the time, how personal the conversation we were having, it was all being recorded. He followed us at our homes, at the rink, everywhere. And there wasn't just the one film crew, there were two, which meant both of us could be filmed if we were apart for any length of time.

Then came the microphones. Eddie wanted us to wear radio microphones on the ice, which we were against. This drove him crazy. 'Look, they're only tiny, see!'

But they weren't that tiny, and you had to have a battery pack clipped on to you. What if we fell on it? We could be injured. There was also a wire leading from the battery pack to the microphone. What if it got in the way of movement?

Because we weren't being particularly good subjects, Eddie wasn't getting the 'drama' he'd been hoping for. But having him there was so distracting, which made it difficult for us to focus on our goal. He was only doing his job, of course; a job that we'd invited him to do. He'd get his drama, though, eventually.

To some members of the skating establishment, it might have seemed like we were just waltzing back into amateur ice skating, expecting to pick up two more gold medals, thinking we could win, but that couldn't have been further from the truth. We had no idea how our routines would be received, and the closer we got to the Olympics, the more nervous we became. Maybe the forthcoming British Championships would give us a much-needed sense of direction?

We should actually have been quite optimistic by this point, as the run-through of *Face the Music*, which we performed for Courtney, Bobby, Betty, Andris and Lawrence, had received a unanimous: 'Yes! That's it, that's what we want!' They all understood the judges and knew of all our rivals, so if they were happy, why weren't we?

For a start we felt like we were diluting what we were good at, which was being original, but our other problem now was nerves. We were actually more nervous going into the British Championships on our return to amateur skating than we had been before Sarajevo.

The difference now was that we had an awareness, which we didn't have back then; an awareness that made us paranoid, bombarding our minds with countless 'what if' scenarios. What if we're being too ambitious? What if we're being too safe? This was also a national championships, which meant it would be televised. What if the international judges saw it? What might they think?

Even though we'd always been ambitious and competitive, we'd never carried such a burden of expectation before. In 1984 we had no idea that we were being watched by 24 million people. That realisation came afterwards. This time, though, we knew well in advance, and were being reminded on a daily basis: '24 MILLION EXPECTED TO WATCH TORVILL & DEAN COMEBACK'.

How we longed for the innocence of the amateur bubble again, when we only ever skated for ourselves, our coach and our families. We skated for our country too, of course, but now we were aware of the level of expectation.

At the practices during the British Championships, Bobby had told us we needed to smile a lot more, which had planted yet another seed of paranoia. Smile? We knew how to smile and had been doing so. Perhaps he was sensing something else?

Then we had Eddie in our face, wanting his footage. Under normal circumstances we like to relax between final practices; sit quietly in our dressing rooms and compose ourselves, and become at one with our thoughts, that sort of thing. These are vital moments if you're to achieve the relaxed concentration required. Eddie didn't just want footage of us sitting around, he wanted reactions, he wanted emotions.

By the time we'd reached the free dance proper, we were in the lead. Well ahead, in fact. But still, the free dance counts for half the marks. What if the judges didn't like what we were doing? This was our first public performance of *Face the Music* and the first time we'd competed for almost ten years. We wanted to be as close to perfect as we had been then.

We gave a good performance and waited for the verdict,

butterflies in our stomachs – Bobby on one side, Betty on the other. And then the marks: eight 5.9s and a 6.0 for technical performance; then nine 6.0s for artistic impression!

We'd won, and won well. This was the first step to where we wanted to be.

It was such a relief and we were now looking forward to focusing on and enjoying our final two weeks' preparation before the Europeans. Even with Eddie and his crew around we should still be able to get through it with smiles on our faces.

The job of bursting this particular bubble would be left to Hans Kutschera, head of the ISU's dance committee. He'd attended the British Championships and had asked to see us back at his hotel. But what for? we wondered. Perhaps to give us his thoughts on what he'd just seen?

So, off we went with Bobby, Betty and Courtney to Mr Kutschera's hotel. After being greeted by him, he gave us several pieces of advice about our performance. He thought he was giving constructive criticism, but to be honest not much of it made sense. At one point during the conversation he even suggested we dance like cats. It was all very strange – maybe it was all lost in translation. According to him, he was only telling us this because he wanted to help us, but he'd made it very clear that he thought little of what he'd seen. In the end, we smiled politely and left – baffled and more than a little deflated.

Jayne was angry, and at the same time depressed by his assessment. Even Betty, who was normally so controlled, let fly 'That MAN!', which for her was very angry indeed. We expected Bobby and Courtney to echo Betty's reaction, but we were in for a surprise. 'You should really listen to him,' they said, 'because he will be the referee at the Olympics. Couldn't you just change that little bit at the beginning? If you did, it would show that you'd listened to him and followed his advice.'

Change a little bit? We were supposed to be leaving for the Europeans in a few weeks' time! Thirty minutes earlier we'd been ecstatic. Our confidence had started to come back and we'd felt able to look forward. Now, we were just downhearted and paranoid again.

The next day got even worse. Eddie was due to join us at practice, but instead of just going ahead as planned we called him up and told him we weren't going in that day. The thought of being filmed for the duration while we felt so down was just too much to bear.

Eddie wasn't stupid, though, and later on in the day he asked one of his crew members to drive up to the rink and see if we were telling the truth. When he found out we weren't, he called Debbie immediately. 'They lied to me! They told me they were having a day off and they lied! I don't think I can go on with this project. They're not keeping to their side of the bargain.'

Later that day, Phil called to see if he could calm Eddie down, but he was still furious. 'They'd had a really bad day, Eddie. They needed some peace and quiet.'

'That's not the way it works, Phil. You know that and they know that. You can't pick and choose which days I come in. I'm sorry but if that's the way of it, it won't work.'

We called Eddie the next day, apologised and promised not to do it again. It was of our own making, as he kept reminding us. We had to fulfil the agreement, just as we would a performance on the ice.

By the time we got to Copenhagen, where the Europeans were being held, we were nervous. Not full of nervous energy, just very, very nervous. This was the big test. The whole competition would be carried live on TV and the place was teeming with press.

Our main rivals were the two Russian couples: the current world champions Maya Usova and Alexander Zhulin, and the silver medallists, Oksana Grishuk and Evgeni Platov. Everyone had seen our free dance, as the British Championships had been televised, but nobody had seen theirs yet. The mood around the Torvill & Dean camp was far from calm. Not just us, but Bobby and Courtney. Even Betty seemed to have a permanently concerned demeanour.

The truth was that they were as nervous as we were, and we could tell that they were unhappy with how things were going, both on and off the ice. Worse still, they obviously couldn't put their fingers on why, otherwise they'd have told us. Bobby was the barometer. He went to every single major competition and had trained some of the best ice dancers in the world. He had done for decades. There was a definite unease about him, though; an anxiety that was far from healthy.

At the practices, things started to become ridiculous, the paranoia forcing us to begin grasping at straws.

'The practice outfits! That's it,' said Bobby, 'they're too dull. For the rumba practice, Jayne had better wear something else. What's she got?'

'Well, I've got a short-ish skirt?'

'OK, wear that.'

But after the first practice word got to us: 'The skirt's not right. The judges don't like it. Don't wear it again.'

Things were even worse off the ice. Bobby said we still had this squeaky clean image and we mustn't let anything affect it. In fact, it was probably best that we weren't seen together with either Phil or Jill too much, and certainly not at mealtimes. 'When you're among the other skaters, make sure it's just the two of you. Better to be safe,' Bobby said.

It felt like they were trying to recreate the Torvill & Dean who had won at Sarajevo, but we were different people now. We had partners, why couldn't everyone just accept that? But we had to play the game, even if it meant projecting an artificial image.

As we worked through the compulsories, our worst fears were confirmed. Although skating well, we received one mark of 5.2, which was astonishingly low for us. Betty hadn't noticed anything wrong with the dance, certainly nothing that would merit such a low mark. What she had spotted, however, was a glaring error by one of the Russian couples, which hadn't been picked up by a single judge.

We didn't understand what was going on. All we knew was that the British press expected us to be out there in the lead, and we weren't. This is when they began touting conspiracy stories about partisan judging. What made matters worse was that, under normal circumstances, whoever was in the lead after the compulsories became the eventual winner. That was how it usually went.

Sure enough, the press were all over us. There were far too many requests to handle individually, so we decided to call a press conference, at which we expressed our surprise, saying that we obviously weren't doing what was expected of us but that it wasn't over yet. We still had a chance of winning. That wasn't what we really thought, though – far from it.

The rumba went well and was greeted enthusiastically by the crowd. Although we got a 5.5 from the Austrian judge this was balanced out by two 6.0s, from Britain and the Czech Republic. We'd won the OSP! This put us equal first with Usova and Zhulin. So, it would all hang on the free dance.

Usova and Zhulin were on before us, and Grishuk and Platov after us. This put Grishuk and Platov in a strategically dominant position as the judges always tended to hold back in marking earlier couples, in case the last ones deserve higher marks.

Our dance went well. Very well, we thought, and the crowd seemed to agree. Even as we were leaving the rink, Jayne was still rushing round trying to pick up all the flowers.

'You're lying second,' shouted a reporter. 'How do you feel?' 'Great!' we smiled, but inside we felt awful.

CHRIS:

In fact, we felt dejected, depressed and run down. We had lost. So that was it, we'd let everyone down.

Before we even got halfway to our dressing rooms, questions were already being asked: Was it all down to us? Was there something else going on? Was there resentment against us making a comeback?

Eddie captured all this on film, which meant he was finally getting some of the drama he'd been hoping for.

It was a horrible moment, listening to Grishuk and Platov do their rock 'n' roll number. Jayne was in her dressing room pretending she was somewhere else, while I was slumped on a bench in the corridor. Grishuk and Platov were good too, very good: three 6.0s, four 5.9s and only two 5.8s.

All we had to do now was find out whether we'd come second or third. As far as the Olympics were concerned, whatever happened here would be fine. The Europeans may certainly set the tone for the Olympics, but there's no cast-iron guarantee that if you won one, you'd win the other. There is, however, less of a chance if you don't.

Not so quick, though. According to Alastair Scott of the BBC sports team there might be a reprieve. If Grishuk and Platov, who were lying third, won the free dance – as they obviously had – there'd be no clear winner. The final result would depend on the tally of the second and first places, which in these peculiar circumstances were treated as being identical. Apparently it was certainly a long shot, but we were still in with a chance.

Alastair was listening intently to what was happening in the arena on a radio earpiece, ready to pass on any information.

CHRIS:

We were only on the ice for a few minutes before we were greeted by Eddie and his crew. Once again he urged us to wear radio microphones. By this time we had no fight left in us, and just agreed.

This was to be one of our worst days ever on the ice. We were both isolated and dejected. Andris urged us on, though. 'Come on, guys, let's work on these leg positions for the compulsories.'

Reluctantly we got into position. After an hour, as we repeatedly tried long backwards edges, I lashed out verbally at Jayne, the pressure finally getting the better of me. 'You're not trying. We may as well give up now if you're not even going to try.'

We drifted over to Andris, who was at the side of the rink, and just stood there, looking at each other accusingly. Jayne broke the silence. 'Don't look at me like that.'

'Like what? You're just acting as if to say, "It's not my responsibility, I'm not changing it. I'm not going to do anything."'

'But I am trying to change it.'

'No you're not.'

'I am!'

'You're not.'

Jayne then shrugged and turned away, which I'm afraid drove me to say something like: 'Yup, good attitude, Jayne.'

Back we went to try again, but still it wasn't right. Eventually we went back over to Andris.

JAYNE:

I can usually take Chris's moods on the ice. It's like water off a duck's back to me. At any other time, I'd have responded to his remark, and that would have put us back on an even keel. But on that particular day, I felt as if there was no escape. No end in sight. I was also aware that every word we spoke was being recorded by Eddie. He was getting his drama now, all right, and on a day when we were feeling least cooperative.

Chris carried on the spat. 'You just don't want to be here, do you?'

'Yes, I do.'

'Do it with me then. *I've* been doing it. The problem is, you haven't even been trying!'

At this point I gave up, stopped responding and struggled to hold back the tears – increasingly aware that it was all being recorded – but it was useless.

'It's no use crying,' said Chris. 'I've got no sympathy.'

That was it. Before he could say another thing I walked back to my dressing room, tore off the radio microphone and threw it on the table. Eddie's sound man must have been almost deafened! It was Chris who came in first.

'We have to work, Jayne,' he said.

By that point I was in the mood to respond.

'Don't you ever have a bad day? I always have to be OK, and just for once I'm finding this hard.'

Eventually Chris apologised and we got back to work, albeit a little bit emotionally bruised and battered.

CHRIS:

When the documentary was eventually released, I have to say I was disappointed by the way it had been edited. That five-minute spat we'd had on the ice was made to look like it was key to our working relationship; as though it was a daily occurrence, integral to our routine. What about the two productive hours that followed the incident? Not to mention all the months of work beforehand. That would have given a far truer reflection of how we worked.

I have to admit, however, that even to this day I still get people chastising me in the street. 'How could you be so cruel to that lovely Jayne Torvill?' they say, usually wagging a finger at me. It makes me smile thinking about it. Now, having worked in TV on *Dancing on Ice*, I understand Eddie's point of view, and appreciate the drama that is required.

JAYNE:

Next on our ever-growing list of 'issues' was my hair. I'd worn it long for over ten years, and in the Europeans it had been in a ponytail. 'Maybe something different would make a better impression?' suggested our coaches.

'OK, how about cutting it short?' I said.

'Yes, that's a good idea.'

There was an ulterior motive behind my proposal, though – I knew that if I had it cut short it would finally put a stop to all the suggestions!

So off I went to get it cut. I wasn't sure it would make a difference, but I was willing to try anything.

JAYNE & CHRIS:

At the end of the day, our new-look free dance, with its flashy new lifts, assisted jumps and bigger, more impressive leaps, had nothing to do with the original conception. But despite feeling like we were betraying our principles, as well as all the advice we'd originally been given, we were told to put everything in, within reason.

But it was no use just following fashion. That had never been our way. If we had to add some razzmatazz, we were going to do it properly.

Towards the end of the four days that it took us to map out the revised choreography, we devised a big trick for the

ending – a final flip that carried Jayne from a piggyback position, clear over Chris's head in a somersault. It was a highlight,
really; a punctuation mark.

There was nothing especially original about the move –
we'd used something similar in *Barnum* after we'd turned
professional – nor was there anything illegal about it, either
in our minds or in the rule book. It wasn't a lift and that was
the main thing.

As soon as we'd finished re-choreographing we performed
a run-through for the coaches. They were unanimous: the dance
was more exciting and the ending spectacular. 'But are you sure
it's totally legal?' we asked.

'Yes,' came the reply. 'It doesn't infringe any ISU rules.'

With the new moves decided, we had just over a week to
perfect them. To put this into perspective, we would normally
give ourselves several weeks to choreograph and rehearse, followed by ten days or so to iron out any imperfections. On our
current schedule, we barely had time to learn the routine, let
alone rehearse and perfect it. If we worked hard enough,
though, perhaps we could still give ourselves a chance of
success?

There was certainly no turning back now. We had two
choices: either we sit and worry about it or we get on and do it.

CHRIS:

Now, as strong as our work ethic usually is, even it couldn't
withstand our next disaster. On the Monday morning, with
just a week to go, I was struck down by food poisoning. But
this was no ordinary stomach bug. I was floored; too weak to
even get out of bed and phone Jayne, let alone take to the ice
and rehearse. Unfortunately, Jill had to ring and make my
excuses.

That evening, my misery turned to fear when a knock at the

door revealed a doctor from the Olympic Committee. I was required to give a urine sample for a pre-competition drugs test – all perfectly routine. 'A sample? But I'm totally dehydrated! I've got nothing to give! What am I going to do?'

Although the doctor understood, he still had to put it down as a refusal, but with mitigating circumstances. He'd be back in a few days' time.

The next day, although still pretty weak, I decided to get back on the ice as we couldn't afford to lose any more time.

Pressured by the time lost through my sickness, we decided to delay our flights to Lillehammer and stay on to rehearse. Thank goodness we did, as when the time came for us to actually leave we'd only managed to run through our new routine three times. At least we knew we could get through it.

When we finally arrived in Lillehammer it was –25°C. I remember walking with our cases across the icy pathways towards the athletes' village. 'It'd be just our luck to slip and break something,' I said. That at least raised a smile.

JAYNE & CHRIS:

Later that day we practised the compulsory dances in the main arena. It was almost full at the time, complete with judges, journalists and photographers. There were no nods of approval this time around; no warmth like there had been at Sarajevo. The atmosphere was as cold as the ice we were dancing on.

Then came the free dance practice. The judges usually enjoyed this session, as it presented them with an opportunity to familiarise themselves with everyone's routine. Unfortunately, given Chris's sickness – not to mention the fact that we'd only run though the routine three times – we decided not to attend the practice. What if we didn't have the stamina? What if we fell? There was a very good chance we might. No, we couldn't risk such a public disaster.

In the later practices, we just performed sections from the dance. The arena had a full audience by now and each time we took to the ice, the onlookers applauded enthusiastically. This helped raise our spirits slightly.

The following day the competition began in earnest. First up were the compulsories: the waltz and the blues. For us, these two dances were the strongest that could have been chosen. We skated the waltz as if our lives depended on it – all turns and big smiles. We couldn't have given it any more and were pleased with our performance, as were Bobby and Betty.

We then watched with astonishment as the marks came through. Some of them were mediocre at best and we found ourselves in third place, behind the two Russian couples. Then we took to the ice for the blues. This also went well, and the coaches were pleased. We were third again.

It was scant consolation (and only added to the mystery) that when our marks came up, the majority of the crowd started booing. Perhaps they knew something we didn't?

After this our minds began to race. Had we been placed third just to make absolutely sure we had no second placings, so that there could be no possibility of another scoring upset, like there'd been at the Europeans? Or was it just our imaginations? Some of the scoring had been bizarre in the extreme.

Next up was the draw for the next day's competition, which was the rumba. Normally we'd go along to that, but as we both felt so dejected we asked the team leader to attend in our place. Betty and Bobby were dead against doing this. 'It'll look bad if you're not there,' they said.

That was enough for Jayne, who gave one of her rare mini 'explosions'. 'Do you really think it will make a difference if we don't go to the draw?'

They didn't say a word, but we could see by their expressions that they meant yes.

CHRIS:

Later that night Jill, Jayne and I all went to Phil's apartment to discuss the day's events. This wasn't a postmortem as such; more a wake!

'Could I have a glass of wine please, Phil,' I said as soon as I entered. 'Me, too, please,' echoed both Jayne and Jill.

After a while we began discussing the low marks we had received. 'We might have a chance to win the rumba tomorrow, as we did at the Europeans,' I said, 'but it's all about the free dance.'

If we did indeed win the rumba – which was worth 30 per cent of the mark as opposed to the usual 20 per cent – we'd go into the final day in the lead. But what if the result had already been decided?

'It's not over yet,' said Jayne. 'It can't be!'

'I'm afraid I heard that it is,' said Phil.

Phil had heard lots of rumours that it had already been decided that we wouldn't win and that we were supposed to finish fourth or fifth.

'We're doing well to be lying in third then, aren't we!?' said Jayne.

'All right then,' I said, a little belligerently. 'Let's just see what happens.'

JAYNE & CHRIS:

Was there any point going ahead? We'd asked that question before out of frustration, but now we meant it. How were we supposed to go on and give it our all if we already knew we couldn't win? But that was ridiculous, of course.

How could we let down millions of people like that? The BBC was still predicting another audience of 24 million – the same as we got for *Bolero* and still almost half the population.

We were devastated that we couldn't bring back gold, but we were going to dance this for them and we were going to dance like we'd never danced before.

The next day was a practice day, and we'd planned to attend the second of the two sessions. The first session was a free dance practice, but we decided not to attend so we could concentrate on the rumba. To us it seemed fairly inconsequential. After all, it was up to us when we practised, and we'd still be putting as much in as everybody else. Wrong again.

Apparently the judges – as well as members of the press – had been there at first practice. Why hadn't we? Eventually the storm died down, and we were left to practise the rumba in peace.

The following day we were back to the competition proper, and the rumba. You know those occasions when something goes absolutely right, except you can't remember a thing about it? *Bolero* at Sarajevo is one example. Well, the rumba was another one of those times. The only thing we remember was the audience, who began cheering and clapping before we went on, and for a good few minutes after we came off.

We also remember the scores, of course, which consisted of 5.8s and 5.9s for composition, and 5.9s and two 6.0s for presentation. We were in the lead, then. Suddenly we started to think, What if all the rumours were wrong? Although it was only a chink of light flickering before our eyes, we couldn't help thinking that maybe we were still in with a fighting chance. It most certainly put us in good stead for the following day – finals day.

Chris couldn't sleep for the life of him, and instead read the book *Schindler's List* from start to finish. Not an especially cheery story!

Jayne managed a good sleep as usual. But we both knew it was adrenaline that would be getting us through today, not sleep.

When we arrived at the arena the butterflies in our stomachs slowly started turning somersaults. The noise coming from inside was ear-splitting.

With about 15 minutes to go, we stretched and paced back and forth up the corridor in silence; Eddie and his crew always beside us, desperate for some kind of emotion to emerge. Our parents were in the audience along with Phil and Jill, not to mention hundreds, maybe thousands, of other supporters. Then there were the millions watching at home, of course.

Usova and Zhulin got good marks, all 5.9s and 5.8s. That would take some beating. Then the Finns were on. In four minutes' time it would be us.

Suddenly we heard a gasp from the arena – the Finns had fallen! That put them out of the running.

We've said that we weren't usually nervy people, but right at that moment we were anxious. It was simply fear of the unknown. What would be the reaction when we took to the ice? What would the marks be, and the reaction afterwards? What kind of reception would we receive back home? What about the future? It was that all-pervading awareness again. It felt like our entire careers were resting on the next four minutes.

Two minutes later the Finns had finished. OK, guards off and wait to be announced. As our names were read out we performed our usual ritual: a quick squeeze of the hand, a nod to each other, and out we went.

Inside, the fear was still burning, but it was slowly starting to be eclipsed by an almost alien nervous energy. Not of the unhealthy variety. This was the kind that we used to feel when we were about to perform at the Olympics; in fact, the last time we'd felt it was at Sarajevo. Our years of performing together meant the old magic was taking over.

For those four minutes we *were* the dance. We lived every single second of it. Then, the final somersault, the quick sideways turn and it was all over. It was, for us, a truly golden performance; as good as anything we'd ever done before.

The audience exploded. All we could hear were screams and foot-stomping, and all we could see were people clapping and waving at us; flowers being thrown from all around the arena. With all the doubt and tension now gone, we were just pleased we had performed as well as we could.

We never thought we'd ever feel like that again. In fact, that feeling alone had made the whole endeavour worthwhile. A bold statement, perhaps, given what you've just read, but there really is no greater feeling in the world than knowing you've competed to the very best of your abilities, making yourselves – and everyone who is associated with you – proud. And that was how we felt.

For a minute we circled the ice, Jayne gathering up the dozens of flowers and bouquets (it took six schoolgirls to help carry them all) until a new and very different reality intruded. In came the marks. For technical merit we received two 5.8s, four 5.7s and two 5.6s. *5.6s?* We hadn't had any of those for a long time, and knew immediately that it wasn't going to be a winning score.

Now we knew we couldn't take gold. It had been exactly as we'd feared, and the audience showed their dissatisfaction. The booing and whistles started, and went on until the next marks came up. We did better for artistic impression, but by then we were safely out of the running.

We made our way up the corridor, and waited for Grishuk and Platov to finish their routine. We knew we couldn't win, but how badly had we lost?

Chris stood against the wall, eating a banana, while Jayne drank some water from a mug before going to her dressing room. A rival passed and touched Chris on the arm, which produced a slight smile. The marks were then announced, which seemed to echo down the corridor.

Jayne came out again. 'Where did we come?'

'Third,' said Chris.

'Who came first?'

'Grishuk and Platov.'

If you watch the documentary, the expression on Jayne's face is dead, but that's exactly how she felt. We tried to escape. 'Let's get away from the camera,' said Chris, before taking Jayne's hand and pushing the camera lens away. 'Can we switch it off for a bit now, please?'

Then came the medal ceremony, which we have to say lifted our spirits somewhat. First to step forward were Grishuk and Platov, then Usova and Zhulin, followed by us. Once again, the moment we took to the podium there was an eruption of clapping, screaming and stomping. There were a few boos and whistles, most likely aimed at the judges. It was wonderful to know we still had the public's support. The audience gave us a rousing reception.

By the time of the press conference, we were beginning to see things in perspective. There was no point being depressed, because at the end of the day *we* had been responsible for our comeback, nobody else. We were the ones who'd chosen the music and who'd asked for advice. Good advice, which was always well meant. In the end, we felt the truest balance we could find between the judges' scores and the audience's reaction was to say: 'We skated as well as we knew how, were happy with the programme, and felt like the audience was our judge.'

The press took things a little further than that and demanded an explanation from the ISU. But instead of simply letting the story die down of its own accord, the ISU called a press conference the next day and tried to justify the actions of their judges. Step forward Mr Hans Kutschera, our 'special advisor' at the British Championships.

'Deductions were made for infringements,' he said, 'and

perhaps they deserved a deduction for that final over-the-shoulder somersault.'

'But that was legal,' came the riposte. 'It wasn't a lift.'

Mr Kutschera deflected the answer and moved on.

'They were apart too long!' was his next throw of the dice.

'Grishuk and Platov were apart longer,' parried the journalists. 'Where was their deduction?'

'The judges hadn't timed the separations,' said Kutschera.

'Well, why not?' came the reply.

Mr Kutschera had no answer to this, which left the journalists to write basically whatever they wanted. He had severely underestimated their knowledge and his performance merited nothing better than a 5.6.

CHRIS:

A medal's a medal, when all's said and done, and although gold is by far the most attractive colour, winning bronze was still a great achievement, especially when you take into account what we had to deal with and where we *thought* we'd end up finishing. Going away for ten years before coming back and doing as well as we did was no mean feat.

In retrospect we are very content with it all and have no regrets. It was something we had to do.

If anything it gave us another lease of life, just as *Dancing on Ice* did another ten years after that. You can actually split our career into roughly three ten-year sections: we had a total of ten years as amateurs, ten years touring the world and another ten doing *Dancing on Ice*.

But the irony of the result at Lillehammer was the reaction it sparked from the press and the public. There were headlines like: 'WE WOZ ROBBED' and 'PEOPLE'S COURT VOTES FOR T&D!'

During our world tour in the wake of the Olympics children

Working with the Russian All-Stars was one of the most exciting and challenging experiences of our professional career. Tatiana Tarasova is on the right of the picture, taken during rehearsals.

Yuri Ovchinnikov, who was the lead dancer and artistic director of the Russian All-Stars, joins us on the ice during a performance in New Zealand. It was interesting to work with the Russians, whose approach was different to ours.

When we decided to try for the Olympics again in 1994, our first major competition beforehand was the British Championships, which we won, but we knew just how high the expectations were that surrounded us. (Getty Images)

In discussion with our coach Bobby Thompson, who was such a help to us, as we tried to negotiate the rules of amateur ice dancing, after having been away from it for some time. (PA)

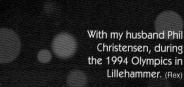

With my husband Phil Christensen, during the 1994 Olympics in Lillehammer. (Rex)

Our Olympic free dance – the audience loved it, but the judges found plenty to fault. (Colorsport/Rex)

Picking up bronze on the Olympic podium, our faces just about masking our feeling of deflation and disappointment. It was a medal – but not the one we had hoped and worked for.

(Getty Images)

Matthew Bourne is one of the choreographers we most admire. (Getty Images)

We were proud and honoured to be asked to carry the Olympic torch in 2012. Needless to say, we took a slightly different approach to the role than most people. (PA)

An emotional moment during the filming of *Piers Morgan's Life Stories*. (ITV/Rex)

One of our favourite moments in the whole of *Dancing on Ice*: Todd Carty shows he still has some way to go before he can turn professional! (ITV/Rex)

Bringing an end to the show. We had loved working with Phillip Schofield, Christine Bleakley and Holly Willoughby. (ITV/Rex)

Thirty years on from winning the Olympics with *Bolero*, we returned to a very different Sarajevo in February 2014. (PA)

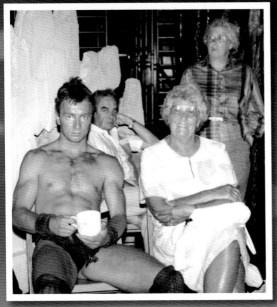

Chris backstage with his mother during *Fire & Ice*, with Jayne's parents behind.

Chris with his two sons, Jack and Sam, who are enjoying life growing up in Colorado.

would make gold medals and give them to us at the end of performances. 'Here, you should have won gold!' they'd say. It was a wonderful gesture and always made us smile. It still does. OK, we didn't win, but with all the support we received afterwards we certainly didn't feel like we'd lost.

11

Touring

JAYNE & CHRIS:

Putting together our own touring company had been a dream of ours even before we turned professional. Michael Edgley, the man who first invited us out to Australia, said he was willing to back the show following the success of our first visit, and so on New Year's Day 1985 we flew back out to Australia to begin preparations.

When we first arrived the company itself consisted of Graeme Murphy, who had already agreed to help choreograph the show, and ourselves. In order to make this work we'd need at least another 14 skaters. We knew exactly who we wanted to approach, and handed our list to Michael Edgley.

Over the next few days we watched as his people made calls, did deals and arranged flights; and that's when the sheer enormity of what we were doing started to hit home. They were inviting people from all over the world, and it was all at our behest. This was a huge gamble at the time because nobody had ever formed a touring ice dance company to this extent before.

This new-found sense of responsibility was driven home even further when the skaters began to arrive. In the first contingent, who'd flown in from Canada, there were three skaters: Gary Beacom, Jonathan Thomas and Kelly Johnson.

When we drove to the airport to pick them up, it all started to become very real. These three people had committed part of their lives to our dream, yet all we had were a few ideas. At that point Graeme had only ever choreographed one piece for the ice, and we had only ever choreographed for ourselves, yet in just a few short months we would have to be ready with a full show lasting two and a half hours and using 16 skaters.

The rehearsal period was going to be two months, but as there was no ice rink in Sydney at the time, the producers had to look for an alternative. When Edgley's team said they'd found somewhere we arranged to go and have a look. We're not sure exactly what we were expecting – a smaller version of Oberstdorf perhaps – but it was certainly nothing like what greeted us.

After being driven through a particularly dingy industrial suburb of Sydney we suddenly drew up outside this enormous building. From the outside it looked like an old warehouse, and from the inside it looked like a derelict old warehouse! The whole place was covered in rubble and dirt and had an old tin roof with great big holes in it.

The ice rink, which had been laid several days earlier, must have been bordering on antique and was being powered by an old and very noisy generator. Apart from that, we just had the basics. There was a tap, some old car seats to sit on and a kitchen area with a kettle and a hob. There were no shops to buy food, though, not for miles.

As soon as the rest of our skaters were in place we arranged to have our first rehearsal, and so one fine morning, in the middle of the Australian summer, we all jumped into our hire minibus and made our way to the warehouse. Because it was summer in Australia, the heat had reacted with the ice and the place was covered in condensation – it was like a thick fog. Oh, the glamour of it all! But we weren't looking for glamour. It might have been a little rough around the edges, but it was *our* ice and we could rehearse there 24 hours a day if we wanted. It was actually just about perfect. And because it wasn't very salubrious, it made you feel as if you were at the start of something unique and very special.

Although there were no shops nearby, we did have a tuck van that visited us each day. This guy must have covered the whole area, and when he arrived he'd sound his horn and we'd slowly pour out of the warehouse. Because it was so hot we'd all be wearing next to nothing, the men in shorts and the girls the same but with vests on. We'd all still be wearing skates, too, albeit with guards on. It must have been quite a sight. Heaven knows what he thought.

When it came to accommodation, once again every expense was spared. At first we thought we were going to be in digs, but in the end they found us some very basic self-assist apartments in the Kings Cross area, which is Sydney's red-light district. We always arrived back just as the ladies of the night were turning out. Then, as we made our way out in the morning, they'd be heading home. It was like a tag team.

This whole period was an extremely heady time for us. We were creating something that hadn't been done before and everyone had bought into it – us, the professional skaters and the producers. We knew it had to make money, which was why we would be skating ten numbers a night, and why we'd agreed to live in basic accommodation, but that wasn't why we were doing it. The buzz of working with a company of like-minded skaters on something completely new was, in itself, priceless.

Once we'd decided on all our numbers, we then had to allocate roles to each of the skaters, which is when we discovered the nuisance of ego ... Graeme Murphy, who was co-choreographing the show with us, treated everyone as if they were part of an ensemble, and had been allocating parts based only on aesthetics. This, we soon found out, was never going to work. In the skaters' minds there was a hierarchy, and each had a different idea of who went where.

'Why is that person getting a solo spot and I'm not?' was one line we heard more than once, together with, 'I can't dance with her. I'm used to dancing with *her*! Why can't you put us together?' Or vice versa.

In the end we held auditions, told everyone to dance the same thing, picked the best, and blamed the decisions on Graeme! 'Sorry, he's the choreographer. Our hands are tied.'

Then, when people started learning how much each was being paid, that opened a whole new can of worms. Especially if somebody doing a solo spot was getting less than somebody who wasn't, which was perfectly feasible. Graeme had allocated roles according to suitability (based on his own opinions), not status.

We left this particular problem to the producers. We were strictly 'ice only'. That said, we did have to learn basic HR skills, and they came in very useful from time to time.

Once order had been restored we carried on rehearsing, and after two months the only bit missing was the grand company finale.

Chris had an idea for this: an adaptation of Gustav Holst's *Planets* suite. A few weeks earlier he'd seen the Moscow Circus on Ice, and it had featured some astonishing wire flying, which had given him an idea for the ending. This would have to be worked out and practised in Oberstdorf, where we were due to finish rehearsals before starting the first leg of the tour.

In the *Planets*, which had been edited down to 25 minutes, our duet was *Venus*, in which Jayne played the Goddess of Love who was looking after the world. The world was a specially made globe that was lit up inside and suspended from a wire. At the end of the duet, Jayne, swathed in a great big cape, had to toss the globe, leaving it to swing in a great arc, before catching it again.

Initially she had no idea how it would swing, and so tossed it as hard as she could. After about 20 seconds or so the globe completed its orbit, landing right on the back of her head. She mastered it eventually.

The number ended with *Jupiter*, in what would be a wonderfully spectacular finale, if it worked. The idea was that we'd all be spinning round like heavenly bodies, some on the ice and some on wires. At the end, all the lights would go out except for some ultraviolet lights, so that the only objects visible to the audience would be the skaters, apparently all spinning round in space. Then, two special effects men, trailing silk tails, would become comets, catapulted by bungee ropes diagonally up into the lighting rig. Nothing could go wrong.

A few days before opening at Wembley, the Edgley Corporation organised a press call. 'Let's give them something spectacular. A real taste of what's to come!' was the suggestion.

'OK,' we said. 'How about sending one of the comets up? That's pretty spectacular.'

'Brilliant, let's do that!'

So the following day we got everything ready, and after the photographers and TV cameras had finished with us, Michael Edgley said, 'OK, gentlemen, you might want to film this, it's pretty spectacular!'

Unfortunately, the bungee rope attached to the special effects man had been tied under too much tension, and when he was eventually blasted off into orbit that's almost where he ended up. Luckily a metal truss stopped him from hitting the inside of the roof, but he got himself a nasty injury. He was limping for weeks. It wasn't exactly the news item we'd been hoping for.

The opening night took place at Wembley Arena on 23 July

1985 and was an extremely glamorous affair. It was a charity performance in aid of Help the Hospices and all 10,000 seats had been sold. The guest of honour was Diana, Princess of Wales and *News at Ten* covered both the performance itself and the presentation afterwards. We'd never been involved in anything quite so glittering before.

After the show had finished a red carpet was laid on the ice so that we could all be presented to Princess Diana. After that we all retired to a huge party, which had been laid on by the producers.

Our initial stint at Wembley Arena lasted for six consecutive weeks and saw us play to almost half a million people. Since then we have gone on to perform at the venue 133 times – a record, according to Wembley. We think that over the years we must have performed live in front of something in the region of five million people worldwide, which is about the same as the population of Scotland, give or take a few. It's frightening, really!

The other highlight of the UK leg of the tour was playing Nottingham. This was a sort of homecoming for us, and we'd been looking forward to it ever since the dates had been announced. Without a big enough venue in the city, it was decided that we'd use a purpose-built tent, which had been specially made by the Edgley Corporation.

At the time it was the world's largest circus tent. It was over 100 metres long and held 7,000 people. It was also 70 metres wide and made up of 20 tonnes of blue PVC, 10 miles of cabling, 36 miles of planking, 100 eight-metre poles and 370 smaller ones.

Once again we played six weeks at Nottingham, and to a combined audience of over 300,000 people. What better way to thank the city that had nurtured and supported us. Our home city.

In turn Nottingham thanked us by granting us the freedom

of the city, a wonderful gesture that we were delighted to accept. In fact, Jayne is Nottingham's first ever 'freewoman'.

When we set off on our first world tour we had no idea when it would finish. It was open-ended. The cost of putting it all together and taking it on the road was immense, so you had to give it time to pay for itself. We just carried on for as long as we could. Once it was rolling, though, it was like a juggernaut that kept going until it ran out of steam. Or, in this case, until Chris broke his wrist.

CHRIS:

With some venues it's more to do with the cachet of playing there than it is the venue itself. Madison Square Garden, for instance, is somewhere we've played three of four times over the years, and is probably one of the most famous venues on the planet. But the building itself was very tired when we last played there. It seemed to be lost in the 1960s. I think it's been renovated fairly recently, so it'll be interesting to see what they've done to it. Hopefully a lot!

Many of those big venues were like that back in the 1980s, quite tired. They were also all run by the unions, which meant if you tried to move something that was in the way but it wasn't your job to do it there would be pandemonium. There'd almost be a walkout.

Things are very different these days, and almost all these venues are run by private companies, usually with big-name sponsors attached to them.

Touring America was always quite rock 'n' roll. You might do 50 shows all in a row, and all at different venues. It'd be a constant round of performing, then jumping on the tour bus to the next town. By the end you were fit to drop. It's an amazing experience, though, touring America coast to coast.

We used to have something called 'the oil spot' on the

American tours. If we were staying in a hotel overnight, everyone would be told what time the tour bus would be leaving, and if you were late, all you'd see is the 'oil spot'. In other words, you'd have to make your own way to the next town.

I remember once when our lighting guy got left behind and had to make his own way to the next venue. As we hadn't got another lighting guy, if he didn't make it we'd have had no lights. Luckily, he managed to turn up.

Jack Nicholson came to see our show once. We were playing the Inglewood Forum in LA, another pretty famous venue, and Andris told us Nicholson was in the audience. At first we didn't believe him but when he told us the actor would like to come backstage at the end, we knew it wasn't a wind-up. So after the show he came backstage with his daughter to see us. That was pretty amazing. When one of us asked if he'd enjoyed the show, he just said, 'I love anything that makes me cry.' I *think* it was a positive comment . . .

We also met Ronald Reagan once while we were over in the States. We were in Washington and our company manager at the time had a friend who worked at the White House. She asked if she could arrange for us to have a look round (as you do) and, lo and behold, she did. We got a tour around the White House. I don't remember going through any security checks, which is quite strange.

Anyway, while we were being shown round the Rose Garden we suddenly saw Ronald Reagan walking past, and he actually stopped and said hello. He told us that when he was a child he used to wait for his local lake to freeze over and then get his skates out and go skating. The most powerful man in the world not only knew who we were (I think he must have been briefed) but he also used to skate!

I think we've only ever experienced one fight on tour (not us, by the way), which happened during *Face the Music*. One of the Russian skaters started dating one of the American skaters.

There was nothing strange about this except that she was married to one of the stagehands and his wife was back in Russia. That got quite nasty in the end, and the stagehand ended up attacking the Russian. Ultimately we had to send the stagehand home. We needed the skater! It took our make-up department an age to get him presentable. By the time they'd finished with him he was wearing enough make-up to play Mrs Doubtfire.

And a few years before that, during the Russian All-Stars tour, two of the couples in the company ended up switching partners. Both couples broke up first, I hasten to add. Then, shortly afterwards, they ended up with each other's ex. That was a very strange state of affairs. It's hard to keep track of all the shenanigans that happen on a day-to-day basis.

We've always been lucky when it comes to alcohol, in the sense that we haven't had many problems with it on tour. Jayne and I are not especially big drinkers, and neither are professional skaters as a rule. However, there was a skater once who caused us one or two problems. He was a speciality act – in more ways than one – and had been around for years, but, boy, could he drink. He used to be able to get absolutely paralytic and still make it into rehearsal. He was a juggler as well, which made it even more amazing. Not all of the balls stayed in the air all the time, though! There were a couple of times when he didn't make it on. He was quite a character.

JAYNE:

The only place we never covered with either of our world tours was Europe, even though we were popular there. At that time there weren't as many big arenas as there are now. There were plenty of ice rinks, but they didn't hold enough people. If it was going to be financially viable, we had to get audiences of about 8,000-plus, and the only way you could do that was in an arena.

These days we could have played everywhere, but back then we were restricted.

The first world tour was probably the most exciting of all the tours. That came on the back of the Olympics and so our popularity was probably at its peak. We also hadn't been professionals for long, so everything in our lives was new at the time. We also seemed to have an almost inexhaustible amount of energy. We felt like we could accomplish anything.

CHRIS:

Even today we're constantly trying to push ourselves, making the shows bigger and better than last time, but there are occasions when we have to be reined in slightly, when our imaginations outgrow the budgets. A few years ago we were planning a number that was set underwater and wanted dozens of huge mechanical fish, some in the air and some on the ice, all moving about. We'd seen something similar in America – airship-type machines that floated about carrying advertising – and had had the brilliant idea of disguising them all as fish.

After all the hoots of derision had died down, tour manager Tony Harpur indulged us by saying he'd work out the cost, and a few minutes later came to the dressing room with a piece of paper. He handed it to us, we looked at it, handed it back and it was never mentioned again. It appeared that disguising airships as fish was an expensive business. Experiences like that never stopped us wanting to experiment, though. We'd still ask the question, no matter how silly.

JAYNE:

At the time we didn't really appreciate the enormity of what we were doing. It was just our job. The fact that we were appearing in front of thousands of people night after night didn't actually register. We were doing the same thing the next night so it just felt like the norm.

Looking back now we can fully appreciate it. As big as the *Dancing on Ice* tours were they never left the UK and would last for around 30 shows. Back in the 1980s and 90s we were playing all over the world and in some absolutely enormous venues. Sometimes there were up to 20,000 people a night.

You really can't afford to get injured in these circumstances. That's the biggest responsibility of all. Although we've had our fair share of injuries over the years, and once had to cancel a leg of a tour, there have been very few other examples of us cancelling shows. On the last *Dancing on Ice* tour we were both very conscious of not wanting to cancel any of the shows through injury. As you get older you obviously become more susceptible to them, and that plays on your mind constantly. It doesn't make you paranoid as such, just quite wary. You become a bit more cautious, and that's not a bad thing. Experience brings wisdom!

12

Parenthood

CHRIS:

Starting a family was a very exciting time for Jill and me. It was something we were both ready for and everything was just right. We felt ready to become parents. Jill was 29 when Jack was born and I was 39, so I was quite an old dad. I didn't feel like it, though, and I don't think it's a bad thing having children when you're a bit older. It meant that I knew for sure it was the right time. I'd done all the conquering and had realised a lot of ambitions. This was going to be the next chapter in my life.

I remember when Jill first told me she was pregnant. In fact, I still have the pregnancy test that showed she was pregnant. It was a life-changing moment. Luckily, she didn't really suffer from any morning sickness, which meant we were both able to enjoy the pregnancy. Watching her get bigger – almost by the day – was a delight.

Being there at the delivery was important to me. I was aware, like I think most people are, that you weren't usually given that opportunity back in the 1940s and 50s. I'm sure my dad was told to wait in the other room, and he probably paced up and down, puffing away on a cigarette. Having the chance to be there for Jill and to see my son being born was something I wanted to do. In the end it was my job to hold on to one of her legs!

Jack was only just 5lb when he was born so he was quite a small baby. We were both a bit concerned at the time but the doctor said he was just a small baby. He was fine. I think he was about 19 inches from head to toe, and I remember he had quite big feet.

I know we men probably put on a brave face about it, but when you leave hospital with your wife and child for the first time it's the scariest thing. You're stepping into the unknown and can't help but think, What on earth do we do now? Where's the instruction book? It's another one of those moments you tend to remember in life, and it's easily the most overwhelming. I remember standing on the ice in Sarajevo with Jayne, waiting to be announced before we performed *Bolero*. We had the hopes of an entire nation on our shoulders then, tens of millions of people. That was nothing compared to the responsibility of a child's welfare.

The feeling of love I experienced when Jack was born was something new to me. I was in love with Jill, of course, but the love you feel for a child is different, it's unique. All I knew was that it was totally wonderful. Best of all, it grows as you get to know them. It's the most beautiful obsession.

I always felt quite isolated as a child. Not necessarily unhappy, but definitely isolated, and that was a state of mind I never want my children to experience. In my opinion children should never, ever feel alone. That's not the reason I'm tactile with them. It feels like a very natural behaviour to me. My dad was never a cold person; in fact, he was extremely warm. But that didn't really manifest itself in either actions or words. It was more a feeling. He had an aura about him. But to me, telling your children that you're there for them no matter what is easily as important as telling them that you love them. It's *all* unconditional.

The dynamic shifts slightly as they become older and less dependent, but by then they're completely part of you. You've been there since day one and they're rooted to you, both biologically and emotionally.

Sam came along soon after Jack, and we were thrilled. Jill wasn't feeling well one day (she was even off her coffee, which is virtually unheard of!) and we eventually found out why. Twenty-one months later Sam arrived, and that's when you start to experience all of those emotions again; all the feelings of love and concern. It's a beautiful time.

Both my boys were early walkers. Jack started at about a year and Sam at about nine months. There was no warning; suddenly they were up and off. The problem being, of course, that when they can walk, you have to walk, almost constantly. Then there's the climbing, the falling and the bumping into things.

The thing that affected me most in those early days was sleep deprivation. It's the same for 99 per cent of parents, I think, and everyone has their own stories. I was getting one, maybe two hours' sleep a night at one point, and then trying to be a dad during the day. I remember driving up to a traffic light one day. I was totally exhausted at the time. Coasting on fumes! I saw it change to red as I approached, so slowed down and stopped. Then I closed my eyes and thought, I'll just have a few seconds. Before I knew it I was woken by a chorus of car horns and moved on. It honestly makes me tired just thinking about that time.

I once had the boys in the back of the car. It was a warm Colorado day and we were going shopping, I think. They were both babies at the time and were asleep. I had to stop off and use a cash machine on the way, and so parked up at the bank. It was probably about ten metres from the car to the cash machine so, rather than wake the boys up and pull out the buggy and everything else – which would have been a nightmare, especially for somebody who hadn't slept in a week – I decided to just make a run for it. They'd still be in full view of me, and I'd wind the window down slightly so I could hear if one of them was crying. What could possibly go wrong?

By the time I made it over to the cash machine a queue had built up, but it was all right, as I could still see the car. I couldn't hear any crying, so I assumed all was well. And it was, inside the car. Outside, a concerned member of the public had spotted the boys alone in the car and had called 911. When I arrived back this person accosted me. 'Are these two yours?'

'Yes, why?'

'I was concerned about them. It's hot and they were left alone.'

'Yes, which is why I wound the window down slightly. I was only over there using the cash machine. They were in full view of me the whole time.'

'But I've just called nine-one-one. They're sending the fire department.'

'Oh well. I've got to be going, I'm afraid.'

As I pulled out of the car park the fire brigade were pulling in. I shudder to think what they said to the 'concerned' member of the public.

Another time the three of us were in a home decoration store called Target, which is a great big barn of a place. Perfect for losing newly mobile children in!

I only took my eyes off Sam for a split second and when I turned back, he'd gone. I had a quick look around and couldn't see him, so I picked up Jack and went to see one of the shop assistants. 'Excuse me, but I appear to have lost my son. Could you help me look for him, please? He must be round here somewhere.' I didn't realise it but they obviously took this kind of thing very seriously. The assistant ran behind the counter, pressed a button, and within about a second every door in the store slammed shut. Nobody could get in or out. There were people running everywhere. It was great that they went to such lengths, but when Sam suddenly toddled round the corner I just wanted to disappear. I could feel everyone looking at me thinking, Oh yeah, Dad's been allowed out with the kids and look what's happened!

You do find yourself doing some ridiculous things, though, especially with the first child. You don't leave anything to chance. There was once a scary moment with Jack, who'd managed, heaven knows how, to get hold of a bottle of Tylenol, which is like the American version of Calpol. I remember just seeing him standing there, holding the empty bottle.

Because it's quite sweet to taste, the first thing I thought was, Oh no, he's drunk the lot!, so I ran up to him. 'Jack, where did all the medicine go? Did you drink it?'

'Yes.'

'Or did you pour it down the loo?'

'Yes.'

'Are you sure you poured it down the loo?'

'Yes.'

'But did you drink any of it?'

'Yes.'

So we were in a quandary. Should we just wait and see what happens, or should we rush him to the hospital? Being first-time parents, we naturally rushed him to the hospital. When we explained what might have happened they tried to make him drink some black charcoal medicine, which would apparently soak up anything harmful. There was absolutely no way this was going to happen. Jack was already a fussy eater, so trying to force charcoal into him would be impossible. In the end, we had to sit tight and see if anything happened. We were there for about six hours before we realised that it must all have gone down the loo. You live and learn.

When *Dancing on Ice* started, Jack was about eight and Sam was about six, so for those first few years I was basically always there; almost a househusband, if you like, and extremely hands-on when it came to things like changing, feeding and burping. I enjoyed every second of it. If I get it in my head to do something, I tend to do it properly, and I really threw myself into parenthood.

My main job of work at that time was choreographing the *Stars on Ice* tours, which feature an array of Olympic medallists and champions. These shows have been touring America since 1984 and are still immensely popular. I eventually became artistic director for a couple of years before starting *Dancing on Ice*, but because it was only a part-time position it afforded me the luxury of being able to get involved in parenthood.

It's sad that my dad never got to meet my boys, and vice versa. Despite not being a great talker I think he'd have made a wonderful granddad. However, they're very lucky to have Jill's dad, as I was and still am. He's a real adventurer and is always taking them away on holiday with him. He says his job is to create memories for them. That's our job too, of course, but we also have the day-to-day stuff. Maybe that's your reward for getting through parenthood. You graduate from guardian to memory-maker.

Personality-wise, my boys are also polar opposites. Jack's a bit of a loner, quite introverted, but very happy in his own space. He's quite like me when I was his age. Then we have Sam, who's probably the most sociable boy I know. He has a lot of big ideas but isn't so good on the detail. He could end up being a salesman, a barrister or the President. He has a definite effervescent quality. Jack's like me when I'm off the ice and Sam when I'm on it.

JAYNE:

When I retired in 1998 Phil and I began having the conversation about starting a family. It seemed like the right time: to begin with, I had plenty of time on my hands, something I'd never known before.

After just a few weeks of trying I fell pregnant, but when I went for my first scan I was told that the pregnancy was ectopic. I had no idea what an ectopic pregnancy was, so they explained that it meant the embryo was growing inside one of the fallopian tubes and not the womb.

'OK, how do we get it out?' I asked.

'I'm afraid we don't.'

In most cases you can escape with only having to take medication, but unfortunately for me there were complications and I had to have surgery.

When I'd recovered we were told that it was all right to try again. We were also told that there was less chance of us conceiving. After conceiving so quickly the first time around we weren't too worried, so started again quite optimistically.

A year or so later nothing had happened, so we decided to go and see a specialist. He asked us all the usual questions: 'Have you done this, and have you done that?' and eventually suggested IVF. We'd both heard of IVF, but had no idea of the process.

The doctor suggested we go away and have a think about it; maybe do some research. That's exactly what we did and the more we found out, the more hopeful we became. In the end we couldn't wait to get started. It has that effect on you. It's also very difficult not to build your hopes up – or at least it was for me. Phil is very good at managing expectations, and so am I under normal circumstances. This time, though, I couldn't help myself.

When the first few attempts didn't work I was distraught to say the least. Then, the next time you think, This one's definitely going to work. But when it doesn't, you start to become desperate. After that you start expecting it not to work, which is hard, not just mentally but physically. All those drugs you have to take have an effect, and I put on quite a bit of weight. So, not only was I not pregnant, but I was also bigger than I wanted to be.

Even before we started IVF Phil had suggested adoption, but I don't think it was something I really wanted to consider at the time. You have to be absolutely ready to adopt a child. It's not simply a case of exhausting all your other options and then thinking, Oh go on, then, let's adopt – absolutely not. It's very different from giving birth naturally and, for the sake of everybody concerned, you have to allow yourself time to get used to it. You have to arrive at the decision. You can't be persuaded.

Phil was always further down the line than me with regard to adoption. His sister is adopted and so to him it was perfectly normal. She'd been adopted as a baby and called his mom, Mom, and his dad, Dad. He never thought of her as being anything other than a sister.

In order to move forward with the idea, I was also going to need some first-hand experience.

When I'd retired I found it difficult to settle into domestic life. I found it totally alien and, if I'm honest, I got bored at times. Then I met a neighbour of ours called Sandra, who was the opposite of me domestically; as comfortable around the house as I ever was on the ice, but who, on a personal level, just drew me in. Sadly, she passed away a few years ago and I miss her every day. She was a kindred spirit and the best best-friend you could ever wish for.

Instead of just ignoring domesticity I thought I'd at least give it a go, and when I announced this to Sandra she very kindly offered to help. 'I'd like to learn to cook first,' I said.

'OK, I'll come up and do it with you.'

And that's the way it was with her – whatever I said I wanted to learn next, she did it with me, showed me step by step. It was like learning to skate again, but with far more laughter and a glass or two of wine!

Around the time I was learning how to become a housewife, a friend of Sandra's called Charlotte, who also lived nearby, adopted a little boy called Aaron. Aaron was about 11 months old and when he arrived Sandra arranged for me to meet Charlotte and Aaron round at her house. Sandra obviously had an ulterior motive, and thank goodness she did, because from the first moment I held Aaron in my arms I knew I could be a mum to an adopted child.

When we left the house I turned to Phil and said, 'I'm ready. I want us to adopt.'

He said: 'I knew you'd get there in the end.'

It was a wonderful feeling. It felt like a new beginning.

Charlotte, who also became a very good friend, put us on to the right people the next day and we set the wheels in motion. Adopting is a lengthy process, but we knew that before we started. We also knew that there was by no means any guarantee of being successful. But this time we weren't relying on drugs or doctors. All we had to rely on was our suitability as potential parents.

After about a year we were accepted by the adoption panel, who then told us that they'd like us to adopt a baby boy called Kieran. We were over the moon.

A short while later we were given some pictures of him. One of the photos had been taken by his foster mum, and because of the angle it looked like he had an enormous head. It was about twice the size of his body. I didn't like to say anything, but Phil's one of those people who'll always state the obvious and he just came out with it. 'His head looks big, doesn't it?' Then we looked at another picture of him and realised that it was just the way the photo had been taken. He had gorgeous big blue eyes. He was such a beautiful baby.

Kieran was eight months old when we first met him. His foster mum lived in Sussex, and I remember when we arrived there our stomachs were in knots. We were nervous but very excited. The adoption people try hard to prepare you before-hand. They told us not to get too upset if he cried when we held him, things like that.

The first thing I wanted to do when I saw him was just scoop him up, but I had to do my best to remain calm and composed. Then, all of a sudden, when his foster mum was holding him, he looked at me and reached out his arms. That was when I first held him. It was just the best moment ever.

Despite my lack of maternal experience, I was never one for reading lots of books on the subject. But I'm good at taking advice, especially from close friends. Fortunately, I had Sandra and Charlotte on hand. They were all I really needed. Also, because I was older and more mature, I was pretty good on the common-sense front. I'm not saying it was easy, because it cer-tainly wasn't, but being used to sticking to a routine certainly helped me. And, because Kieran was adopted, I also had the support of social services, if I needed them.

But regardless of how confident I was with my support net-work, I was always fearful of being judged, of not doing the right thing. That was put to the test once when I was out and about with Kieran, who was about two and a half at the time. We were in the Early Learning Centre in Tunbridge Wells and when I said it was time to leave he decided to throw an enor-mous tantrum: kicking, screaming, flailing arms, the works! I did what I thought I was supposed to do in such situations, which was to walk away and ignore him. At that moment a chap came in through the door. 'Hello, Jayne, how are you?' I didn't recognise the guy and was getting flustered. Not wishing to be rude, though, I stood there and made polite con-versation, all the time trying to ignore the fact that my child was going absolutely bananas.

'Is he yours, Jayne?'

'Yes, I'm afraid so. He's not usually like this!'

With that, he just smiled and left. About a week later, John

Barrowman, who was appearing in *Dancing on Ice* at the time, came up to me in the studio: 'Hi, Jayne, I believe you saw my agent last week.'

'I'm not sure, did I? Where did I meet him?'

'In the Early Learning Centre in Tunbridge Wells.'

'Oh my goodness. How embarrassing!'

'How's Kieran?'

'A lot calmer, thanks.'

When Jessica came along I was much more relaxed. I think most people are with second children. There's a kind of process of elimination that takes place and you cherry-pick what was necessary from the first time. It leaves you with more time and less stress. I remember when we adopted Kieran I'd spend ages making up his bottles. Then, by the time Jessica arrived, I realised you could buy milk ready-mixed. I just heated it up in the microwave, then gave it a good shake to remove any hot spots. Amazing!

When we first went to meet Jessica she was crawling on the floor. Again I was holding back, trying to remain composed, but Phil couldn't help himself and he scooped her up; so he got the first hug with her. It didn't take long for me to have my turn, though.

We then had to make sure that Jessica and Kieran bonded, and that was quite a worry. You never know how they'll take to each other. They were fine and are as close as any other brother and sister. But whenever they fall out, the first thing he says is, 'Mum, when's she going back?', which makes us all laugh.

When we had Kieran I wasn't working, but when we had Jessica I was, and I felt quite guilty at the time. I'd been able to dedicate myself to him, yet couldn't do the same with Jessica. The first couple of weeks were fine as I was able to be at home, but then I was away every other day or so, and it was hard going. I was concerned that she might not recognise me as her mum, but I needn't have worried.

As is often the way, our children have very different personalities yet complement each other perfectly. Kieran's quite a sensitive soul and is the one who requires the most attention, whereas Jessica is far more laid-back and gregarious; a typical second child, in fact.

People sometimes ask me if I regret not having children naturally, but I can honestly say, with hand on heart, that I don't. The IVF and the ectopic pregnancy were both very difficult experiences for Phil and me. All I know for sure is that had they not happened, we wouldn't have Kieran and Jessica, and that is an unthinkable proposition. I wouldn't change them for the world.

13

Dancing on Ice

JAYNE & CHRIS:

This chapter has been divided into two parts, as before *Dancing on Ice* there was an eight-year period during which we were, in effect, no longer Torvill & Dean.

Not too many people are aware that we once retired from skating together, which is why it's important to talk about it here, and even though we eventually acclimatised, the uncoupling itself was deeply painful.

What brought us back together was, of course, *Dancing on Ice*, a show that for ten years turned our lives into one big adventure.

Take our word for it – there's no finer way to spend a decade.

<u>NOT</u> DANCING ON ICE

CHRIS:

The reasoning that led to us retiring was actually quite logical.

After competing at the 1994 Olympics our profile was quite

high again, and the world tour that followed went on for well over a year. I remember it as an extremely productive period. We were brimming with creativity. The trouble was that, once the tour had finished, our options would not be as exciting.

Ever since first getting together we'd spent the majority of our time either competing or touring. There had been other, little things in between, such as the odd TV appearance, but tours and competitions had always been our livelihood. That's all there was.

As we've previously mentioned, before deciding to compete again in 1994 we'd reached an impasse. We'd won the Olympics and had toured the world several times over. Being allowed to go for gold again had kept things fresh for us, and had – we thought – extended the life of our partnership by a good few years. So, come the end of the tour in 1995, we couldn't really see what the future held for us, save for guest spots on tours, and that's exactly what came to pass.

JAYNE:

Both of us were happily married and either starting or thinking about starting a family. So it came naturally to the point where we had to devote time to making that happen. Being away on tour and apart from your partner isn't conducive to having children. We might have been naive and slightly innocent at one time, but even we knew that you needed two to make a baby.

We never actually announced our retirement or made it official. It was only between us and those closest to us. I think people realised as time went on, but by then we had adapted and were no longer in the limelight.

But in addition to family planning there was also the geographical issue. Chris was now based permanently in America, whereas I was still in England. Since moving out there he'd been making connections and had received some invitations to choreograph.

There was a way this could have been resolved, though. Phil, my husband, is from America, and he asked me if I'd be interested in moving over there. I was quite open to the suggestion, so much so that we even spent a few weeks looking at houses and different areas. But I was never entirely convinced that I could settle in America. For one thing, I didn't want to leave my parents. I'm an only child, and if I went they'd be on their own. Phil understood, and in the end we simply gave up on the idea. Had it happened, then perhaps Chris and I might have thought differently about retiring, especially as ice dancing is a lot more popular in the States than it is in the UK. Who knows what opportunities might have come up?

But with things remaining the way they were, we decided that it was time to call it a day. There was always going to be an end, and this was most probably it.

CHRIS:

The bizarre thing was that we never formally agreed to retire, just as we never formally agreed to become partners. We'd started with a trial period back in 1975 and had been extending it ever since. When it came to retirement, a similar attitude applied. It was just suggested almost in passing one day, and we said OK.

We'd been guests on the *Stars on Ice* tour, which was due to end in May 1998. After that I was going back to Colorado and Jayne to Sussex, so that would be that. We didn't talk about it until after we'd done it, as strange as that sounds. We just had a feeling that it was what we were supposed to do. It was almost as if we'd been led to it. We both knew it was time for starting families.

I recently watched a recording of our last dance together, which took place in Vancouver, and it almost brought me to tears. Jayne was in floods of tears at the time. It was probably one of the most emotional moments of our lives. Then, a few days later, when we were sitting there on opposite sides of the earth, it suddenly dawned on us what we'd done. That was it – we were no longer Torvill & Dean. We were Chris in Colorado and Jayne in Sussex.

Actually calling a halt to Torvill & Dean as performers meant that we no longer thought or planned (professionally at least) as partners. We were now living as individuals, which took us out of the public eye almost immediately. People only recognised Torvill & Dean, not Jayne and Chris.

TV wasn't an option for us back then, apart from interviews, so the majority of the ideas – the tours and shows – had always started with us. It was the same when we were competing as amateurs, when it was all about self-motivation and long-term goals, the pinnacle being the Olympics. Then, as professionals, we decided we wanted to put on our own show and tour the world. But that's the point: it was something *we* wanted to do. Nobody called us up and asked us to do it. So, if *we* weren't thinking about what Torvill & Dean were going to do next, nobody else would be.

In hindsight we should simply have taken a sabbatical, which would have meant we'd continue to think as partners.

We'd been in each other's company almost every day of our lives for the last 23 years – ever since that Thursday morning when Janet Sawbridge had told us to get in hold and stand eye-to-eye and pelvis-to-pelvis. Since then we'd always been Torvill & Dean, our competition billing, because competition was what we lived for until we turned professional. By then we were synonymous with each other, not only in the eyes of the public but in our own too. We'd been apart from time to time (I'd been living in Colorado for a few years prior to this) but the difference was that we always had something planned, something to look forward to.

JAYNE:

I found the first few months really hard to deal with, and felt quite depressed at times. One day we were appearing in front of an audience of thousands, surrounded by people I'd worked and lived with for years – not just Chris, but an entire company – and the next I'm flying home with nothing at all in my diary. No plans and no partnership. I was unemployed.

Phil and I had recently moved house so I didn't have any friends in the area. In fact, I had very few close friends in the country. Leading a nomadic lifestyle meant you made friends all over the world, and the only way to keep all that alive was to carry on being nomadic. So, on top of no longer having Chris and our partnership, I had also said goodbye – or it felt like it – to all of my friends, people I'd known for years. I felt extremely lonely. Empty, even.

Not long after the split Chris had to come back to the UK for a few days to clear out his old house. That was the final nail in the coffin for me, as it felt as if he was severing his ties with the UK, and with me.

When I took him and Jill to the airport on the day they left I just burst into tears. I promised myself I wouldn't but I couldn't help it. That's when it really hit me, the enormity of what we were saying goodbye to. It was almost like losing a limb.

JAYNE & CHRIS:

Calling time on Torvill & Dean is something we have vowed never to do again. We're both believers in fate, though, and although we didn't go about it the right way, taking a break did result in us each having two beautiful children. If we'd carried on touring we might not have been so blessed. And the eight years wasn't all separation anxiety and depression. As we've said, we did learn to adapt in the end and we each carried on working. There were even occasions when we did things together (although not on the ice): we delivered a seminar in Nottingham once and we also put together a skating gala for the Queen's Golden Jubilee celebrations. Most importantly, we remained friends. As painful as it was to break up our partnership, it was never going to affect our friendship.

DANCING ON ICE

JAYNE & CHRIS:

When it dawned on us that we might start working together again it was like receiving a huge shot of adrenaline. We'd obviously remained friends since the split and still saw each other three or four times a year, but the dynamic of our relationship was different – we had no future projects to discuss. We still talked about skating from time to time, but as friends. So when *Dancing on Ice* moved beyond being just a pipe dream, we were both fit to burst.

But in order to go back to doing something, you first have to evaluate whatever it was you were doing previously; and during those eight years apart we'd had time to do just that. This had left us with a sense of pride and appreciation that we'd never really felt before. We'd never had time to smell the roses. It had all been such a rush.

That, apart from our experience and our enthusiasm, was what we brought to the table: our history. And whenever we went out on to the ice, it all came with us.

So coming out of retirement was in itself a positive move for us, and we were able to carry that positivity through to *Dancing on Ice*. The format of the show was right for us and the people we worked with were wonderful, but that was all underpinned by an acceptance that our first 23 years together had been worthwhile. The anticipation about working together again became almost tangible.

Like *Bolero*, *Dancing on Ice* is very dear to us. It's probably been the high point of our professional careers so far, just as *Bolero* was the high point of our career as amateurs.

The difference between the two is that for just over ten years we ate, breathed and slept *Dancing on Ice*. It was what we got out of bed for and it enriched our lives almost beyond recognition.

Getting back on to the ice and being Torvill & Dean again was fabulous, but then transforming that into nine successful series and seven sell-out tours was light years beyond anything we thought possible. Best of all, the friendships we've made over that time have been many, varied and lasting.

We feel it's only right that we take you through the whole story of *Dancing on Ice*, just as we did with *Bolero*.

In 2004, out of nowhere, we received an enquiry from a development producer. He had an outline for an idea similar to what eventually became *Dancing on Ice* and wanted to know whether we thought it might work. It was only a 20-minute conversation and we thought little of it at the time.

A couple of weeks later we had a meeting with a different producer, but about the same idea. The meeting took place at Jayne's house in Sussex. The producer was supposed to come with her boss but he'd apparently been waylaid. After about half an hour of talking about nothing she pulled out a camera and took a photo of Jayne, which annoyed her as she hadn't even asked permission. Jayne had been out of the public eye for quite a while so the producer had probably been told to find out what she looked like these days. It wasn't a good move.

Then, a couple of weeks after this, we were contacted by London Weekend Television, once again about exactly the same idea. This time we went to see them and had a 'professional' meeting about what might be possible. In the end we asked both the second company we spoke to and LWT to put a proposal together, which we could then go away and discuss.

Both proposals were good, but there was something very unrealistic about the one from the second company. They were offering silly money, providing it went ahead, which made it feel less likely it would actually materialise. It was like they were trying too hard. They were promising everything.

LWT's proposal seemed far more realistic and they had definite lines that they weren't prepared to cross. It was much more businesslike.

On top of this, the first proposal, if it went ahead, would be made for the BBC, and the BBC already had *Strictly Come Dancing*. Why would they want *Dancing on Ice* too? There were too many similarities. What would they do with it? Where would they schedule it? *Strictly Come Dancing* is made by the BBC *for* the BBC. It's a flagship show. *Dancing on Ice* would be almost an outsider. If the BBC wanted *Dancing on Ice*, why weren't they speaking to us direct?

LWT were pitching the idea to ITV, who are part of the same company and who at the time had nothing similar within their schedules. The money might have been less, but it was a clearly defined proposal and, in our view, would be pitched to a channel that was far more likely to take it seriously. So in the end it was a fairly obvious choice – and, of course, the right one.

JAYNE:

LWT were inspired to produce *Dancing on Ice* by *Strictly Come Dancing*. It had started a couple of years before but Chris had never seen it, as he'd been living in Colorado. I remember trying to explain the format to him over the phone, how professional dancers teach celebrities to dance, but he wasn't impressed. 'Well, that's just dancing,' was the initial reaction. Then I tried to explain how we'd be responsible for transferring this on to ice, and he suddenly became interested. 'Hmm, possibly. I suppose it could work.' Deep down I think he knew it could work. I did.

CHRIS:

Yes, I suppose I did. It certainly got our creative brains working again, which had been pretty much dormant for what seemed like the longest time. Then, as things progressed, we started to buy into it more – 'Maybe we could do this and maybe we could do that' – and it gradually became more and more exciting. It got to the point where we'd have been shattered if it hadn't gone ahead.

Phil is very much a realist, and I remember when he, Jayne and I were having all the initial meetings about the show. Phil said: 'Don't get too excited just yet; these things don't always happen,' whereas Jayne and I were like children in a candy shop. We were totally wrapped up in it all; the possibility of working on a major television series, being part of something new and original. And because we were there right from the beginning, it always felt like a joint exercise, marrying our expertise on the ice with the expertise of those producing the show. Usually you're just there as talent, as a performer, but with *Dancing on Ice* we were also part of the creative team; intrinsically involved and so ultimately partly responsible.

There was no single person in charge. We knew as much about TV as the producers did about ice dancing, so we had to mentor each other. It was a coming together of a popular medium and a sport that we were trying to turn into an entertainment art form. Learning how TV works from the inside out has been a real journey, something we've thrived on.

We couldn't have done it back in the 1980s. We weren't yet mature enough, not as ice dancers and choreographers or as people. In order to be in a position to transfer what we did on to

TV, we had to be at the very top of our game. The competitions, the world tours, the TV specials all contributed to our training. Then and only then were we in a position to begin work.

The amount of creative freedom you get working on a project like *Dancing on Ice* is something that you could never achieve while performing on tour. TV is geared to feeding the imagination, and it can be as intimate, grandiose or intricate as you wish. Provided you have the budget, of course.

Then you've got the challenge of meeting and working with all the celebrities. It's such an intense period, like running a school.

We now feel totally at home working on TV. It's extraordinarily hard work but hugely gratifying. It brings out the best in us, not just as performers but as choreographers, teachers, coaches and human beings. You try to be the best at everything, and you have around you this amazing team of people, all working towards the same goal. It can create an electric atmosphere.

JAYNE & CHRIS:

But as we got further into developing *Dancing on Ice*, we really tried to emphasise to the producers that in order to make it happen we had to have time. It wasn't something we could sign up for and have ready the following week. If it was going to be done properly we'd need at least three months. First the contestants had to learn how to skate and, second, we'd have all the choreography to work out, not to mention rehearsals and everything else.

On a dancing show, each routine can be classed as just that, a routine; whereas on a skating show, they're more like a 'production'. They often involve all manner of props and special effects. Fortunately, the producers trusted us and gave us the opportunity to experiment and do things that had never been seen before. If we were starting the show from scratch again today, we're not sure we'd be given the same leeway. Budgets are so much tighter these days.

We think that over the years we've probably had more injuries than any other show on television. But things could have been a lot worse if we hadn't taken the care and attention we always did. The contestants' safety was always paramount to us, and to the producers, but as you now know, ice can be a very unforgiving surface. And, as for health and safety, it'd most likely all be considered too dangerous to do!

JAYNE:

When we first started rehearsing there were two concepts for how it might work. Because Chris didn't live in the UK it didn't matter where he was based when he was over here, and so the first idea was to split us into two teams, with Chris up in Blackburn choreographing 'Team North', and me down in London choreographing 'Team South'. That was great from an entertainment point of view, but because of the budgets and timescales involved (which were significant) efficiency was crucial, and so it was eventually decided that a joint effort was the only way it was going to work. Chris and I had been choreographing large numbers of people together for well over ten years, and in doing so had been able to demonstrate both the male and the female roles.

The next idea, which is the one we went with for the first series, was for us to teach all of the celebrities the basics. Nobody realised it at the time but the workload involved was overwhelming. Yes, we were used to working with groups, but only accomplished skaters. Teaching ten celebrities to skate from scratch is a very different proposition. For a start, people progress at different paces, so you end up basically having to teach everyone individually. And, because the contestants are inexperienced, they're also far more likely to incur injuries.

A solution was needed, so by the time it came to begin filming the second series, it was decided that Chris and I would do
a kind of 'meet and greet' with the celebrities. This would also
include us having two or three days on the ice with them, after
which they would work with a professional coach who'd take
them through the basics. That left us free to concentrate on the
production itself, the opening numbers and things like that.
Then, once the celebrities were at the required level, we'd pair
them up and begin choreographing them.

CHRIS:

The person who was perhaps most crucial during this early
period was Katie Rawcliffe, the show's executive producer. She
was our Betty Callaway on TV, if you like, and helped us
understand and appreciate not only the possibilities television
can present, but also the pitfalls.

Until then we'd only really made guest appearances on television (apart from the two *Omnibus* episodes), and so had never
had to do anything more than turn up on the day – the only other
exception being a TV special we made in 1986 called *Fire & Ice*.
That was a full-length company piece – a ballet on ice – and was
the closest we've ever come to making a movie. It sounds quite
glamorous – and the finished product was – but the process of
actually filming the piece was both slow and stifling.

The idea for the narrative came from a discussion between
Jayne, Graeme and me while we were devising the programme
for our first world tour. There was no music at this point, it was
merely a synopsis, and we soon realised that it was going to be
far too long to perform as part of a show. It would have to be a
stand-alone production, and the music would have to be commissioned if and when the piece itself was. Fortunately, London
Weekend Television loved the idea and so, after their involvement had been confirmed, we decided to approach an

extremely eminent musician named Carl Davis. Not only is Carl a conductor with the London Philharmonic Orchestra, but he is also a BAFTA award-winning composer, responsible for scoring (among many others) two of John Hurt's best-loved films, *The Naked Civil Servant* and *Champions*. I was, and still am, a great admirer of Carl's work, so was thrilled when he agreed to score *Fire & Ice*.

The narrative is set between two planets: the Planet of Fire and the Planet of Ice and is basically a love story featuring the rulers of the two planets – the Prince of Fire (me) and the Princess of Ice (Jayne). The piece opens with some conventional ballet danced on a studio floor, not on ice, and features me and members of the company wearing nothing but G-strings. This took some getting used to and it was a while before we all felt 'comfortable', shall we say! The rushes were fun to watch, though. I seem to recall there having to be quite a few cuts!

Filming took place in Germany and was a long, arduous and fragmented process, totally at odds with the natural flow of ice dancing. This had nothing to do with anyone involved, of course. It's just the way it has to happen. But I remember that it made for an often fractious environment and so wasn't something we were desperate to get back into.

Fire & Ice was, nonetheless, extremely well received and became one of the most-watched TV programmes of Christmas 1986. It also won the Bronze Rose at the prestigious Montreux Festival.

Dancing on Ice was a whole different ball game. There was a lot to take in; it was like learning a different language. Katie seemed to have a knack of recognising exactly what we needed to know and at what stage. She made what could have been an extraordinarily stressful experience into something enjoyable and fulfilling.

That's not to say we didn't still get nervous every now and then. I remember watching a playback of some of the rehearsals from the first series. All the ITV executives were in attendance, and none of us really knew what to expect.

In hindsight this was a mistake, as we were at the very start of the process and so the majority of the footage was of the celebrities learning the basics – skating back and forth, back and forth, back and forth. Pretty boring stuff, save for the odd fall. It left the executives in a state of panic: 'What have we done? We can't show this!'

We had to explain to them that in order to take part in the show, the first thing the celebrities had to do was learn to skate. It was as important as learning to walk. Once they had a handle on that, we'd be able to stylise and choreograph them; then, come January, they'd be ready to perform in front of the cameras. This wasn't what the executives were used to, however. They expected things to happen 'now', so it must have been a nervy time for them. For us, too, to a certain extent.

Our approach to *Dancing on Ice* was the same as our approach to amateur skating or touring as professionals, in that every show should be better than the last. We were always looking to up our game. That desire for steady, constant progress certainly hadn't deserted us.

It took a couple of years before we properly acclimatised to TV. The first two seasons were extremely hard work (in many cases unnecessarily so), but a gradual and continuous process of refining took place until we were left with a well-oiled hit show. Everyone learned as they went along and each year we became more and more efficient and adventurous.

At first we were pretty sure it was going to be a one-off series, especially with the budgets and rehearsal time involved, so we were thrilled when it was recommissioned for a second series.

JAYNE:

Getting back on the ice full-time was pretty daunting. Not only had our bodies changed – some of the strength we'd built up over the years had gone, as had some of the muscle mass – but we were also older, of course. We'd kept in shape, but were nowhere near as fit as we'd been in order to skate professionally. All those muscles I hadn't used for years. The day after the first session I was in absolute agony! It was a very rude awakening.

But because it was touch and go as to whether the show would go ahead – even up until a couple of weeks before production started – I still wasn't taking the whole 'getting back into shape' thing that seriously. It was only when we got the green light that I really started to panic a bit. After that I just lived in the gym.

Before the very first show went on air, ITV had said they'd be happy with an audience of about six million viewers; in fact, it ended up attracting closer to ten million. Everyone was so happy; totally ecstatic.

The first couple of years were tough, though. Probably the hardest we've ever worked.

After the first series we were asked by the Australian arm of ITV to go out and make a series there, which meant another eight weeks' work, not including rehearsals. Then, when we arrived back in the UK we went straight into rehearsing the second UK series. After that had finished we started working on the first *Dancing on Ice* tour. It had been two and a half years of almost constant work.

Just before that first tour started, we sat Phil down and said, 'We can only do this once, OK? We're exhausted. We can't carry on doing a series in the UK, a series in Australia and then a tour.'

Although we didn't make any more shows in Australia, that eight- to ten-week period was soon eaten up by the UK series and the tours. In fact, it would be another seven years before we took a proper break. Seven more series on TV and around 250 live shows. To be honest, after the first tour had finished we didn't take much persuading to carry on. We'd really missed being on the road, the fun you have and the camaraderie it creates, not to mention the buzz of performing in front of a live audience. Sure, you're away from home for weeks on end, and it's extremely hard work, but that's what I'd missed most about my life with Chris (apart from him of course) – the nomadic lifestyle. It can be addictive. Things are different now, and I think we've got it out of our system again, but I wouldn't bet against it coming around again!

JAYNE & CHRIS:

As each year went by the technology became more and more advanced, which meant the possibilities became endless. Twenty years before you wouldn't even have thought of these kinds of ideas, let alone suggest them. They simply weren't possible then. That candy shop just got bigger and bigger.

The production team on *Dancing on Ice* were, and still are, an enormously talented team of people. It's all well and good having the technology at your disposal, but you also need people who know how to realise its potential.

One of the highlights from a creative point of view was making the promos for the forthcoming series. These were usually put together around October and would be aired in December, about a month before the series started. This was our opportunity to showcase what was to come and so we really went to town. It all became quite cinematic, in fact. Everyone turned into Steven Spielberg for a couple of weeks.

When it came to choosing our contestants, we obviously had to have an audition process, which some of the celebrities must have found strange. Usually you'd get a straightforward offer to appear on a celebrity talent show, and that's how it was with *Dancing on Ice*; except that this offer was on the condition that you could learn the basics of skating. But we soon realised that it wasn't just about ice skating. We had to include contestants who might struggle a bit, the plucky triers! Ultimately, it's all about personalities and their journey. However, there are some people who, no matter how hard they try or how long you coach them for, simply don't take to it. You can usually tell after the first half an hour if somebody's going to be able to progress.

Then you need to achieve a balance between those who are going to be good skaters and those who are going to be, shall we say, entertainers. What mattered to *us* most was always a contestant's skating ability; whereas the producers tended to be guided more by personality and profile. The fact is, people like to see celebrities fall over; it's as simple as that.

But for every Todd Carty and Joe Pasquale – who, despite not being natural skaters, made an awful lot of people laugh – you need to have a Ray Quinn and a Beth Tweddle, contestants who could have become professionals had they started skating earlier in life. They provide shows like *Dancing on Ice* with a competitive element, and as the series wears on they invariably rise to the top.

The audiences at home wanted to be entertained, but ultimately they also appreciated what they were watching. If we'd wanted a show full of mishaps, we'd have called it *It'll Be Alright on the Ice*!

But even we recognised that having a show full of brilliant skaters wouldn't have been as entertaining or as interesting. It just involved a bit of give-and-take. Once again, by the second series we'd got the balance just right.

The one element that transcended skating ability was the relationship that developed between the professionals and their celebrity partners. They usually became very close very quickly. It's not like appearing with somebody in, say, a sitcom. It's a very tactile thing. You're holding and touching each other all day and from there a trust develops. Not just the celebrity trusting the professional. The professional has to be able to trust the celebrity. They need to know how far they can push them. It's so easy to get injured and, if that relationship isn't there, the chances are something will go wrong. That's why a lot of them are still very close.

One of the highlights for us on *Dancing on Ice* happened during series four, when Bette Midler sang on the show. We skated to her singing 'From a Distance'. That was amazing. At the end of the song we were happy with our skate, and as far as we were concerned Bette had been note perfect. She wasn't happy, though. 'I'm not sure about that note at the end, should we run through it again?'

'Nooo, it sounded wonderful, Miss Midler!'

What might have sounded not quite right to her had sounded perfect to the rest of us. She's such a big talent. She was OK with it in the end.

CHRIS:

I'd like to think people will remember *Dancing on Ice* for what it was as a TV show, as well as for some of the people they saw who went on to become champions. But, ultimately, I think the majority of people will always remember, initially at least, incidents like Todd Carty whizzing off the ice towards the end of 'Help!' It's amazing how one instant can capture everyone's imagination. It doesn't matter if that's in a positive or a negative way; the fact is, it became TV gold. It's one of those moments that you can't recreate and people will probably keep referring to it for decades to come. That was our *It'll Be Alright on the Night* contribution!

Some people could look at it in a negative light, as something that belittles all of the routines that went well – but I don't subscribe to that. Most people appreciated what *Dancing on Ice* was, and I think everybody realised how difficult it was. It didn't matter how proficient you became, everybody started at the same level, and so although the Todd Carty moment was laugh-out-loud funny, I think people appreciated that he'd also achieved something. After all, he finished the routine.

Jayne always wanted David Beckham on the show – David Beckham or Robbie Williams. We knew we'd never get them but Jayne always held out hope. She'd have enjoyed coaching them!

One of the biggest shocks was when we got Pamela Anderson on the show. The company were all like, 'Wow! How did they get her?' She certainly brought a bit of glamour and physicality to proceedings. I had the onerous task of going out to LA to audition her. It was such an inconvenience. Then, when she went out on the first show, the producers were absolutely devastated as she must have been an expensive booking. You can't argue with the viewers, though. If nobody votes for you, you're out!

Working on *Dancing on Ice* was like being part of a big family. We obviously had a different class each year, but the people who worked on the show full-time became our constant. We really enjoyed working with Phillip Schofield, Holly Willoughby and Christine Bleakley. There was a real cama- raderie and the atmosphere was always very warm and enthusiastic. It wasn't an easy show to bring together, and everybody had to work extremely hard, but that's what helped create the close environment. We all felt like we had ownership of it.

As we said, there's no finer way to spend a decade.

14
Choreography

CHRIS:

My interest in choreography came as a direct result of working on the ice, and started when Janet Sawbridge began encouraging us to choose our own music, make up steps and start to put our own moves together. That was all we did with Janet to begin with, and from then on I became hooked. The possibilities were mind-blowing. There were thousands upon thousands of different records in existence, and each one would trigger new ideas. I began to see choreography as a kind of infinite world of creative possibility.

I started watching musicals on TV. Fred Astaire was my big inspiration. Watching him helped me to understand choreography; why certain steps worked in certain places. His elegance and ease of movement were mesmerising. Even now when I watch him, I still love his style. He has that certain *je ne sais quoi*. Then add to the mix the likes of Gene Kelly and Bob Fosse – people with different styles to Astaire but no less engaging. I wanted to be like all of them.

Then there were all the big Busby Berkeley films, which I used to tape from the TV or rent from video shops. I've still got about 20 of them on VHS somewhere. From a choreography point of view they're timeless, and had such big productions.

The aesthetics of movement are so important. I'd always been into gymnastics as a child, and dance took that to another level. I began to appreciate it as an art form, or as a form of entertainment, and just absorbed everything: the music, the steps and the movement. So my initial training in choreography came from Fred Astaire, Gene Kelly, Bob Fosse and a whole host of other celebrated performers.

JAYNE:

Early on in our relationship I used to chip in with ideas for choreography, which Chris would always take on board. It was very much a joint effort back then, but as Chris became more confident about what he wanted to do, as well as being able to express himself more – far more than I ever could – I decided to take a step back and allow him to grow as a choreographer.

The process began when we chose the music. We'd sit down and listen to it together, over and over again, until we literally knew every beat of it. As you do that, images and ideas start to form in your head – a kind of 'virtual choreography'. This could be a productive and sometimes quite exciting time. Then, when we were ready, we'd take all the ideas on to the ice and start work. Even after this, nothing was ever done unilaterally. If it was included, it had been agreed by both of us. But I realised very early on that Chris has a genius for choreography.

CHRIS:

The year I think we matured as choreographers was in 1982, with our *Mack & Mabel* routine. People often cite *Bolero* as being the first single piece of music used for a free dance, and in the strictest sense it was. *Mack & Mabel* was an overture, which, despite being made up from a variety of pieces, is still actually classed as one single piece of music. These days it would probably be referred to as a mix or a mash-up.

That was a big jump for us, and some say for ice dancing as a whole. The overture still adhered to tradition, in that it featured a variety of different pieces and tempos, but as they all came from the same musical – which had a beginning, middle and an end – it provided a narrative, with each piece telling a different part of the same story. It also featured the same two characters, Mack Sennett and Mabel Normand. Once we had that in our minds we were able to immerse ourselves not only in these two characters, but also in the story itself: the magic of the silent movies and the melodrama of their romance. It was a very, very different experience from simply skating to three or four pieces of music, and obviously a lot more interesting. It added depth to our choreography. A sense of realism. Things would never be quite the same again.

The following year we did *Barnum*, which was also pretty ground-breaking. Not to mention a lot of fun.

About halfway through the 1982 ISU tour – which took place every year after the World Championships and featured all the competing couples – we were offered some tickets to either the Bolshoi Ballet or the Moscow State Circus. Tickets to the Bolshoi were like gold dust back then, just as they are now, so everyone else plumped for the ballet. Not me, though. As soon as I heard the word 'circus' something clicked in my head. Jayne was apoplectic. 'What? You've been offered a free ticket to see the

Bolshoi Ballet – the greatest ballet company in the world – and you're going to the circus?'

'That's right.'

'The circus? Are you serious? Well, if you're sure. But I'm surprised.'

We were already pondering our new programme for 1983 and I thought we might be able to use a circus theme: the jugglers, trapeze artists, clowns and the rest. It was just an idea, but I wanted to explore it further.

The circus in Russia was very different to the kind of thing we were used to in the UK. There, it is a profession and there are circus schools and a genuine career structure in place. It's a Russian heritage.

The Moscow State Circus is world-renowned, and I'd really been looking forward to it. I was interested to see how my idea might translate on to the ice, so when the others made their way to the ballet, I made my way to the circus.

There was no tent involved. The circus was a permanent fixture in the city and was housed in a huge stone building, complete with rows of seats, huge drapes and sawdust on the ground. This was *real* circus.

When the lights eventually came up, the band – which was situated above the entrance – suddenly began to play and out came a procession of talent: the ringmaster first, then the trapeze artists, followed by the jugglers, the strongman, the high-wire act; even bears and tigers, which was old school.

From the moment the procession began I knew that this could turn into something. The next day I told Jayne about my idea.

'Aah, so that's why you wanted to go. Yes, I like it!'

We always had to have complete agreement on everything we did on the ice, so I was relieved that Jayne seemed keen.

'Where do we take it from here?' she said.

'I'm not sure yet,' I replied. 'Let me have a think.'

A few weeks later, when we were back in the UK, I noticed in the papers that the musical *Barnum* was playing at the Palladium, starring the great Michael Crawford. In order for me to be able to explain my ideas more succinctly, I suggested that Courtney, Bobby, Jayne and I get some tickets and go and see it.

As we took our seats in the stalls, Michael – who had been peering through the house-tabs to get a look at his audience – spotted us, and duly sent somebody round to invite us backstage after the show. This was a real honour; we couldn't wait.

The show, as you can imagine, was inspiring, and we all went backstage enthused by what we'd seen. We've said this many times before but Michael Crawford is a circus all on his own. He has a huge smile that never seems to leave his face, and he acts with broad expressions and exuberant gestures. He has immense charisma.

After telling him how much we'd enjoyed the show he asked us what we were up to. 'Funny you should ask that, Michael. Have you got a couple of minutes? We'd like to pick your brains about something.'

After telling him about our plans he asked what we'd need to move it to the next stage.

'About four minutes of music,' we said.

We knew that this would be no easy task with regard to *Barnum*: the musical had no overture, and the majority of the numbers had vocals in them, which was not allowed within ISU rules.

'OK, let me see what I can do. I'll get back to you as soon as I can.'

We didn't have to wait long, and within a couple of weeks Michael had invited us down to London again, this time to meet Mike Reed, the show's musical director. He suggested to us that he might be able to do a special arrangement; actually create an overture for us. All we'd have to do was get it recorded.

We were thrilled at the offer, and so within a couple of weeks we had our music for the 1983 free dance. It had only been recorded on piano at that point, but was enough for us to be able to rehearse over in Oberstdorf. When it came to the recording we only had to pay for studio time. Every single musician gave their time and talent free of charge, which was a remarkable gesture.

Thereafter, although just for a few months, Michael Crawford became our mentor. He helped us to mime trapeze artists, high-wire walkers and jugglers. 'Juggling is a circular motion with the shoulders. Not just the hands going up and down. Here, watch.' Then he taught us backflips, as well as all the different expressions we'd need. For example, the intensity of our smiles was something we had to master. 'It's no good just smiling, you have to actually *become* the smile – like this. You've gotta go out there and sell it to the audience!'

This was the first time we'd ever worked with an actor, and the experience was enlightening. But Michael Crawford is so much more than just an actor. Thanks to him, my initial idea went from being a pipe dream to reality in just a few weeks. But it was his actual day-to-day involvement that made the difference. It was a pleasure working with such a special man – he's a huge talent.

So *Bolero* was the next step, really; the culmination of everything we'd done previously. From a choreographic point of view it was a very bold move, skating to just one continuous rhythm. Where were the contrasts?

JAYNE:

The routine I'm most proud of when it comes to choreography would have to be *Bolero*, for the simple reason that it's become almost timeless. When we went to Australia after Sarajevo we'd decided not to do *Bolero* again. As far as we were concerned it was done; our mantra always being to move on, reinvent and progress. We didn't want to put on some kind of 'retrospective'.

In our minds, each tour would be treated the same as each round of championships – new routines performed to new pieces of music. When we first mentioned this to Michael Edgley he almost fell off his chair: 'Have you any idea what would happen if you didn't perform *Bolero*? There'd be a full-scale bloody riot! Everyone would want their money back. If you want to be indulged with new routines you also have to give people what they want, and what every single Australian wants is to see you two doing *Bolero* – live!'

He was absolutely right, of course, and it wasn't just the Australians who demanded *Bolero*. Every country we've ever visited has been the same, which is why almost every professional show we've ever put on has featured it. Leaving it out would be like the Rolling Stones not playing 'Satisfaction'. We'd be lynched!

When it comes to people I admire within the world of choreography, I'd have to say Matthew Bourne is probably my favourite – after Chris, of course. I worked with Matthew very briefly about 12 years ago when I was asked to help recreate a scene from *The Nutcracker*. It was for a charity event at Somerset House, where they'd erected a temporary rink. He was choreographing and asked if I'd help him out, which of course I was delighted to do. Maybe he could be persuaded to put the whole ballet on ice?

CHRIS:

We did *Fire & Ice*, a ballet on ice, but that was made for TV and was choreographed by Graeme Murphy. Actually putting a ballet on to the ice for a live audience is something we would love to do. Who knows, maybe it could happen one day?

Back in 1996 I was commissioned to choreograph a ballet for the English National Ballet. The artistic director at the time was Derek Deane and he wanted to bring some guest choreographers in for the forthcoming season. I bit his hand off.

The piece was called *Encounters* and was semi-autobiographical. It was split into six sections, each illustrating a different part of my life: the contrasts between my marriages and my wives, my relationships with my mother and my stepmother, as well as my professional partnership with Jayne. For the music, I decided to use six songs by Paul Simon.

After it had all been choreographed I received a call from Derek Deane. 'Chris, I've got some bad news. Paul Simon won't let us use his music.' Apparently he's extremely protective when it comes to his music (so he should be!) and wasn't about to let it be part of something over which he had no control. It was a fair argument. In the end the ballet company made contact with Paul's agent and he said that Paul wanted to speak to me personally. It was quite a surreal experience, talking to Paul Simon about his music and about ballet; helping him to reconcile the two in his mind. At first he was very reluctant but in the end I managed to assure him of my integrity.

I loved working with the ENB, and perhaps I should have tried to do it again. But I viewed it more as an ambition fulfilled than as a career move. And, besides, it's a very difficult industry to get into. Being asked to choreograph as a guest is hugely different from actually becoming a 'ballet choreographer'. Programmes are planned years in advance, and so to be in with a chance of employment you have to live the life; immerse yourself totally. But I'd also had no formal training in ballet so was never meant for that world. It was a thrilling place to visit, though.

JAYNE:

In 1989 we created a routine based around two songs written by John Lennon, each with contrasting forms of choreography. First of all, we used the Beatles' 'Revolution'. The choreography here could be described as action-reaction, as when one dancer instigates a move, the other either recoils or reacts. It has a very staccato feel to it.

The inspiration came from a Montreal dance group we'd seen in Sydney called La La La Human Steps whose rapid, staccato movements were unlike anything we'd seen before. Chris thought the technique might be adapted for the ice, if we replaced the dancers' lifts and throws with quickfire upper-body movements. It was long, fast and very testing, of our abilities not only as dancers but also as actors.

At first I didn't like it. I'm not an aggressive person, so I had to go completely against character, using vicious movements and displays of anger. But it was good that Chris pushed me through it, because it brought out another side of me, another character that I could portray. To the best of our knowledge, nobody had ever done anything like that on the ice before, so it was as new to ice as it was to me.

CHRIS:

It can put you at risk with the audience, though, as it's not a particularly warm form of expression. It's far more thought-provoking, in fact. But we felt it suited both the tone of the song and the narrative.

This was based around a young couple who are having marital problems. They've been together for years, and the fairy-tale life that they started off with has begun to turn sour. As it all starts to go wrong, tension builds and anger grows within that. And that's what I wanted to get on to the ice, that raw aggression, and completely overstate it – so that it was as real for somebody sitting in row Z as it was for someone sitting at the front. After this the routine goes straight into 'Imagine', which is, of course, a much softer song, promoting peace and harmony. It was the calm after the storm.

Here I wanted to explore a possible resolution of their troubles, but not necessarily a happy ending. Maybe there is something else? Maybe there is a compromise, or at least an understanding of their situation? They may still end up parting, but at least they've analysed that they have a problem and perhaps there is something to work towards. Again, it was a narrative for us to choreograph and dance to.

We used this piece at the 1990 World Professional Championships, and despite making a slight mistake just before the end, we still received six 10.0s and went on to win gold. A couple of weeks later we received a letter from John Lennon's widow, Yoko Ono, who told us that she'd really enjoyed our interpretation, and that she was sure John would have said the same. We were touched by this, especially as the choreography was so avant-garde. Perhaps it would have suited John's sensibilities. It's nice to get affirmation from somebody so close to the source.

After we made the decision to go back to the Olympics, we were given the opportunity to do a Tom Collins tour in the USA, which comprised around 50 one-night stands in nearly as many states. It was normally only open to skaters who were still competing but, as with the Olympics, it was now open to professionals. We thought it would be a good way of reminding people that we were still around, so agreed to take part.

The routine we worked out for the tour was something called *Drum Duet*, which is a track by Genesis. It's literally a four-minute drum solo featuring Phil Collins and Chester Thompson. The whole thing is continuous, relentless even, and extremely rhythmic – and our routine was exactly the same: highly energetic and almost impossible to keep up with!

For us it was a chance to demonstrate how fit we were and that we still had originality. In an exhibition tour a lot of the skaters would do relatively easy numbers, but we were trying to showcase ourselves. But a few nights in, and we were thinking, Why did we do this? We must be crazy! We used to come off exhausted and dripping with sweat. It was like running a four-minute mile every night.

Oscar Tango was a unique piece, as we started the choreography without any music. This was all about timing: sometimes we'd have our backs to each other and, with no music to guide us, we had to make sure our timing was spot-on. Then the music would come in partway through, before disappearing again. It was a very innovative way to work and, when it came to performing it live, you could hear a pin drop. It was a real contrast as it was all about silence. We had to rely on an inner metronome throughout the number.

One of my personal musical favourites was a routine we did originally for Sport Aid called *Shepherd's Song*. The music was written by the French composer, Joseph Canteloube, and was from a collection of folk songs he wrote for soprano entitled *Songs from the Auvergne.* The recording we used featured Dame Kiri Te Kanawa and is still one of the most beautiful pieces of music I've ever heard. I'll probably have it played at my funeral.

The routine went so well at Sport Aid that we decided to adapt it and take it on tour with us. Debbie Roberts, who was working as our PA at the time, wasn't such a fan of the piece. Whenever it was referred to on tour, she'd say, 'Oh no, not *Sheep Shit* again!'

I don't regret a single piece of choreography we've created. One or two haven't aged particularly well, but they were right at the time.

JAYNE & CHRIS:

We've talked about being the subject of two documentaries. The second is the more famous of the two – the one that followed our return to the Olympics – but the first one, which was made three years earlier, in 1991, concentrated purely on our choreography. It was called *Bladerunners* and is something we're both very proud of.

The people involved in making the programme were a great team. They were basically allowed to do whatever they wanted. For a start, time wasn't an issue with them, so they could take as long as they wanted getting a shot right. And it was all shot on film as opposed to videotape. The whole operation oozed quality.

The idea they approached us with was to make a programme about ice skating as an art form. We were only too happy to oblige as this was exactly what we were trying to achieve.

It was indulgent. We were able to concentrate purely on the dance and, because it wasn't a competition or an exhibition, we could do anything we wanted. The only people we had to please were ourselves. It was purely about the movement, utilising the speed and flow of the ice. It was a liberating experience for us.

The programme culminated in us choreographing and dancing to a six-minute piece called *Ice Works*, which featured music that had been written specially for us. It was pure indulgence and was well received.

We're both also immensely proud of our collaboration with the cellist Yo-Yo Ma, who is the most amazing person to work with. He was a child prodigy who went on to become probably the most celebrated cellist since Jacqueline du Pré.

Yo-Yo first approached us back in 1994. His intention was to make six films, each accompanying one of Bach's *Six Suites for Unaccompanied Cello*. Each film would be in collaboration with a different artist using each of their respective disciplines. As well as us, he would feature a landscape designer, a choreographer, an architect, a director and an actor. He described it as a multifaceted celebration.

Our film would be the last of the six, accompanying Suite No. 6. His vision was to combine images of him playing in various locations with our skating sequences, which we would choreograph. These would all be interwoven with an actor reading J. S. Bach's first-person narrative. It was all about investigating Bach's personal and professional history, while linking his life and music to the modern world. Essentially, we had to bring Baroque music to the ice. It would be unique!

The first time we met Yo-Yo was in Boston. We were on tour at the time and he'd asked if he could come and see us and have a chat. Of course we were delighted, and so invited him to see a show one evening. After that we could go back to our hotel and talk.

When we met Yo-Yo after the show we noticed he had a cello with him. This intrigued us. Perhaps he was going to play? We later discovered that this was no ordinary cello. It was the world-famous *Davidov Stradivarius* cello, made around 300 years ago. Jacqueline du Pré had owned it before Yo-Yo and so it was priceless.

When we got to the hotel Yo-Yo started telling us about the six films he was planning.

'Which of the suites have you got in mind for us?' we asked.

'Yours will be the sixth suite. I'll play some of it for you.'

So there we were in a hotel room in Boston with Yo-Yo Ma, the world's most celebrated cellist, playing Bach's Suite No. 6 for unaccompanied cello, which is a beautiful piece of music, on what was probably the world's most expensive cello. It was absolutely breathtaking. One of those moments we'll never forget.

When we walked him to the foyer later on, he spotted a

friend of his. 'There's Teddy Kennedy, let me introduce you to him. Hey, Teddy, come and meet Torvill & Dean.' It felt surreal!

It took two years for the project to eventually come to fruition – two years of chats and ideas. But that's what made it so rich: the details that went into it.

JAYNE:

The shoot itself was extremely hard work. It was made at this freezing cold ice rink in Canada. It wasn't very inspiring when we first turned up, and still seemed pretty sparse even when they'd dressed it. Watching it back, though, it definitely works.

To tell the truth I found it all a bit of a chore. We hadn't done a lot of TV work then and were more used to a live situation. If we did it again today, I'd probably enjoy it a lot more, but going into it not knowing much about the process made it all a bit laborious.

The problem was that we'd choreographed it on our own in London. Then, once we got to Canada, we had to try and explain the choreography to the director, before she went away and decided how to film it. And that was obviously going to be different to how it had been originally planned. None of this really dawned on us until the cameras started rolling. We were used to directing our choreography with a live audience in mind, and so had to become aware of the camera very quickly.

For the beginning of the piece we'd worked out some hand choreography. When the director began filming it, we assumed the camera would be only on our hands, but in fact it was covering us full-length and we hadn't choreographed the rest of us! We were just standing there. We almost had to re-choreograph as we went. It was a very difficult process. The finished product looks great, though. It's a fantastic piece of work.

JAYNE & CHRIS:

The series went on to win a Primetime Emmy Award, as well as a Grammy nomination. We weren't at all surprised, as although we're extremely proud of our own contributions, the rest of the films are beautifully and artistically made. They are indeed works of art.

The icing on the cake for us came shortly after the films were released. During an interview to promote them, Yo-Yo was asked the question: 'Why Torvill & Dean?'

'I think they're extraordinary,' replied Yo-Yo. 'They did for ice dancing what Bach did for the cello.'

We were very humbled by his remarks.

15

Torvill & Dean on Torvill & Dean

JAYNE & CHRIS:

This partnership of ours, which first began almost 40 years ago, is easy to examine – fun, even. But one thing's for sure, it's almost impossible to categorise. Many have tried over the years – including us – but there are just too many elements to it. It's a real hybrid.

First and foremost, we're friends – the best of friends. We always have been and we always will be. But there's a bit of husband and wife in there, too; not to mention brother and sister. Then there's colleague, of course. We've been colleagues for as long as we've been friends. Some people have even suggested that we might be a bit like identical twins. We're not entirely convinced of this as neither of us can ever recall sensing that the other might be in trouble. Saying that, we do finish each other's sentences on occasion!

But at the very heart of our relationship, what underpins it all is commitment and trust. From the earliest days of our partnership, everything we did on a day-to-day basis relied on our commitment to each other, and through that commitment an unquestionable trust was formed.

What makes it even more unique is that this was all established with very few words being spoken. For the first few weeks of our partnership we hardly spoke to each other, such was the severity of our shyness. But as time went on, and as ice skating began to take over both our lives, we came to rely on each other totally, and we've never let one another down. We spent almost every waking hour together. If we weren't skating, we'd be doing something associated with skating; whether that was travelling or talking about choreography, or choosing some new music. The only two constants in our lives were skating and each other.

After a while this all became perfectly natural to us, but to the outside world – in particular the press – there had to be more to it. To this day, people still ask us if we ever had an affair. We had a kiss on the back of a coach once.

CHRIS:

This only came to light in 2013. It was during an interview with Piers Morgan. He kept on asking the usual 'did you or didn't you?' question and before I knew it the word 'dabbled' had fallen out of my mouth. 'We'd dabbled on the back of a coach once.' Well, that was it. The next morning it was all over the papers. 'TORVILL & DEAN FINALLY ADMIT THEY "DABBLED" ...' We're the dabbling duo!

JAYNE & CHRIS:

We were very prudish back then, but as time went on we became subconsciously aware of what a physical relationship or a romance might do to our partnership. Also, if you become romantically involved, there's always a chance that the feelings you have for one another might change, which is when things like fear, secrecy and betrayal start rearing their ugly heads. Once they come into play you're finished. You see it all the time in skating. Couples skate together, fall in love, split up and another one bites the dust.

The more we saw this happen the more guarded we became, and so a romantic relationship was completely out of the question.

In the early days, though, we made a point of neither confirming nor denying a relationship. It was like a game of cat and mouse, except there was never anything there to catch. We also dreaded interviews, which meant that nine times out of ten we'd just give a yes or no answer. We couldn't wait for them to finish!

That particular line of questioning has followed us around for decades now; the only difference these days is that the questions are always worded in the past tense.

Back in the mid-1980s you could hardly go a week without there being some kind of new 'revelation'.

JAYNE:

I remember we were being interviewed by a newspaper once shortly after the 1984 Olympics, and yet again the same old question arose. 'Are you going to get married?' To which Chris replied, 'Not yet.'

That was a little bit different to the usual answers, as it implied that we perhaps intended to. It wasn't like fanning the flames – it was like pouring petrol on them!

CHRIS:

It wasn't done intentionally. It just slipped out, really. Jayne thought I was making mischief, but I wasn't.

JAYNE & CHRIS:

The next day the papers were full of it: 'LOVE ON ICE! Sources close to Jayne Torvill and Christopher Dean have revealed that it is only a matter of time before they name the day.'

The word 'sources' meaning 'made up on the spot', we presume . . .

The vagueness was, however, genuine to a certain extent. If a journalist asked us if we'd ever get married and we answered, 'We don't know', it was partly because we genuinely didn't. We had no intentions to, but that wasn't to say it would never happen. It wasn't impossible. We were just being honest. We were far more naive than we were devious.

There was definitely an attraction between us in the beginning, though. Not a straightforward physical attraction, but something more representative of our relationship, in that it encapsulated everything – every aspect of what made our partnership work. It was as much about the fact that without each other we'd have been lost. There was a definite sense of belonging.

But the kind of marriage we were referring to back then was completely different to a conventional marriage. It was something very pure, really; no more than just a word and a few preconceptions. And it certainly didn't involve sex. It was all extremely innocent.

Below are two excerpts from an interview we did in the early 1980s. We'd been asked by John Hennessy, who was writing a book on us, what we meant to one another; and the result, we think, exemplifies the innocence of our early relationship.

JAYNE ON CHRIS:

I can understand why women's heads are turned by Chris. Mine was once. I have a deep affection for him. I could not skate the way I do with him if it were otherwise. But where does deep affection end and love start? I don't know, but it's not a question that troubles me – for the moment – not while we are training for the Olympics.

I sometimes wonder what the future has in store for us both. I am pretty sure I will marry one day, but don't ask me when or to whom. If we turn professional after the World Championships in 1984, I cannot see it would work if one of us formed an emotional attachment elsewhere. But then I cannot imagine getting married to Chris at the moment. Don't bet against it, though.

CHRIS ON JAYNE:

I have to see Jayne in a special light. Our skating is so all-absorbing that she has to be a friend and partner. Other men see her as the attractive female she is, but I have discovered by experience – we both have – that romantic commitment would interfere with all we have worked for. That is in cold storage at the moment and neither of us knows what we'll find inside until we unlock the door.

We were very close at one point but it was difficult to define because we were so young at the time. There was no sudden heartbreak, no discussion about it not being able to work. It is a strange relationship we have, a mystery to most people, including ourselves.

JAYNE & CHRIS:

Some might say that those paragraphs are loaded with all kinds of mixed messages, but they'd be wrong. They're simply the words of two very young and inexperienced people, who spent a lot of time together and who were asked the same questions day after day after day.

By the time we *were* ready to form relationships – which, as you know, wasn't until we were in our late twenties – we no longer felt like that about each other. Also, where would the romance be, the excitement of getting to know somebody? We knew each other far too well by that point!

The only time the whole 'will you/won't you' scenario ever became a pain was when the paparazzi got involved. You could usually decline to answer a question, or at least deflect it, but if you ever had a paparazzo standing in front of you, there was little you could do to escape.

In our experience, the best way to get rid of them was to say nothing and look as blank as possible – something that came quite easily to us in the early days! One of the first times we ever encountered a *true* paparazzo was at the 1984 World Championships in Ottawa.

All the skaters were staying in the same hotel, and the organisers had laid on a shuttle bus which would take us from the hotel to the ice rink. Just after getting on the bus one day a paparazzo jumped on and sat opposite us. Heaven knows how, but he'd managed to get hold of some accreditation that allowed him to be there. It was a bizarre experience; unnerving at first because all he did for the first few minutes was sit there staring at us both. He didn't smile or say anything and showed no emotion whatsoever. He just stared.

Then, all of a sudden, out came the camera, and that's when he started taking photos. There was no permission asked, he just held his camera about a foot from our faces and began shooting, one after another. We were wary not to ask him to stop, as we knew that would potentially spark controversy, so we just sat there, Jayne looking out of the window and Chris staring at his shoes, both of us looking blank. Not miserable, as that would only have garnered a 'TORVILL & DEAN – LOVE ON THE ROCKS!'-type headline. No, blank always worked best. Get a story out of that!

The second time was just a few weeks later while we were on holiday in Barbados. After the World Championships in 1984 we were exhausted, and so our new agent, Michael Linnitt, had suggested that we go away for a week.

Once there we rather naively thought we'd be free from the paparazzi. How wrong were we? There was not one but four of them – three from the UK and one Bajan photographer.

The local chap was by far the most determined. He'd leap out in front of us as we were out walking – snap, snap, snap – then run off back into the bushes. We found it quite funny in the end. How on earth would he sell that to the tabloids? Where was the headline? 'TORVILL & DEAN OUT HAVING A WALK. WHATEVER NEXT?'

After a few days we got used to him and ended up being able to spot him a mile away. He may well have been a decent photographer, but he wasn't especially covert. To be fair, he did manage to get one of his photos published: a snap featuring our beach shoes outside a door, which of course begged the question: 'WHAT ARE TORVILL & DEAN UP TO NOW?'

We could never really understand the interest in our relationship. We'd always considered ourselves to be fairly boring characters. It fascinated us, though.

JAYNE:

Our relationship is not without its difficulties and conflicts. One of the longest-running of these would have to be timekeeping; one of Chris's favourite subjects and something he takes very seriously. He says it came from his time in the police. 'We were taught that if your shift started at eight in the morning, you were there by seven-thirty!' he used to say.

I'm afraid I've never really subscribed to that particular pearl of wisdom, much to Chris's annoyance.

'You're always late, Jayne,' he'll say, tapping his watch before an interview or a photo shoot.

'Ah, yes, but NEVER on the ice!' Which is true.

Once, when we were in New York, I had arranged to meet Chris and he actually called the police. He thought I might have been attacked or something, but I was only in GAP, doing a bit of shopping. He was absolutely furious. 'I thought something had happened to you!' he said. I couldn't help laughing.

Chris did become quite devious at one point. Back in 1981, when we were due to collect our MBEs at Buckingham Palace, he told me we had to be ready to go by 9am. It turned out that we didn't have to be there until midday and were only a 15-minute drive away. We ended up sitting on The Mall for hours. He called it an insurance policy.

Another thing he likes to do is critique a dance as soon as it's finished. We'll be coming off the ice after a good performance and he'll suddenly remember something that felt wrong, such as 'Can you stretch your leg more here' or 'Can you jump a bit higher there'.

CHRIS:

I'm right, though; you have to get these things sorted out. If I don't say anything there and then they'll get forgotten. Saying it is like writing it down.

JAYNE:

This is all routine stuff and has never come close to affecting our underlying trust and commitment. That's rock-solid.

The fact is we complement each other almost perfectly. Chris is the creative force – the perfectionist who is never satisfied, always pushing and coming up with new ideas – and I'm the interpreter, there to help him make these ideas a reality.

After all these years together we've created a kind of short-hand way of working. There's an almost telepathic understanding; an instinct that allows us to move very quickly through the creative process.

CHRIS ON JAYNE:

People have best friends throughout their lives, and when you're a teenager that usually refers to a person you hang out with and have fun with. So to have somebody from that age who you share everything with, and who you would genuinely trust with your life, is pretty unique. But when that relationship then blossoms and endures over a 40-year period it becomes more than just a friendship. It becomes a blessing. And that's what Jayne is to me – a blessing.

We've got to a place now where we don't even have to say things. It just is. We don't have to put on any airs or graces. We can also talk through glances; through eye movements and facial expressions. We can be at opposite ends of a room but still communicate without having to vocalise what we're thinking. It's obviously quite difficult to get over on paper, but it's almost like a form of sign language. We can genuinely hold a conversation just by moving different parts of our faces!

Jayne has a limit when it comes to attention span, especially in meetings. Sometimes our *Dancing on Ice* meetings would last anything up to two or three hours, but she'd only ever be good for about an hour and a half. Then it's like a switch that goes 'click', and that's it, you've lost her.

I can't think of two people in the world who've spent as many waking hours together as we have. Even people who've been married for 50 or 60 years will have spent a lot of that time either asleep or at work. Not us, though. For the first 23 years we were together almost constantly, come rain or shine.

We've been in Oberstdorf for six or eight weeks at a time before, often just the two of us, and despite the odd spat on the ice we've always gotten along. Kept each other from going insane! We were in each other's company from shortly after getting up in the morning through to just before going to bed. I don't know many people, married or otherwise, who would be comfortable spending so much time together.

So perhaps the most exceptional thing about our relationship is the fact that it has never faltered. We've never fallen out in a big way. We've had a few cross words – almost exclusively on the ice – but nothing that hasn't been forgotten after a few minutes.

We've been conditioned to each other to the point of being almost identical in the way we think. If one of us makes a mistake during a routine, the other can feel it happening and will compensate immediately. It's as if we're instinctively one on the ice, inextricably linked.

As well as a very deep love, I have an immeasurable respect for Jayne. Nothing fazes her. She takes everything in her stride.

One rather comical but nevertheless salient example of her stoicism happened at Madison Square Garden back in 1988. We were performing with the Ice Capades revue at the time, a show that was predominantly child-orientated; all Smurfs and cartoon characters. I think we were the adult relief. The routine we were doing was a piece called *Eleanor's Dream*, which was based on 'Eleanor Rigby'.

Jayne was wearing a very avant-garde outfit and during one

of the lifts I thought I saw one of her breasts. I couldn't be absolutely sure because we were moving at the time but as soon as we got off the ice I said, 'I'm sure you just flashed. You should get your dress checked out.'

'Nooo, I did not. There's nothing wrong with the dress, thank you very much!' She was totally indignant at the time, so I just left it.

About a week later she came running up, waving a photo at me. It turned out that a friend had actually taken a photo of us both at that exact moment and, sure enough, there it was! She'd flashed. Jayne's mood had completely changed by this point and she actually seemed quite relaxed about it. As I said, she takes everything in her stride.

Something else you've probably realised by now is that Jayne is a power-shopper. She's a professional. Interrupting her mid-shop is like interrupting a pilot trying to land a plane. That old question: 'What would you be if you weren't a skater'? Well, for Jayne it would have to be personal shopper. She'd make (and spend) a fortune!

One of the only times I've ever seen Jayne pushed to one side was when Tom Cruise came to see our show. We were in Toronto at the time, and I think he was filming *Cocktail*. The producers had invited him to come backstage after the show and he'd agreed. This, as you can imagine, caused a not insignificant amount of excitement, especially among the female cast members, and in particular Jayne.

Everyone wanted to meet him, of course, and as they all filed out of the dressing rooms they made a beeline for him. But it wasn't just cast members who were interested; it was cast members' families, members of the crew, you name it. Jayne was one of the first out, but being quite a bit smaller than most quickly got pushed out of the way. I remember looking at her getting more and more annoyed! A group photo was taken but poor Jayne was nowhere to be seen. She did her best to look as if she wasn't bothered and probably had everyone else fooled. Not me, though! She laughed about it afterwards.

When she does get angry, which is probably once every ten years or so, it comes from inside and you know about it. Then she just freezes you out. She can be an ice maiden.

JAYNE ON CHRIS:

The last time I had to describe Chris was to a journalist. I forget what I said exactly but it was no more than a few words. Actually writing it down is something completely different.

The Blond Prince, as I used to call him in the old days, is a perfectionist, both on and off the ice. When people ask us who the boss of the partnership is, I always say that I let him believe that he is, to which he usually replies, 'That's right, she's actually working me from behind, like a puppet.'

He sometimes stresses over very small things, and I'll have to say to him, 'You've got to look at the bigger picture, Chris.' He doesn't like that!

Chris is so impatient, though. Not irritatingly impatient, just amusingly impatient. For example, he'll ask me to give somebody a ring. 'Can you call so-and-so about something or other', and I'll say fine. Then about an hour later he'll come back and say, 'Don't worry, I've already called them.' Once he's got something into his head, that's it. I've no idea why he asks me in the first place. He knows it'll take me ages.

It's the same with things like gadgets. Chris loves gadgets. He'll call me up and say, 'I'm thinking of buying a new phone, could you go and have a look at one and let me know what you think.' Then, when I eventually get round to looking at it, I'll call him up and he'll say, 'Oh, I bought that ages ago.' He can't help himself. Everything has to happen now.

If I'm ever upset he'll always do whatever he can to make things right. That's probably the sweetest part of his character.

He's also a peace-maker. If anybody falls out on tour or in the studio he's always first to help smooth things over.

He might be quite demanding sometimes, but that's because he's a perfectionist. His main priority, however, is to make sure that whoever he's working with is comfortable and happy. He won't start work otherwise.

On the ice, his three main qualities are his enthusiasm, his creativity and his energy. I find them infectious and it makes working with him a joy. Sometimes he comes up with ideas that at first glance seem ridiculous. I just don't see it. Then, as he explains himself and we begin to work it out, it all becomes apparent. 'I see what you mean. That's fantastic.' He's a very clever guy; a genius, in my opinion, but don't tell him I said that.

He does have another side to him, though. I'm probably one of the hardest people in the world to wind up. It's just not within my nature to bite, never has been. It doesn't matter what you say, nine times out of ten I'll be able to ignore you and walk away. Water off a duck's back to me. Unless your name is Christopher Dean. He's the only person in the world who can do it. Why? Because the only thing that winds me up is being told I'm not up to doing something on the ice, and the only person qualified to tell me that is Chris. 'You're just bailing out, Jayne. You haven't got the courage to do it, have you?' It's just back-handed motivation, of course, and will almost always result in me getting it right. Sometimes I wish he'd try and motivate me in the traditional way, but I think it's probably too late for that. These days it's slightly different, as we're obviously older and more susceptible to injuries, and so he tends to go a bit easier on me. But he still knows what buttons to press. He loves it, of course. Thinks it's hilarious.

Believe it or not Chris is quite chirpy first thing, which always makes you want to work. He doesn't need anywhere near as much sleep as I do. I need at least seven hours, otherwise I'm useless. He's a thinker, too. I'll ask him how he's slept and he'll say, 'Dreadful. I was thinking about this move or that routine.' If there's something unresolved in his head, he can't switch off. Taking your work home with you – I always prefer not to.

When Chris got together with Jill I was thrilled for both of them. Jill's a very warm person, very giving. It seemed like a perfect match, and even though they're not together any more, I'm glad they're still close.

Jill was a friend of mine before she and Chris became involved, and the only problem I find in a situation like this is when the inevitable questions start: What's Chris like? Does he do this? Does he do that? It compromises my relationship with them slightly, because I won't let it compromise my relationship with Chris. I have to take a step back.

We're very protective of each other. On the very few occasions people have been unkind about him in front of me they've been given short shrift. It's something I won't allow. I'm not saying he's perfect, and neither am I, but he's as close to me as anybody and my respect for him is immense.

We share quite a few interests off the ice. We both like musicals and ballet; anything with dance in it, basically. We're both fitness fanatics, too. We have to be. He's got a trainer over in Colorado and I have one in the UK and we quite often compare notes. This extends to us both owning racing bikes. I recently completed my first duathlon, which was fun. Chris had been nagging me to buy a bike for ages, so when I was asked to do a duathlon I thought, Why not? I didn't set out to win (Chris would be horrified at that!); I just wanted to finish. That's what drove me on – even if I ended up walking, I had to complete the race. Chris, on the other hand, has to do everything at 100mph, and he has to win!

I do worry about him sometimes. I always have. There's a real vulnerability to Chris. In many ways he's an extremely strong person, but in others he isn't. For a start, he's no good on his own. He can get bored very easily and always needs to be doing something. He also thrives on having people around him and is very gregarious.

He's very good at practical jokes, although I'm not sure if 'good' is the right word. Years ago, when he was still in the police force, he chased me in his patrol car, lights and sirens blaring. I was absolutely terrified! It was all planned before-hand. He and his colleague waited for me to leave work one day, then followed my car for a while. Suddenly, all hell was let loose. I couldn't think of what I'd done wrong. I should have known it was him! It was only when I started to pull over that the penny dropped. I looked in my mirror and there they were, PC Dean and his mate, clearly howling with laughter. He thought it was hilarious but I was furious at the time, and told him so. It must have seemed strange to any onlookers: a woman in a Mini telling off a policeman.

This might sound a little bit strange (I promise you it isn't!) but he once decided to put his police handcuffs on me, before pretending he'd lost the key. I was so gullible back then (a weakness not lost on Chris) and I fell for it. 'Oh my, what are we going to do?'

'I'll have to call the police and get them to bring a spare key.'

'You can't do that! How's it going to look?'

'They won't mind, they're very broad-minded. Only kidding, here it is!'

'Aaaaaggh!'

All in all he's a good guy, and I love him dearly. I couldn't imagine life without him. Although I'm slightly older than him, he's like a big brother to me.

16

Present & Future

JAYNE:

Chris is far more forward thinking than I am. He's really ambitious; whereas I'm happier sitting back and letting things happen. I'm a great believer in fate. It felt like that with *Dancing on Ice*, with just a phone call out of the blue one day. Chris is much more inclined to actually make something happen.

I have got a small bucket list, though. For a start, I'd like to run the London Marathon one day. I keep saying that I ought to try and do it. It seems like such a huge thing to so many people and I wouldn't mind being part of that. The amount of money they raise year after year is staggering. It's such a worthwhile event. Keeping fit and raising money for charity is a great mix. Maybe I'll do it next year.

I've had a couple of offers to go skydiving in the past. That's something I could never do. It's not the distance to the ground that terrifies me; it's being pushed out of the plane. I prefer to keep my feet firmly on the ice, thank you very much.

It might sound a bit clichéd but as long as my family are all right, I'm happy. Professionally we'll probably slow down a little bit now that *Dancing on Ice* has finished. Having said that, you just never know, do you? I might not be as forward thinking as Chris is, but I still get excited by the prospect of a new venture, and if something came along that was right for us – well, you never know.

CHRIS:

The days of being away for five or six months of the year are over. It has to be like that. My children are actually two young men now, and they're forming very definite ideas of who they are and what they want to be – and I want to be around for that part of their lives. I don't necessarily have to help them make decisions, but I want to be there if they need me. If they make mistakes I want to help them get over it, and if they succeed at something I want to be there to help them celebrate. That's what being a parent is all about – being there.

I like doing new things, and I've always thrived on variation. But for the time being this is my new thing – being there for my children.

We've got a few things in the pipeline work-wise, which are all based in the UK, but instead of disappearing for months on end, I'm hoping to break things up a lot more from now on, perhaps only going away for a couple of weeks at a time. I love England and I've got a lot of friends over there, including Jayne, of course. Coming over more often but for not as long will hopefully work well for me.

Looking to the future, there are a couple of ambitions I'd still like to fulfil. For a start, I'd like to get involved in skating on a national level. Not day to day, but perhaps as a mentor to some of the young upcoming skaters. Future champions, perhaps. Jayne and I have a huge amount of experience and it would be a shame and a waste if we didn't try and share it. We're also both parents now, and are used to interacting with young people. I'd really enjoy imparting some of my knowledge to them. And, dare I say it, wisdom. I'm sure Jayne would too.

A couple of years ago I was contacted by the Canadian entertainment company, Cirque du Soleil. They had a few ideas they wanted to discuss and I have to say that the whole proposition got me really excited. I love their work and to create something with them would be a dream situation.

They actually formed not long after Jayne and I got together and were also helped out with a grant from their local government. These days they have shows running all over the world and have completely revolutionised live entertainment. They gave it a unique look, and started to ignite people's imaginations again. They certainly did mine.

They're also very adventurous with regard to developing artistic form, and they make everything look stunning. It all has a slightly surreal quality to it, and it astounds me how they manage to achieve that. It's very much like ice skating in a way. People see the flow and the freedom of movement, but to actually make that happen you need all the rest; the nuts and bolts, if you like. It's like making a film: behind the superstars and multi-million-dollar contracts, you've still got the cleaners and the catering vans. It's all about creating an illusion. Marrying Cirque du Soleil with ice would be a fantastic enterprise.

I'd like to see more live entertainment generally. People's attention spans are becoming shorter these days and everything seems to happen on a screen in front of you. It's all so readily available, yet at the same time disposable. The fact is you can't beat the thrill of attending a live performance, and people need to be reminded of it. In fact, a lot of young people need to be introduced to it.

I've got three more ambitions at the moment. The first is a musical based around ice skating. I've already written a treatment for it and have even had one or two tentative meetings. Skating rinks are a microcosm of life itself: all the characters, all the politics and all the emotions. It's potentially an extremely powerful subject. I'm not sure who'll be scoring it yet, either Andrew Lloyd Webber or Stephen Sondheim. If only.

My other ice-based ambition is to create a sitcom, once again based around life at a local ice rink. It's actually more of an idea than an ambition but it's definitely something I can see in my head. As well as drama and politics, you also get a lot of humour at ice rinks, not to mention characters. I've witnessed so many things that have made me laugh over the years, not least the old man on skates being pulled around by a tractor when resurfacing the ice. None of that was done with any humour intended yet was one of the funniest sights I've ever seen. You've also got a lot of people falling over, of course, although that would probably lose its lustre after a while. That said, it all depends who's falling over, I suppose.

On a lighter note, my final ambition (for the moment at least) is to get a part in *Coronation Street*. I'm a huge *Corrie* fan and have been for years. I even created a role for myself a few years ago. I was to be the new gym owner. Six months later they actually created the role for real and someone else (who could act) got the part. But you never know – stranger things have happened.

Acknowledgements

First and foremost we must once again thank our mentors: Janet Sawbridge, the late Betty Callaway MBE, Courtney Jones and Bobby Thompson, Graeme Murphy and Andris Toppe. Without whom . . .

Our memories have served us surprisingly well while writing this book. Even so, there are four people who were invaluable when it came to filling in the dates and details. They are: Courtney and Bobby, Sharon Morrison and Tony Harpur. Thank you, you four!

Last but by no means least we would like to thank those responsible for making our book a reality, in particular: Phil Christensen, James Hogg, Tim Bates, Ian Marshall and everyone at Simon & Schuster.

Index

Note: 'JT' denotes Jayne Torvill, 'CD' Christopher Dean.
Subheadings are in chronological order, with the exception of lists
of proper nouns, which are in alphabetical order.